Diverse Career Paths
And Things You May Encounter
Along the Way

By Kurt Tyler

Copyright © 2017 by Kurt Tyler

All rights reserved worldwide.

No part of this publication may be replicated, redistributed, or given away in any form without the prior written consent of the author/publisher or the terms relayed to you herein.

Kurt Tyler, dcareerpaths@gmail.com or Twitter @kurtkattyler

ISBN: 978-0-9994043-1-7

Art design by Kurt Tyler

First Edition

Dedication

Thank-you God for helping me find the words.

Dedicated to my father Homer Duke Sr., my mom Delma Louise, who as a team created the foundation for me to feel confident in my ability to pursue diverse career paths. Prof. J.L. Lane, who challenged me to emerge, evolve, and to recognize the potential of my composite skill set.

And all the ones whom I found to be prolific and/or just brutally honest, which I often needed. I truly appreciate you! Uncle Sylvanus, Aunt Addie, Uncle Dan, Aunt Gert, Aunt Hazel, Uncle Walter, Uncle Alfred, Joanne T, Dr. Judy, Dr. Rudy, Daniel Jr., Homer Jr., Bruce, Finis, Emzy, 'C' & Deborah T, Sylvia & Dr. George, Bo, Big Mike, Kevin J, Mike 'Leroy' A, Keith S, Bird, Chuck, Porter, Joe J, Tim V, Dr. Turner, Dr. Watkins, Ikaha, Slajana, Mary S, Noreen, Marvo, Rev. R.Grady, and Studs Terkel.

About the Author

Kurt Tyler, is currently an active Business Technology Consultant, with over thirty years of experience working with small through large businesses including corporations like GE and Freddie Mac, both of which utilize diverse workforces whose efforts impact economies worldwide.

Kurt's business experience includes merger and acquisition capability planning and integration, IT governance and compliance, client and vendor relationship management, health care, finance, e-commerce, and virtual reality conceptualization technologies, process improvement, behavior modification, mentoring, thought leadership, corporate strategy, collaborative team building, crisis management, conflict resolution, initiative management, music, media and broadcast production.

Author's Note

This book includes a number of true experiences and observations that I have selected with the belief they will empower those who are in the midst of making critical career decisions, with a heightened sense of awareness that can strengthen their abilities to develop effective strategies as they plan their steps throughout their careers. I decided to be brutally honest when writing about the beneficial and unfavorable experiences because only by having the awareness of both can one create well rounded plans. That awareness can increase one's ability to perceive when an opportunity and potential risk is in your

path. This book shines a spot light on a number of work place challenges that are often overlooked during formal education, and could lead to dreams deferred. Planning a strategy that includes more than one source of income is just one of the types of antidotes presented in this book.
– KT

Contents

Purpose 7
Chapter 1: Introduction 20
Chapter 2: Needs and Character Types 33
Chapter 3: What's in it For Me? What Job Options Do I Have? 58
Chapter 4: What's the Point? 75
Chapter 5: World Cultures 81
Chapter 6: Know Your Own Core Values and Moral Compass 104
Chapter 7: Your Value, Salary, and Income 121
Chapter 8: Career Market Indicators 142
Chapter 9: Search Approaches for Finding a Job 152
Chapter 10: Adversaries in the Shadows 163
Chapter 11: Be Good to Yourself, Along the Way to Success 177
Chapter 12: The Dead-End Job Blues 186
Chapter 13: The Rules of Discrimination 196
Chapter 14: A Look into Being a Team Player 208
Chapter 15: Social Responsibility 227
Chapter 16: Preparing Your Stand Against the Face of Deception and Avoiding the Five Major Risks 236
Chapter 17: Conviction, Strong Faith, and Confidence 264
Chapter 18: The Blame Game 271
Chapter 19: Increasing Your Odds of Having a Successful Career 281
Chapter 20: Acknowledge Those Who Help You, Your Business and Your Career 298
Chapter 21: Leap of Faith 311
Chapter 22: Perspective 316
Appendix: Summary of Recommendations 328
Appendix: Sample Career Theme 335

Purpose

The purpose of this guide, is to provide assistance to: 1) students who are developing their skill set to be used for a specific profession requiring special training, or developing a broader set of skills which can be utilized progressively over time, for various careers within one or more industries, 2) individuals who are already employed or currently seeking employment, and 3) anyone in parental, guidance or instructional roles where someone confides in you as one of their trusted advisers with whom they are comfortable talking about their dreams, goals and aspirations.

My goal is to help you envision potential career paths through a clearer lens, to become aware of potential pitfalls, and to provide you with some tactics for you to consider, which will hopefully increase your odds of developing a successful diverse career strategy that's totally your own.

At times, I will approach ideas from a high-level perspective, as if you are floating above a city, looking down over the landscape so you can see the road or path you are currently on. But more importantly, you should begin to see some additional paths, routes, or options, currently available, and opportunities for new paths that can be created, all of which, can be under construction with your own hands. This means that your career paths that are now under construction could end up changing in any direction, leading you to encounter points along the road that require decisions. I suspect that you'll also encounter adversaries who jump into your path for unknown reasons and you'll wonder, what is their freaking problem? You may have dreams deferred, temporarily, and have unexpected influences which may or may not be under your control, but could require you to make adjustments to overcome them.

In this guide, I will share with you some scenarios that I've personally experienced, some I've witnessed as a third-party spectator, and some that others have shared with me. My hope is to help you successfully navigate your own diverse path by increasing your awareness, and to assist you in becoming skilled with tactics for constructing your own diverse path. And just to be perfectly clear, I believe my success has been due to my partnership with God, who I believe guided me, provided insight, put me in contact with key people and ultimately invoked favor on my behalf. But by no means is that a requirement for using what I will share with you in this guide. Your beliefs are up to you. I can only provide you some tools that you can pull out of your backpack as needed. These are the gifts I will share with you in this guide.

You Should Know

In this guide, I use my own conceptual definitions to distinguish between what is a job, a profession, and a career. I state these knowing that others may have their own definitions, and that's fine. But as I write, by referring back to how I define these, hopefully it will bring better understanding of my point of view at that time. In my writings, I consider a job as being different than a profession, even though some will consider them one and the same. Also, a *"work-for-success"* opportunity could be a job that is used as a stepping stone within a career strategy. In many cases, we take a job so that we can get something, with no thought-out plans that the job will lead to something long-term or more beneficial.

In this guide, I consider a *profession* to be an effort you choose to do that requires years of specialized training or knowledge. Yes, being a lifeguard at a swimming pool requires training, as most jobs do. But when thinking about specialized training or knowledge, I'm thinking more about years of training before you can go into a profession. For instance, becoming an orthopedic surgeon is a profession that requires years of specific training. I want to clearly distinguish how I define what is a profession, from how many refer to all work as being a job.

In this guide, I consider a *job* to be work you take on to get money for something, *but will not require years of extensive specialized training*. Hopefully, surgeons don't think of what they do as being a job in this sense.

In this guide, a *career* is the result of a focused plan concentrated on maintaining a profession or targeted jobs, long-term, where over time you enhance your viability with remaining in a targeted job, profession, or multiple professions within an industry. You can build a successful career as a surgeon within the healthcare *industry*. But you can also have more than one profession or careers within an industry. This concept of strategic planning is the basis for how you target specific *"work-for-success"* opportunities.

For example, you can begin a *career* in the healthcare *industry* by having a profession as a surgeon. Years later, you transition from being a surgeon to begin a second career and a new profession as a hospital Medical Director. You could look at this as having one career that includes varied targeted opportunities, or multiple careers with a totally different set of opportunities, all within the healthcare industry. I believe when people are in their early stage of career planning, while in grade school or even college, your ability to envision having one career with multiple professions, might be a challenge. I believe if you are already employed, the realization of having multiple career paths is more easily realized if you are more knowledgeable of available roles in your industry. In the case of a surgeon, you probably have substantial industry knowledge, and have added, enhanced, and perfected skills over time, all within the healthcare industry. Those skills can now be applied to a new profession or career path as a result.

Conceptual Clarity

This is important because as you move along a diverse career path, the odds of your success can increase when you consider the goal of: 1) always enhancing your skill set; 2) creating multiple options; and 3) beginning your acquisition of skills, early during your basic education stage, and continuing over the course of your career. If you decide to be laser focused on one and only one industry, you can begin to identify various skills that can be transferable within that industry. Over time the result can provide you the option to transfer into similar or related professions. Others may simply call this "changing jobs." But to change professions requires specialized skills, even if remaining in the same industry. And even if you choose to remain viable in one profession, you will also need to enhance your skill set as the demands of industry evolve. Determining your industry of focus and related industries early, could become the fundamental defining motivation for how you develop your diverse career path.

For instance, can the health, medical, and wellness *industries* relate to the food *industry*? How many intersections might there be? How many *professions* might be related or interchangeable across on another? What might be some transferable skills that would allow you to move between each *industry*? In your career plan, which *job* or *profession* would be beneficial as a starting point to your career and could facilitate opening the door for opportunities within the four different industries? And if you were to consider the global stage, which countries could benefit the most from someone having the transferable skill set you just identified? Will that require additional language skills and cultural awareness? So, I hope that provides a bit of clarity and something to think about.

When thinking about a diverse career path, plans, or strategy, I hope that you will begin to think beyond what you are currently learning in school or have already learned, and begin to envision where your plans might lead you over time. Normally you can envision working in one or maybe two industries. But there are some "power skills" that are transferable across industries. I hope that you would take time to find them so you can have some of those within your skill set to facilitate morphing to another profession or career, if so desired. Even if your plans are to become an eminent surgeon, there is no way you will be able to ride a lifetime on just the skills learned in medical school. With new discoveries come new training, tools, and procedures. You must evolve to remain viable, and evolution begets opportunities over the course of a career.

"Work-For-Success" Opportunities

What are some good examples of one opportunity followed by similar types of opportunities, which in turn can be part of a plan to build a career?

Being a life guard could be called a summer job. It could also be a strategic starting point into the health fitness industry, making the job now a *"work-for-success"* opportunity.

Being a multilingual professional swim coach/instructor, fitness specialist, or physical therapist could be professions that, through planning, could result in building multiple careers internationally within the health fitness industry, all from having the experience of being a life guard in concert with a forward-thinking career plan.

How about you obtain an airplane pilot's license? From working support at an airport, you can expand to being a charter pilot, to a test pilot, to a commercial pilot, become an air traffic controller, then move into airport supervision, airplane design, air safety, outer space transport, or aviation-related training. All of these could be considered careers within the aviation industry.

You Should Also Know

Some people may have their dreams deferred or experience roadblocks and detours along the path of building a career or careers that align to their personality. Hopefully as you become more in tune with who you are, you will continue to develop stockpiles of personal support which you will be able to utilize at various times to remain on track as your path takes a detour, then straightens and new opportunities present themselves.

Formally, my hope for this guide is to act kind of like a supplemental insurance policy by:

- Empowering students, graduates, and those in parental, guidance or instructional roles, with awareness of some *recurring business cultural practices* that are unspoken and ingrained in the workplace.
- Facilitating discussions on workplace-related challenges that some may not be aware exist.
- Facilitating the reader's ability to create *risk and issue mitigation plans* that may have not been considered when strategizing on their career plans.
- Acting as a policy conversation starter for schools that may not have mechanisms in place to provide students with tactics for *conflict resolution* focused on handling discrimination and unethical actions experienced in the workplace. Given the high volume of conflicts that individuals face in the workplace, in their personal relationships, and when dealing with the public, it's amazing that conflict resolution training is not a focus in middle school through college.

- Providing readers with some *recommendations* to be considered, and hopefully motivate those interested to develop their own innovative and unique tactics that they can use while navigating their own individual career paths.
- Providing *reference material* for readers to refer back to after leaving the classroom and while moving along their career paths.
- Providing readers with *hope and reinforcement* that while they are working on developing successful careers, they are not alone. There are others out there who have awareness and experience that are available to them.
- Providing readers with some *tools* that I believe can assist them with determining professions and career paths that align with their personality.
- Helping readers begin to become more conscious of their personal *character traits*, with the goal of helping them determine *"work-to-success"* opportunities that better align with their individual character traits.
- Providing readers with information focused on assisting in developing and implementing unique career strategies in the private comfort of their own controlled space.

The challenge of landing a beneficial *"work-for-success"* opportunity after you've identified a viable service or skill you can offer can be one of the most stressful hurdles many will have to face. When thinking about planning, the truth of it is, many will have to face and overcome this hurdle not once, but multiple times along their career path. So, I suggest you continually dedicate time to fortifying and enhancing your strategies and the skills you've already learned. In combination with the learnings presented in this guide, I believe you can empower the ground-level foundation of your own diverse path in ways that no one can obstruct, unless you allow it.

Many people might have dreams deferred, but if you have the will and conviction, dreams will only be deferred or postponed, *not stopped.* If you want it, you can create a fortified path to obtain it. A diverse path not documented in any book, but one you create, and one that you will be the governor of, to change, adjust and control as you see fit.

Also, I highly suggest that you try to apply the suggestions and observations in this guide continually and *more than once.* As time goes by, you should become skilled enough to design unique tactics that become a natural part of your own abilities to maneuver on this game board. In other words, you begin to make some of the rules for this game, and easily manage any obstructive actions against you achieving your career goals, with professionalism and ease. And if you are making some of the rules, I'm confident that you will make them so that you achieve your goals, at least the majority of the time.

In reading the various bits of wisdom, actual experiences and information to help you determine your own individual path, I want to level set with you from the very beginning.

The more you are aware of the potential challenges coming your way, the more you have opportunities to research, prepare, and implement plans, to minimize, control, or totally block the impact of risks before they become an issue that could hurt you. Key to this preparation is knowing that there will be risks introduced by the people you work with, report to, or are your clients. Along the diverse career path, you will run into businesses that expect to see high levels of success for their stakeholders, including you. Some will speak of risk management, while on the flip side, those who don't engage in risk management will be the ones who when the unexpected challenges arise, will need to make reactionary decisions instead of thoroughly researched decisions. Those quick decisions could initiate a ripple effect, that could result in more issues. Over time, it's not unusual to see adverse financial impacts result downstream in employee layoffs, client business relations severed, negative impacts on the bottom line, or impact to multiple downstream relations. Why? Because they didn't engage in proactive risk management planning.

After you've begun visualizing a couple of target professions and potential career paths (I do hope you will consider more than one), you will want to think about what you can do to strengthen your probability of success when you encounter obstacles that disrupt your movement along your career paths. Obstacles could come in the form of emotional stress, inappropriate behavior, discriminatory actions, or the lack of inclusion. So even though most would like to dismiss these realities, it's our diversity values that influence how each person determines who they choose to be around, and what they will do to make that a reality. It's our diverse beliefs that make us all unique, but can also present steep challenges, which often require strategies for how you will overcome antagonistic roadblocks, and continue along your career path.

Knowing these points puts you in a position to strategically map out more than one approach for you to develop, prove, and test, which ultimately, when applying along with your archive of lessons learned, should make it easier each and every time you have to face that hurdle or roadblock. As you begin to utilize more and more of your lessons learned, you begin to realize that part of the stress associated with landing beneficial *"work-for-success"* opportunities is self-inflicted and often the result of not having information or tactics. Yes, information is essential.

And for those who don't have much patience, those early yearnings for immediate gratification to take whatever *"work-for-success"* opportunity you can get or the first offer that comes your way should remind you of a similar impulse. And that is the one when you purchased something just because you wanted it, not taking into account if it's really the best thing for you at that time.

What many soon discover is that when taking the first opportunity that lands on your plate, even when it doesn't come close to something you really like, things often don't turn out well. That impulse or reactive decision can be similar to buying a car, or clothes to impress someone other than yourself. If only you had put in a little more effort to vet, using a few additional checks and scrutiny, you might find something that truly benefits you, and others will begin to acknowledge your ability to make sound decisions, which then builds on your public reputation. Other impulsive decisions many make include moving into a place to live that they really can't afford or that looks good from the outside. Or traveling somewhere your friends, family member, or coworker bragged about and you paid for the trip on credit before you could actually afford the trip. That's all your impulse, not based on information you've gathered and assessed to determine what will be the best value for you. For those that are initially not afraid to ask for advice from their elders or from someone having more experience than you, the feedback received will at times, be something you really don't want to hear, and so you might avoid returning for additional advice. However, those with wisdom are often the ones who can communicate a warning, especially when it comes to making impulsive decisions, and I concur.

Warning: Falling Rocks Ahead

One of the most challenging hurdles many might experience when reading this guide, is the need to *be honest with yourself.* This alert will be critical for you throughout this guide. In order to figure out the best *"work-for-success"* opportunity, profession, or career for you, you must be honest with yourself. In the quietness of reading the scenarios, suggestions and observations in this guide, you really don't have to tell anyone, what you're thinking or what you discover to be your true self. But you must accept the reality of what you like, and don't like, your tendencies, and your behavior propensities, which, *as a whole, make you who you really are.* I urge you to be you, and be proud of who you are. Through your self-awareness, you will begin to easily know the most conducive and beneficial *"work-for-success"* opportunities that align, or don't align to who you are.

Remembering over time as you have more experiences throughout your life, more definition of your character will emerge. You will realize some things about yourself as you interact with people and engage in situations that result in decisions, and also forge how you feel about things. Some people say that they changed after the birth of a child, the loss of someone special, or any traumatic event. Maybe someone you least expected, saved your hide. But rest assured, many people change over time, with an increase of experiences, or with misfortunes. Wisdom arrives early, in small bits and pieces. But we often ignore them or don't acknowledge each separate block, until years later.

The *second and even more challenging* hurdle of being honest to yourself, is centered on a common premise that is assumed, but rarely vocalized or openly discussed. The assumption is that most people *are willing to pay other people money, if they can help them in some way*, physically or psychologically. The "help" part is very important to remember. If I need something done to help me achieve a goal, I will communicate my need, and then seek out someone I believe can best achieve what I want. So, at that time, it's my need that creates the value. "*Work-for-success*" opportunities can be revealed by understanding *what is the need that someone wants resolved*. Is sounds simple enough, and yet so many focus their plans to obtain what they need personally, regardless of the need of the payer. Behold, when there is mutuality, there can be mutual rewards, fulfillment, and success. This is why you need to be honest about knowing who you really are. Then seek out payers whose goals are focused on fulfilling needs, mutually aligned to who you really are. Knowing this concept early may help you avoid some painful "*work-to-success*" choices.

Can you impress me enough that I begin to visualize you being able to help me achieve my goal, or fulfill my needs enough that I pay you? And if after hiring you, and I begin to feel that you are not helping me, obviously I will seek ways for separation and stop paying you. This is where you might see some creativity from the payer seeking separation.

Ideally it would be great if during the early months after starting a new opportunity, in addition to you actually helping me fulfill my goals, you also show me additional value. But keep in mind that you need to achieve my original goals before providing what you think is additional value for me. *Remember, people will pay you for helping them. If you can't help them*, it's extremely probable that you will experience turmoil, not have perceived value to others or be able to build a respectable, legally acceptable career.

Your challenge will be to figure out how you can *provide value by helping someone* and you get paid based on the perceived value of the help you provide. Keep in mind that you can influence your perceived value in many ways, that are outside the scope of this guide.

This guide will be focused on helping you develop your own approach that will ultimately help you identify legally accepted careers.

Chapter 1: Introduction

Greetings, everyone. I hope you are well and have started your journey toward working on creating an environment where you will be able to live in some semblance of enjoyment and happiness.

I've written this book to give back, with the hope that it can facilitate some long-lasting blessings for you, your family and your friends.

I invite you to read with an expectation that you will need to mentally process, apply your own reasoning, and not blindly accept everything I've written without challenge; but instead, be consistently aware of the need to filter according to your unique situation, and consider any contemporary issues, practices or policies of the day, along with any experiences that might be an influence on you. You will need to ponder, debate, and challenge what I present to you with the hope that you will discover some value from the message and adjust as needed so that it can best apply for you. In this case, selective cherry-picking is in order.

I hope you will be able to take on a mindset where you can visualize us having a casual conversation where I'm sitting at a table across from you, with a glass of Cabernet Sauvignon, and we are about to talk about a whole variety of career-related stuff. In this conversation, I'll share with you some of my actual experiences, some of which where I was the participant, while others I was fortunate to have observed events, like a fly on the wall. More importantly, I'm interested in what is your perspective and point of view. What are you concerned with or thinking about? What challenges or questions you might be trying to figure out. And so, in my writings, hopefully you will notice that I'm trying to answer some questions which I think you might have. And that empathetic perspective is the result of me having similar questions at some point while moving along my own career path.

But let's be real: I'm not God, and would never profess to be. But I believe the Spirit is in me, and so, I'm confident that I will be able to answer some of your questions, but not all. But I can tell you, as I write, I'm thinking about the curiosity I had when I first began on my path (a path I'm still on at the time of this writing) and the curiosity I still have. And so, I'm thinking empathetically, and will be sharing with you my consciousness that allowed me to navigate boldly along my path with the confidence instilled from my parents, faith from my beliefs, and conviction resulting from having goals and plans I had thought out and believed in. My faith and curiosity helped me discover priceless gems of knowledge and uncover various obstructive strategies planted upon an ever-changing game board where I plotted my career path. I hope you noticed the game board analogy because it's game time; it's on, and you are in it. I truly believe by having a mental visualization of your career planning and strategies as being a FUN game, may, be just the mindset that will enhance your strategic thinking. Make it fun, not work.

Earlier I mentioned that I wrote this book to give-back with the hope that it can facilitate some long-lasting blessings for you, your family and your friends. My belief is by sharing good things from my heart, they will in turn bring forth good things for you. My expectation is there will be something that hits home and you will then be a wiser individual to manifest additional good things, which I hope one day, you too will give back.

I hope you can put on the lens that you will gain some wisdom by seeing, through reading about some of my mistakes, or from becoming aware of information I will share which comes from the book of *"If Only I Knew Then, What I Know Now."*

So, I'm going to share with you many experiences so you will know in advance, well before you actually encounter the issue. In doing so, you can have the benefit of pre-planning multiple chess match moves or basketball drives to the hoop, and have the capacity to develop your own proposed solutions to something yet to come. And in the event the situation gets real, you can then finalize a valid solution based on the exact details of the challenge you are facing.

As mentioned, this book includes a combination of actual experiences, lessons I learned as a result of roadblocks I encountered and had to figure ways to overcome the impediment in my way, and I've also included some experiences I observed or witnessed from a third-party perspective, like that proverbial fly on the wall, or like a ghost floating above the fray just observing without being noticed.

For me, the third-party observations helped me to realize, and have validation that some experiences were not unique to me, but others were actually going through similar experiences. But often the missed "teaching moment" is that so many choose not to discuss or expose their embarrassing moments, except to their close friends and trusted confidants. Well, in this book, I will share with you some of those experiences, some of which will stir up the emotions of some, because of me exposing some areas that some may want to remain untold. For comfort, I've decided not to identify parties that may or may not have been involved. I will neither confirm or deny, since in some cases you may think I am talking about you; but how could that be?

I decided to bring to light both the positive and negative scenarios. They will be available for you to think about and possibly use to obtain your own validations by retaining what I've pointed out, and then thinking if it is similar to what you are tussling with, or has been on your mind.

Also along the way I will offer a few, no actually a lot of recommendations for you to consider. Keep in mind that I'm sitting across the table from you, not as a sibling or parent, but as a concerned friend who has no value in judging you, but can only offer humble recommendations based on the little bit of information you've shared with me over a glass of wine. (Right?) I really don't know what's your favorite drink, strong, social, or cordial, so I need to stay mindful of not really knowing you that well, and not having a lifetime of interactions I can refer back to and say, "You know, I've seen you do that before." None of that has been shared so please realize that this is a purely objective discussion where I can only rely on my own experiences, influences, values, principles, and beliefs. All of which I'm comfortable having a respectful conversation and open to acknowledging that we might and probably will disagree on some points, the same as what actually happens with my close friends and family, who have their own perspectives. And believe me; I already know that I will hear from them all. So why should you be any different? Let's agree to disagree; but where we agree, let's work together.

I encourage you to challenge what I recommend, to ask yourself if my recommendation makes sense to you, or if there is a better path that fits your unique goals or situation. Either way should make you stronger, which is one of my goals. And if you can derive a better way, then you will be empowered with wisdom, without having to wait for the actual experience to smack you in the head, but be in the driver's seat. Being able to perceive the situation before it can impact you. And, if one day you find, "Wow, I've seen this before," or "I know this picture, and I know what I'm going to do here," then once again, the blessing is revealed, this time through you, and just for you. If and when that happens, and I believe it will, then you will have validation of the blessing upon you. If not, oops, sorry; I tried. But I would however suggest you hold on to this book, since the blessing may not be realized until the perfect time for you to use it. Sometimes it goes like that. But strong faith is what gets you there.

So, let's get started. I'd like to start with a visualization to get your mind stimulated on what at times, I would like for you to be able to see my situation as though it was yours, or as though you were the third-party, watching and thinking. I hope you will refer back to this and recall this first telepathic teleportation. Also, now would be my first recommendation to take a sip of whatever you have on the table in front of you. Here we goooo-oh!

Empathetic "Wake-Up" Scenario:

Imagine you are lying in bed, your head sunk deep into the comfort of your soft pillow when suddenly you begin to hear a ringing in your ear. You are slowly awakened by the sound of the wake-up alarm on your cell phone which you placed next to your bed, as one of the last tasks you completed yesterday, before jumping in bed. But now, once again, it's time to get up; it's the start of a new day. Slowly as your brain begins to get up to speed, those first thoughts begin to tumble and then slowly come into focus, more and more, beginning to get clearer in your mind. You begin to think about all the tasks you need to complete today. And if you are like some, included in those first thoughts are a glimmer of feelings around remorse and sadness. Maybe you're even pissed off that you have to get up. And almost simultaneously while stretching out your arms and yawning, that little voice in your head says, *I sure don't feel like going back to work today*, or it may say, *I sure don't feel like going back to school today*, or *I wish I had taken school more seriously when I was young so I wouldn't have to struggle so much now*. And for some, the realization of not having a sufficient income to do what you want, when you want, is now starting to piss you off.

But then there's a moment where you snap out from slumber and the cold taste of reality hits you square in the face. You command yourself, *well, let's get moving*. So, you pull yourself up and slowly drag yourself out of bed to start your daily morning routines: The 'good morning' to family routine, the wash-up routine, the breakfast for family routine, the communication of actions you'll need others to complete routine, the get dressed routine, the check your phone and email routine, the attend to the pet routine, maybe an exercise routine, and there may be a few more. All these routines are focused on preparing to get back on your path towards making that money, going to a dead-end job, or going to school, to work on building skills for your career, or what about, going to a fun job that you planned to be in.

Wouldn't it be great if you could eliminate those *remorse thoughts* and replace them with, "Oh it's on, I can't wait to get started on where I left off," type of thoughts? I'll ask you one more time. Wouldn't it be great if you could eliminate those *remorse thoughts* and replace them with, I can't wait to get started thoughts? This is the start of another day, another day with maybe only a small bit of remorse and sadness. Okay, now it's time to snap out of it. </*End Program*/>

Let's get some downloading and self-analysis going.

If you felt that any of that *Empathetic "Wake-Up" Scenario* included something about you, then this book will be some fun for you. For the rest, since you wake up having glee, joy, happiness, birds singing and can't wait to get out and make stuff happen, this book contains a different set of perspectives for you, as well as a number of mental provocations focused on stimulating your innovation genes, psychological growth and moving toward achieving and strengthening your self-actualization. Ultimately, I hope that all of you reading this book can also reach a point where you, too, wake up having glee, joy, happiness, and hearing birds singing. Being able to get out of bed and being able to smile. Looking forward to getting up and out, ready to make stuff happen. Keep in mind that to achieve this presents different challenges for different individuals, but part of your journey includes building a viable career plan and knowing that you are on it, strong.

I think it's fantastic and outstanding that all of you are pro-actively taking steps to build a successful career. And you should know, the "wake-up" scenario was a bit of a self-analysis exercise to get you a bit further. Part of the "wake-up" scenario was to help you practice visualization, and the other was to help you bring to the surface some idea as to how satisfied you might be at this point. If you wake-up with a sense of glee or a sense of remorse, you will find that book presents different interpretations and value propositions woven into this book, depending on if you wake-up satisfied, or seeking satisfaction. You'll know. And so, I challenge you to not give up. There may be some cross-over, because of your unique mix of motivational needs.

But take note: if you are a procrastinator, and I know plenty of them, even if you may not want to admit to yourself that you are, your thoughts have already told you there's no point in going any further, or you really don't have time right now. So, you might be thinking that you should just put this book in a corner of your room and walk away from it. Or better yet, why not donate it to someone who might, unlike you, truly could use it. Because you believe that you personally, really don't need it. You are happy and there's nothing any book can do for you. I added this message in the introduction section specifically just for you so that you won't waste your time. You probably have better things to do. And I wish you well, for this book is written for the ones who *want* to transform into stronger individuals.

But for those of you who found there was something in that empathetic "wake-up" scenario teleportation that made you think, *Hmm, I've felt something similar to that before*, what you are about to experience from this point forward, is a whole download of blessings. I'm not sure which ones are for you, but I believe and have confidence you will get some. It's time to get yours.

At the time of me writing this book, I am three decades along my diverse career path and still out there moving along my path, having fun, using what I've learned and it feels good. I now wake up hungry to achieve, which was not always the case. Now I'm navigating a path that I actually thought about and made strategic adjustments, but also recognize that there's opportunities which I'm looking forward to discovering. Along the way I've also encountered a number of surprises, fun and some things that were not so much fun.

But if you were to ask what's the secret to my success, I'll have to tell you, after taking another sip of wine, even though this may turn off some of you, but this is really me, and you have the ability to disregard this. But I credit the primary secret to success is the result of having favor from God, being blessed, having a diverse set of skills, being comfortable with change, and having a personal mantra that boldly proclaims:

1. No matter what you do, you can't stop me! (as of date, for those who are thinking about it, I'm already there).
2. Its over only when God says it's over.
3. I define what is success for me, not based on what others define is success.

So, if you see success as being some specific set of acquisitions, and if that's not how I define success, well then. What if my success is defined by being able to grow the tastiest heirloom tomatoes and most beautiful orchids, while yours is being on the cover of a major magazine, having the most expensive car in the world and owning a one-of-a-kind piece of art? Think about that for a second. I'm going to revisit how you define success, later in the book.

I alluded to earlier that one focus of this book is to spotlight some workplace practices that, for some reason, people are embarrassed to discuss, or believe should not be discussed. I happen to acknowledge and accept that each generation, has different ways of doing things as well as different sets of values and etiquette. This seems to happen every generation, so we can all learn from it and be entertained by the uniqueness and creativity of each generation. I'd like to personally thank the "Daisy Dukes" generation as well as the coolness fashion styles coming out of the forties generation. There's no sense in trying to curtail or belittle the differences which pop up from each generation, that ultimately contribute to defining who they are and how they will leave their mark on the on-going history, of the humans of planet earth. I already mentioned I will be providing recommendations, but I also want you to be vigilant for any opportunities unveiled, for I will not be able to call out, what they might be for you, so I suggest you should feel free to mark up this book with your own notes.

Along my career path, I encountered all types of games, antagonists, demons, brain-deads who didn't realize they were already dead, and angels who whispered in my ear, "Hey, stop. Don't go that way; go this way," or do this instead of what I was initially planning. Along my path I became aware that this is *my path, and my purpose*. At no point do I believe that all of my decisions will apply for you. My decisions were the result of the situation I was in at that time. But because blessings are blessings, I don't believe they will become un-blessed. So, although I am going to share with you some of my successful game board moves and failures, some of you may believe you are not blessed or not even believe in God for that matter. This is not a problem for me. But this is where you *can* receive blessings through becoming more aware. I'm not one who is going to say you must believe, in what I believe, in order to achieve (hey, that rhymes). A blessing is just that, and could possibly have various levels of impact; but I don't control that part, so I will not worry about it. I just let it flow out from me. What happens after that, well now.

What I'm making available to you is the *knowledge* of some recurring moves and tactics still being played in the work environment today. They are the ones that throw so many off track, so why would anyone change them since they work? As I share them with you, they will become yours to customize or have as tools should you encounter similar tactics being played on or around you, while you are moving along your own path. You will become aware of some missteps and pitfalls. You will be empowered to plan safer steps, strategies, and counter measures. For as you move on your career path, you will be on a game board. That's a visualization. You are on a game board, whether you want to play or not. Go on then; don't play. But you'll get played. No matter how you look at it, the game will be played whether you play, make moves, or allow the ball to keep hitting you square in the face before you learn to move, prepare how to evade, dodge, weave and proceed forward on the game board. While it is totally your choice, please don't let the ball keep hitting you in the face. You could get very dizzy and dis-orientated.

All jokes aside, this is where many choose to self-medicate in order to manage their emotional or physical pain. That ball can make you dizzy and you might eventually choose to get some pain relief. The challenges of the work environment are real and can make you drink, or self-medicate. You want to avoid this at all costs. But this is where some are dropped to a lower game board level, having higher walls and many more roadblocks to overcome before you can possibly get back on track, and résumé on the previous level from where you fell. One actual high-walled game board is referred to as jail. In this case, jail is not a code word or metaphor.

One of my driving forces is visualizing exactly what winning teams and players experience during the course of a game. There will be rules and cheaters who ignore or seek to circumvent the rules. There will be joy and let downs. There will be obstacles, set-backs and bonuses awarded while new clues are unveiled after achieving certain levels or points.

I believe most of us have watched some type of sports events. If not, I recommend you find one that you can build interest in. Anyway, there comes a time in tight games when a referee may become reluctant to issue a penalty when the other team or opponent breaks a rule. Maybe they become fearful of being involved with making a decision that influences the results, like having a finger on the scale, and oh so slightly, assisting a team with loosing. So, the referees begin to look the other way when there is an obvious foul, kind of like allowing the game to be played without any of the minor rules being called. For example, a basketball player is going for a basket and is hacked, fouled, or tripped right in front of the referee. And there's no call. At that point, there is an emotional explosion from the team and fans. But what does a good coach do? He/she protests the missed call but more importantly, rounds up the team to keep them *focused* on the rest of the game, and *focused* on recovering and keeping their heads together so they can continue to run their strategies successfully. If their anger remains to be more influential than the strategies they practiced all week, there is a higher probability they might lose the game. This scenario actually happens in the workplace. A foul, a no-call or ignoring by managers, an emotional response, and a need to stay focused toward your goals. You need to have S.M.A.R.T. goals.

Recommendation: Please run a search on the meaning of S.M.A.R.T. goals.

It's extremely important when you get on the game board and begin to make moves along your career path, you must try to manage (not suppress or eliminate) your emotions, stay on your game, carry out your strategies, put bandages on your wounds, and get back in the game. No matter what they do, remember, no one can stop you!

This is your first blessing. Think about it. Take some time to think about the game. You'll need conviction to win. You'll need skills to maneuver. You'll need to believe in your strategy. You'll need to obtain bonuses and new clues so you can keep developing successful strategies and making adjustments. Keep in mind, it's always hard to stop someone when they don't know what's your next move.

Behold, that was blessing number two. You are the owner of your strategies. There is nothing wrong with listening to advice or recommendations, but ultimately any decisions are your intellectual property. You will be accountable to complete, manage or delegate.

These are my initial gifts to you. A few foundational gifts for you to add into your thoughts and think about as principles to help you to stay focused. Please keep in your mind to set a goal to diminish any thoughts of remorse (wake-up scenario) while increasing the levels of positive outcomes, possibilities and hope. I truly believe hope dies last. Everyone has a unique path, and we all travel along *diverse career paths* leading toward reaching any number of goals that we, as individuals determine. Making that money, leading toward your own self-determined and defined state of satisfaction. Pause and ponder. Get a bowl of snacks, have a cool drink, and let's get started.

Chapter 2:
Needs and Character Types

Character types are one of the key psychological concepts you'll need to keep in mind from this point forward. Specifically, you will begin to identify what are your own character types which as a whole, make you unique. Everyone has a combination of types that collectively forms how people perceive you, and how you perceive yourself.

Honesty plays a critical part for both perceptions. For instance, if someone does not like you, is a bully, or is jealous of you, you probably shouldn't put too much value on statements they make about you since you can't rely on their statements being objective, and there's a chance their statements might be false. They are not someone to rely on for anything unless you seek failure and disappointment. You should not place much value in their statements, opinions, or advice. On the other hand, those you can trust can often be helpful with helping you realize a part of your character that you may not be aware exists.

Early during a point when I was trying to build stability in my own career, I realized that often some of *my peers* seemed to wait for me to give direction, take charge, or make recommendations on a course of action before they would start working toward completing our project tasks. After some frustration with them repeatedly waiting on me for direction, I confided in a friend to get his opinion as to why these grown adults can't seem to proactively work towards completing our project tasks until I gave some direction, even though I perceived all of us having similar roles. The reply I received that day was a turning point for me. He told me, some of us see you as someone that we trust will be more thorough than the rest of us when it comes to planning, and as such we unknowingly, perceive you as a leader, who can provide insight, regardless of whether you see yourself in a leader-type role. It was my friend's trusted objective counsel which helped me to realized that I naturally lead by urging teamwork and collaboration, and that I try to be considerate of the input from those I collaborate with. Up to that point I had very limited understanding about the various character types of leaders. With a little research, I discovered that leaders can be autocratic, authoritative, democratic, dictatorial, consultative, coach types, manage by walking around, persuasive, chaotic, laissez-faire, or paternalistic. Each of these management styles are distinctly different and have strong and weak elements, but align to specific individual character types. I gained an important lesson that day, just because I asked for an *opinion* from *someone I trusted*. His response turned out to be objective and profound.

Your Needs

When I first entered high school I really needed to find someone who could answer a number of questions. I needed someone to just tell me in plain English, what actions I needed to take which could help me figure out what would be a suitable career for me, what I needed to do to prepare for that career, and what high school courses I should concentrate on to help me get there. What I got were counselors who gave me general direction, but didn't really take into account my own, individual personality character traits. Asking me what I would like to do as a career at a time in my life when my collective experiences were that of a teenager, really was not a productive approach for figuring out what might be a suitable career path to take. As adults, we have to keep in mind that no matter what age you are, no one can ask questions about something they are not aware exists. This really calls attention to the need for much more extensive career counseling for students in middle through high school. And if a school system is facing budget cuts, students are left trying to gain awareness without really knowing what might be available to them, or what exists. So, I was pointed toward the curriculum for college-bound students, not really knowing what would be a direction for a specific college degree, especially when I liked science, math, and concert band. What degree would that be? What profession would that be? And, what career would that be?

As I got closer to my graduation day, I began thinking more about what should be my college major. Should I make my selection easy and just go for what my parents did, or my brother, or maybe like some of my friends? How about just go for the careers known to pay respectable incomes? That meant doctor, lawyer or engineer. For many this is that moment when either you have chosen a profession, or you go for anything you like at that point in time. And, for many people their career plan only included one step after high school graduation. That one step was either going to college to major in one field of study, going into the armed services, or going right to work. And if the choice was to go on to college, there was probably no other strategy other than relying on the preset course of study presented by the college of choice.

While in high school, students just want some guidance from someone they can trust to help them gain better understanding of what they would like to do as a career and what they might enjoy doing that aligns with their personalities and targeted lifestyle. For me, I just picked two areas that I enjoyed: music and technology. As you might imagine there were a lot or options to choose from in the technology and music categories. So, I did a bit of both, and my self-designed diverse career path training was on.

During that course study, I began thinking about the next steps, in my career plans, and so I decided to volunteer at the campus radio station on the broadcast engineering team, where my concert band experiences helped me realize I was a good music recording engineer. I also decided it might help to have a Master's Degree, to reinforce my options, and so the plan continued to evolve. After the Master's degree and finding a job, which was not really what I had expected, I began night school to add a marketing diploma. Later I added a degree in Information Technology.

Needless to say, my career strategy was being developed on the fly, as I fought to obtain a more respectable income. Over time and with much research, I began to evolve into a "Creative Technologist," a producer, and consultant, being able to fulfill the needs for purely creative projects, purely technology projects, or a combination of both. Oh, how I needed someone who could describe an example of a big picture career plan. Oh, did I need this guide then!

Where is the Path?

So many people are discovering at the very point when they need to make those important cross roads decisions, the much-needed guidance is elusive. And although you may receive suggestions from various sources, those directions need to account for your specific personality traits and goals, so you as an individual can begin to *develop a forward thinking thought process* which you can use to begin mapping out your own journey. You should also take into account that your journey will probably require regular adjustments and customizations, possibly over a good portion of your career. So, there is a strong probability that *your journey will evolve* as your needs, beliefs and personality evolve. But at least, once you gain better understanding about who you are, what you want to become, and the lifestyle you seek, you will become better at drafting plans that meet your specific needs, goals, personality and character traits.

I remember when I was a teen, I really didn't have clear thoughts on what profession I would like to do for a living, but I did however have some clear thoughts on things I enjoyed, and things I just really did not enjoy. I recognized that I was beginning to understand my style and my character. Some basic character traits. Without question the types of women I was attracted to definitely became clearer during my college days. Also, without question I now could reflect and recognize the thoughts I had at an early stage would drive a number of my future actions. For example, I loved creative activities and later became employed by businesses requiring creative resources. I loved music and later worked as a producer and recording engineer. I had interests in gadgets, science, sci-fi and later worked as a technology manager. I loved traveling and sports. Today I travel often and stay actively involved with working out and attending sports events.

So, the likes and dislikes one has at an early age should be earnestly explored and taken seriously, as character traits.

Who Are You Really?

As you now might imagine, in order to determine a profession or a few careers that best suit you as a unique individual, you will need to think about who you really are as a person. Therein lies the challenge; the same challenge I had in high school. Until you begin to truthfully answer some questions about yourself, become willing to self-analyze, and be truthful with acknowledging your good and bad traits, likes and dislikes, preferences, strengths and weaknesses, the path ahead and decisions you make can be unclear or misdirected. You will have difficulty determining what might be a good profession, career path and suitable roles. For those in high school, it probably would help if you can recruit your parents, relatives, or a high school counselor to help guide you through this discussion.

For example, if you are a selfish person, but choose not to admit it to yourself, you will probably have difficulty working in roles focused on dispersing benefits, philanthropic roles or roles helping underserved communities. If you don't have patience, going into a profession or *"work-for-success"* opportunity where you will be working with children or the elderly could be frustrating for you. If you don't like to be around people, having a customer service role will probably leave you uncomfortable every day. But if you find you really enjoy helping people you probably will excel in medical, educational or problem-solving professions where you focus on helping people. I recall a couple of situations where I needed to speak to customer service associates and afterwards, wondered if they were just having a bad day or if not, what they were doing in that specific job.

Have you ever had an experience when you spoke to someone in customer service and that person did nothing to help you solve your problem? Or maybe they just sent you to another customer service person, later to find out you had to go back to the first person, where you started? And then you wondered, why are they in the customer service department. Well their predicament could also be the result of their manager not understanding the character traits and capabilities of their resources, the regular customer service person being off that day, or the only resource available was assigned temporarily to customer service even though they were not suitable for customer service. Hopefully you get the point why it's so important to be honest with yourself, even if not admitting publicly to others. You absolutely need to be honest with yourself when conducting career planning and targeting a specific profession, or you could face finding that you are in a dead-end job, doing something you don't enjoy doing. And what a waste, if after you dedicated time and money toward acquiring specific skills.

Traits

So, let's get started with a few basic questions to help you begin to paint your own picture, create your selfie, and begin to render the evolving snapshot of you. As you build, you will also begin to uncover just what makes you make the decisions you make, and why you choose the people you hang out with.

For this I would suggest you save, date and keep secure (private) your responses to the questions below since I can almost guarantee some of your responses will change over time. As a result, I also suggest that you try to keep track of what you believe was the cause of each change.

For example, I found that I get bored with a task when I have to do the same thing all the time. As a result, I enjoy being able to set my own hours, work from home when I want and have varied assignments. I really enjoy having varying assignments and challenges.

Remember, the purpose of answering these questions is to assist you with self-awareness and identifying your true self. So, it will only hurt you if you are not honest with yourself, and that could create problems for you and building a viable career strategy, unless you choose a profession or *"work-for-success"* opportunity where integrity is not needed.

Also, please keep in mind that the below questions should be only used to *facilitate your own individual self-analysis.* The statements following the questions should not be viewed as actually pertaining to you specifically, but as *generalizations* just to make you wonder. The statements may be far from your sense of purpose or potential. In reality, your answers, which I have no idea what they might be, should be considered just like the outer skin of an onion: having many more layers to peel back to understand who you really are and all of the unique qualities, characteristics and values which in combination, make you who you are. We all have strong and not so strong traits. But in being aware of them, you can then have some awareness of the types of *"work-for-success"* opportunities that would be more enjoyable and fulfilling than others. In reading the questions, try to visualize an actual experience you had.

You should also be aware that there are actually formal, more extensive personality tests available through various organizations. I actually signed up for a couple of sessions which were offered as an alumni career service benefit where the tests focused on career assessment and determining my personality traits. Tests are available which focus on helping you determine your strengths and weaknesses, what motivates you, your current and future areas of interests and also list various careers that seem to align to your test results. The tests are designed to help you get a better look at how you think, judge, your like/dislike preferences, what types of people you should be more compatible to work with and how you would tend to react to various scenarios. In going through the questions below, also try to consider other related character traits that you believe might apply to you personally.

1. Do you like crowds? Generalization: You may like working on a team.
2. Do you prefer being in smaller groups? Generalization: You may like working alone.

3. If you have been asked to complete a big job would you rather recruit friends to help you, or would you rather just do it yourself and make sure it gets done, based on what you believe is correct? Generalization: You might desire to utilize all available resources and subject matter experts, or tend to be a perfectionist or micro-manager. Micro-managers are not easy to work with.
4. Do you seek opportunities to have fun or some form of entertainment away from home every week? Generalization: You may desire a healthy balance between work, and fun. You might also believe it is important to consider the health of those you work with.
5. Do you seek to impress others? Generalization: You may be driven by obtaining rewards or maybe desire a special title that sets you apart from the rest.
6. Are you more concerned with being verbally acknowledged or monetarily rewarded? Generalization: If more concerned with being verbally acknowledged, you may be fulfilled by how your image looks to others or the level of your prestige, regardless of monetary rewards.
7. Do you desire to travel? Generalization: You may enjoy working outside of an office setting or having the opportunity to work at different office locations. Some organizations have 'hotel' work areas for employees to temporarily work at different locations.
8. Would you consider yourself a curious person, wanting to understand about things you don't already know about? Generalization: You may enjoy investigations or figuring out how to manage crisis situations. You may be more engaged working for international and multicultural organizations.

9. Are you comfortable going places you know nothing about or may present a sense of danger? Generalization: You may like covert or investigative work. Maybe work that requires international communication skills.
10. Do you seek adventure? Generalization: You may enjoy work that involves exploring, astronomy, oceanography or archeology.
11. Are you a lush, excessive, or moderate when doing things? Maybe you continue to eat well after you are full, drink well after you are buzzed, or have a strong desire to self-medicate? Generalization: You may be a workaholic or excessive at work.
12. Are you quick to reach a conclusion? Generalization: You may not be perceived as being thorough.
13. Do you consider multiple possibilities before reaching a conclusion? Generalization: You may like research or discovery areas related to the sciences, scientific method and explorations where multiple scenarios need to be analytically ruled out.
14. Do you like to work on a task until others are satisfied or until you are satisfied? Generalization: In both cases you probably take your work seriously, but one sway more toward ensuring customer satisfaction over your personal satisfaction, which could be beyond the approved project budget.
15. Do you volunteer to help get something done, or wait until you are asked or invited to help? Generalization: Either you are proactive, self-managed or not. You could also be adhering to cultural practices even when the client doesn't require them to be in place.

16. Would you prefer to give directions to a team or are you more comfortable relying on trusted individuals to provide you direction? Generalization: You may tend to be a leader or an individual contributor who carries out the directions provided.
17. Do others acknowledge you as a leader? Generalization: Your actions may result in others trusting in your suggestions or decisions.
18. Do you usually come up with suggestions for solving a problem, where to go, or how to get something done? Generalization: You may tend to be a leader or not so much. These could be signs of leadership tendencies within you.
19. Do you rely on others to make suggestions on what you should do to get a problem resolved? Generalization: You could be a go-getter and like seeing tasks resolved.
20. Do you feel comfortable answering truthfully even when the answer may make you look bad? Generalization: This possibly speaks to your level of integrity and your value system for whether the gravity of the situation warrants telling the truth which results in hurting someone's feelings, or avoiding the truth to protect their feelings.
21. Are you someone who relies on people to get the job done? Generalization: You could be a user, lazy, like taking the path that obtains the most benefits for you at all costs, or maybe you have a sense of entitlement.
22. Are you someone people call when they are in trouble, need help or need advice? Generalization: You may be considered a reliable person.
23. Do you manage and save your money well or spend it soon after you get it? Generalization: Either you plan for the future, live for the moment or need some serious money

management training. You may be focused on long-term growth or short-term gains.

24. Do you try to keep current with trends and new ideas or tend to avoid change? Generalization: Either you like or dislike change. You also may like to have a trending self-image and just look good.
25. Are you someone who shares the benefits you have? Generalization: You could be a considerate individual.
26. Is personal hygiene important to you? Generalization: This potentially speaks to your self-esteem and/or how considerate you are of others around you. This could also be a result of your cultural practices.
27. Are you considerate of others or is that not your concern? Generalization: Either you think of how a customer would feel, or you don't. You may or may not be customer-centric.
28. Do you tend to stand up for others who can't defend themselves? Do you get angry when you see injustices or someone being treated unfairly? Generalization: You may enjoy being a lawyer or community organizer and feel good when you win a case that results in actually helping someone.
29. Do you seem to stay upset when you lose, or things don't go your way? Generalization: You may be unhappy in sales or roles where your success depends on your ability to persuade, since it doesn't always go your way.
30. Do you like helping others? Generalization: You may enjoy being a lawyer, firefighter, police officer or community organizer.
31. Do you enjoy the companionship of having a pet? Generalization: You may have a nurturing nature and enjoy roles in which you help others.

32. Do you like games? Generalization: You may like entertainment or need to draw on the need to develop higher skills over time.
33. Do you enjoy being challenged to overcome mental or physical hurdles? Generalization: You may like problem solving. There are many opportunities for problem solvers in many different areas of concentration. You'll need to dive deeper into what floats your boat.
34. If you enjoy sports, which do you enjoy more. Team sports or sports focused on individual performance? Generalization: This could translate into the work environment you would prefer.
35. Do some people call you "bossy?" Generalization: You may enjoy leadership roles, but could also desire to be in control. This is good as long as it is not excessive with little concern for others.
36. Do you have a strong desire to own expensive things? Generalization: Personal aspirations, peer pressure or psychological needs could be driving this desire.
37. Do you like making things from scratch? Generalization: You may be a creative thinker who enjoys design, building, and specialties.

With any personality assessment, you should always *keep in mind* that the results can only *generalize*, not conclude, what options could best work for you, based on your truthful responses to the questions. There will be many options, so you'll need to keep track of and periodically monitor *how you feel* given the scenario, the "*work-for-success*" opportunity or profession you are actually in. This presents a strong defense for engaging in one or more *volunteer and internship* opportunities as early as possible, so you can assess how you feel, before making the decision to commit to one career path or another.

The Jack of All Trades

I once heard the phrase, "jack of all trades, master of none." But what I've discovered is that the opportunity to enjoy more than one career during one's lifetime is 100 percent possible *when you think long-term and do the math.* During the course of moving along a career path, we start out curious as a child, go through entry-level, mid-level, and senior level and then in retirement years we continue to seek to be useful and hopefully keep our minds entertained. In each of these stages we have opportunities to do something different.

By today's standards someone with *ten years of experience* is considered as having *senior-level* experience. So, by age forty, you could potentially have developed a senior-level of experience *in at least two different areas of focus* if you began your first career at age twenty and second at age thirty. You could be a chess master and sous chef in twenty years. How about an interior designer and architect? Maybe an app developer, game developer and yoga instructor. Learning a second language or developing an artistic ability at a young age while learning science could easily result in having two senior-level and marketable skill-sets by age thirty. You could also learn a new language while you are in the midst of your career. Basically, there is nothing stopping you from planning for an exciting career path just like making early plans for a journey to distant lands. You only need to start by being honest with yourself, and keeping track of the things that you really like and dislike. Keeping track of your emerging personalities and how you interact or don't interact with people. Simultaneously, in years twenty to thirty, continue to proactively investigate the careers aligned to what you like and aligned to the values that are aligned with those careers. Today we are seeing an emerging trend of individuals who retire earlier than those in past trends, beginning a new career focused on something they always wanted to do, but maybe it didn't pay a salary needed when they were younger.

Just remember; at any time, you can use the internet to initiate your search for details like training and skills needed, and to find out how strong is the demand for the career you choose to pursue. For innovators, you may need to figure out ways to market unique ideas to the people who have not yet realized they need something. Innovative endeavors will probably include research and development (R&D), identifying target markets, developing disruptive delivery solutions, introducing the new product or service, and marketing and advertising in which the art of persuasion is needed.

Always Be Your Own Coach

I once heard former Vice-President Joe Biden state during a 2016 speech, "We own the finish line." When it comes to building your career, God knows the finish line, but you and only you own the finish line, for being you. Don't allow anyone to change who you really are.

Key Problem 1:

Unless you have a financial benefactor or can draw money from a trust fund most people will need to figure out how to earn an income, or as some say in the street: how to "get paid." Your path will lead you one of two ways: some type of post-secondary (high school) school training, or minimal additional formal training.

For many who have aspirations of going to college, they may reach a decision point where they really *don't have a clear idea of what will be their major field of concentration.* As a result, they may choose to major in liberal arts with the hope of figuring out what they want during the first two years of working on a liberal arts curriculum. It's not unusual to encounter difficulties when attempting to figure out a career path strategy. And you can expect that some of those liberal arts courses may or may not prepare you for what you will be doing in the future, but they are intended to get you some type of job. But after you have researched opportunities, have an idea what they are, the steps you'll need to make and the courses you think will prepare you, the opportunity exists for you to adjust your major to something more aligned to your character traits and goals.

For others who choose not to attend college, you still need to figure out an approach for what will be a career that best matches your personality. There is really no guarantee in which path will best suit your personal needs but college may surround you with a high quantity of options for you to try in a short amount of time, and should provide you easy access to a wide variety of counselors and advisers. Unfortunately, many college students don't realize this benefit until after they graduate and begin to seek guidance to help them with a critical decision process.

Key Problem 2:

In order for someone to be able to assist you with determining a career that best matches your own unique personality, you will need to be able to communicate to that person your likes, dislikes, beliefs, strengths and weaknesses, etc. They need to understand who you really are at this point in your life. In addition, you will want to develop a process that you can continue to use over and over again, as you become more in tune with your personality.

For example, many energetic people are motivated to protest against authority figures and rules that constrict one's actions for one reason or another. Later in life as they become more in tune with their personality and character traits those same people may choose to become politicians or form socially conscious community non-profit organizations because of their love for helping others, or as a vehicle for fighting against injustices. They may also choose to become lawyers to defend others and fight for judicial change.

The Risk

The person who counsels you needs to be someone you can trust and will keep your best interests in mind. There is always the chance that some counselors may have preconceived opinions of you, make inaccurate assessments of your potential, and may not spend much time getting to know your unique personality. Some will just give out the same advice they give to others. Some have been known to steer students toward a path *well below* their potential or some could potentially take advantage of you once they learn about some of your weaknesses. Stay alert. If someone falls into any of these categories, look for someone else to assist you. You must recognize that the construction of a viable career path is serious, and you need people who are serious about helping you.

If you ever have the opportunity to receive career coaching or counseling from someone, you should keep in mind that only people who take into account your specific character, goals, beliefs, personality and needs will have any chance of helping you as an individual. This means they have to take the time to really get to know you and you need to be able to communicate your character traits. This also means that you need to keep in mind that if you let someone really know you, *they can also take advantage of you* if they are not a person of integrity. So, don't be gullible; always assess if you feel like you are moving forward and getting results. Just like instructors give out tests to assess what you've learned, you should also set realistic time boundaries for your adviser to meet goals. With your career, you must consider that you are the person who must have positive results and outcomes. You have to consider that *your career is the product* that has immense value and must be protected. Work with your adviser to set goals and a realistic amount of time to see results and achieve your set goals.

Friends

Unfortunately, we all get burned, used, hurt, or taken advantage of by someone we thought was our friend. Have you determined a set of measures to help you validate who should be considered a friend? Can you tell the difference between a friend and an acquaintance? Keeping it real, have they actually proven to you that they are someone you can trust? Are you able to determine who are friends under consideration possibly because your paths collided after a life-changing and bonding experience, or you have emotion-related reasons of your own? Remember, awarding someone the title of "BFF" or friend is not a title that you should just give out blindly. Over a lifetime most people only have a small set of best friends, while others who meet a lesser criterion may be ones you might hang out with, but not trust enough to share private details about your life. And then there are acquaintances. So stay alert for how someone treats you while you share and as they learn more details about your personality, beliefs, and needs. Having true friends who respect you, whom you can trust and rely on, and who you are there for when they need a friend can be rewarding experiences, as you move along your career path. Friends are extremely valuable, so be mindful with how you treat people and how they treat you.

For predators, this is an opportunity to take advantage of you or recruit you into a false belief by claiming they know of others who believe in the same things as you. Watch out and take time to vet individuals who you award the coveted title of "best friend."

Regarding friends, they might exhibit one or more of the traits listed below:

- Best friends are often those who have proven, over time, that they can be trusted. It's the compilation of shared scenarios or experiences that will reveal their character.
- Although at some point a friend could hurt your feelings, you should keep in mind, they usually try to avoid actions that hurt you.
- A friendship should be a two-way experience, often not balanced, but hopefully there are mutual efforts to maintain and build the friendship, respect, considerations and loyalty.
- Friendships will attempt to endure and overcome various types of challenges.
- Friends will try to protect each other from painful situations and adversities.
- Friends try to help each other.
- Friends can be known to guard each other's secrets.

Please consider the above traits to facilitate your thinking on your criteria for determining various levels of friendships. Ultimately, only you should determine the value-based measures for determining who are your friends.

Determining Your Economic Needs: What Does it Cost to Be a Relatively Satisfied You?

Throughout this book, I make a point of bringing economics to your attention from various perspectives. In one perspective you should be aware of, when your living conditions or your need for being "relatively satisfied" becomes an increasing area of focus, it can become more challenging for you to concentrate on achieving career goals. That doesn't mean you can't achieve your goals; just that it may require increased dedication, conviction, and effort. And I say "relatively satisfied" because I believe each person has their own economic state in their minds based on previous experiences, expected lifestyle and/or desires that they aspire to achieve. For example, if you grew up in a four-bedroom home with a backyard, it may be a bit depressing or a mental let down if you can only afford a one-room unit having a shared bathroom. People often have a clear vision of the lifestyle they want to have, and will try to obtain it, even if their economic status doesn't allow it. Also, in this discussion I want you to keep in mind that I can't take into account all of the unique measures for how every individual defines their success or expected happiness. Only you can determine what is the state that will allow you, as an individual, to comfortably pursue your career goals with a minimal amount of stress. That state could be a one-room unit, a two-bedroom unit, or a house with a yard, etc. Only you know what will help you to be "relatively satisfied."

To help you have a better idea as to what might be your *realistic* tolerance-to-comfort zone, I highly suggest you determine your basic 'core' economic needs. This is really simple once you can visualize your minimum comfort state. For example, I've met individuals who boldly proclaim they don't need much to live on. Well, the reality is that many people can survive on bread and water, but I guarantee there will be many who will realize that living on bread and water is not enjoyable, and in that living condition, it *can be a bit of a challenge* to *successfully* achieve your career goals. So, let's keep it real when trying to assess your *realistic* tolerance-to-comfort zone.

The focus of determining your basic 'core' economic needs is to increase your probability of successfully achieving your career goals.

Understandably, there are some who will proclaim that they plan to focus their career plans toward a humble profession, and as a result, don't find any value in considering how much money they will need to pursue their career path or profession. My response would be that staying healthy requires investment. You *need to eat fresh food* to stay healthy. You need to live somewhere you can be relatively *secure and safe from physical harm* and adverse weather. You need economics to safely travel to and from locations, potentially early or late. Without convenient transportation, you may need to account for additional travel time, which cuts into your rest, re-charge, and recovery time. Eventually, your lack of rest time could introduce physical and mental fatigue, along with stress. According to numerous physicians, stress can introduce multiple health issues. Plus, at some point, there may be others who rely on you for support. It could be an elderly parent, sibling, offspring, or significant other, all of whom can impact your economics. If you are only thinking about what you alone will need when working toward even a humble profession, I suggest you take into account during your effort to move along your career path, there might be others in the picture. Without planning you could experience some dreams deferred moments.

A Simple Plan for Determining Your Economic Needs
1. It will be helpful if you have some type of transportation that can be used throughout good and bad weather. Depending on

the climate where you live, and considering a basic, as opposed to an extravagant solution, a used, rental or inexpensive bicycle, motorcycle, scooter, public transportation, or compact car might be suitable.

- What is the monthly cost for your transportation solution?
- What, if any, is the monthly cost of insurance for your transportation solution?
- How much for transportation-related costs (car gas, tolls, or public transport fares)
- How much, if any, might be needed for licenses, maintenance and fuel costs?

2. It will be helpful if you have a secure space to live where you can have privacy, be able to come and go without interrupting others, and is quiet enough for you to comfortably work, study, and relax any time of the day or night.

- What is the monthly cost of having a secure place to live?

3. You should gather information to assist you in determining your food consumption plan focused on keeping you healthy and keeping your energy levels high. While moving along your career path there may be times you may not get adequate rest, or find that you are experiencing stressful situations. Having a plan to stay healthy can provide enough benefits that can carry you through adverse situations. Early in my career I decided that I could live on a diet centered around lunch-meat and powdered drinks. I was able to do that, but I also experienced unexpected challenges that I soon had to reverse. As I became more knowledgeable of healthy eating, I found that there were options which were relatively similar in costs when compared to my lunch meat food plan. Just as a motivator for your own quest

for information: Did you know that there are daily maintenance vitamins which contain food? Did you know that there are specific fruits and vegetables that are high in nutrients? A salad with these, along with drinking water could take you far and not cost much. A good health food store or nutritionist can help you find a beneficial path, but you need to be curious and ask.

- What is the monthly cost of your healthy food plan?

4. There will be a number of basic utility and personal support needs: cell phone, internet service, subscription streaming content bill, electric bill, gas bill, apartment insurance, etc.

    - What is the monthly cost of your basic utility and personal support?

5. When considering a long-term career plan, hopefully you will not overlook keeping physically healthy to provide you higher probabilities of overcoming physical and stress related challenges brought on by the work environment. This suggests the need to consider incorporating, along with eating well, a fit program that might include a health club membership, jogging, cycling, yoga, martial arts, walking, swimming, or any fun physically challenging activities you can do to remain physically fit, tuned up and in shape. You should also include health insurance to handle the unexpected and to keep you informed of public health concerns that may be impacting your area. Did you know that there are some chronic disease states that many people don't know about until they have some type of adverse health event? With awareness and having periodic low cost or free health screenings included as part of your fit program and long-term career plan, you can have opportunities to deploy preventative measures to battle against the onset of some disease states that can be easily detected and managed before reaching an adverse state. Unfortunately, many people are working on building

careers, not knowing they could have a manageable health issue which could impact their careers. Some of the more common disease states are high blood pressure, high cholesterol, diabetes, asthma, kidney failure, hepatitis, and HIV/AIDS.

- How much will it cost to keep yourself fit and to manage your health?

6. I found that when seriously involved in conducting a consistent and sustained effort to try and achieve one's career goals, at some point, stress and possibly fatigue can creep in if you are not mindful to include relaxation and entertainment activities. Depending on the individual, the cost for entertainment and relaxation can be minimal or excessive, depending on what makes you happy and allows you to decrease stress.

- How much do you need to spend each month on entertainment, traveling or relaxation to ensure you don't build up stress? (This cost could be combined with your fit program)

7. When thinking about longevity, and being in it to win it, you'll need to have some type of long-term investment strategy to mitigate unexpected issues, minimize large credit balances and to plan for growth. Although deploying investment strategies can take time to implement until you reach a point where you believe you have enough discretionary cash to invest, the sooner you can begin, the sooner you can enjoy benefits.

- How much can you save or invest each month?

8. I would highly suggest creating a "contingency" discretionary cash fund to have available should an unexpected expense come up. Otherwise you face the risk of having to rely on a credit card, which for many, results in needing to pay an increasing monthly bill if you keep a balance on it. Also, it can be a challenge to avoid using a credit card to help fulfill your vision

of the lifestyle you want to have before you actually can afford it. You definitely want to avoid putting yourself deeper into debt.

- How much can you set aside for quick emergencies?

Above, I've listed only a few typical items for your consideration, but I recognize that you may think of additional items to add to your list.

Your Estimated Cost to be Relatively Satisfied

Now, total up the monthly costs (questions 1-8), and multiply by twelve. This will give you a rough estimate of your costs on a monthly and annual basis (total x 12), to be *a relatively satisfied you*. An economic snapshot perspective focused on how much it will cost for you to put in place a basic, non-extravagant level of support that can facilitate your ability to strive towards achieving your career goals, with minimal stress. Again, the cost should be based on your own truthful numbers you estimated. I can personally attest that after realizing my comfort support levels and putting them in place, my ability to move along my career path and achieve goals increased. On a personal note, I remember when I first did this exercise for myself, I was quite surprised at my monthly costs. This gave me some additional motivation toward revising the steps in my career strategy.

In addition to this simple way to capture an economic snapshot of your happy state, there are other tests to take and additional questions to ask to gain a deeper understanding about yourself. But more importantly, you should now have a growing, documented list of your desired needs, likes and dislikes.

Chapter 3: What's in it For Me? What Job Options Do I Have?

I'm willing to guess that when trying to answer the question asked by a family member, teacher, or close friend, "What do you plan to be when you grow up," or "What would you like to do in life," the response has rarely been thought out. At some point, after some contemplation, many might consider what types of things they believe will make them happy, fulfilled, or wealthy. Others may have derived their response as a result of someone influential in their family who either presented a "weighted" speech, or you just accepted wanting to be like them, without really knowing what will be required or if the career will actually be a good match with your character type and goals. I'm also going to guess that whatever might be your answer, there is a strong probability that your initial choice will fall into a group of opportunities where there are already large numbers of applicants in those fields. And the numbers of those interested are still increasing, which, as a result, creates increasing competition in those areas.

Other factors that contribute to increased competition for job seekers within a region are the migration of people leaving their areas because of increased taxes causing a higher cost of living, fewer opportunities in their town, residents escaping from high crime areas, or the creation of new opportunities when a major organization moves into the area. In addition, government contracts, grants, pork barrel projects, ear-marks, incentives to fund work specifically for a government representative's constituents or to encourage organizations to offer new job opportunities are also influences. We also can't leave out all of the students arriving from various locations worldwide to attend educational institutions, and business practices that rely on low wage earners to support their operations. In addition to all of the factors mentioned above, there will be job seekers migrating from various international locations to any country believed to have higher job opportunities and safety. For entrepreneurs, locations having larger customer markets also motivate people to migrate to a new region. And when taking into account the worldwide stage, whenever countries have economic problems and their unemployment rate rises, the countries believed to be striving will always appear inviting to job seekers. When you focus on the popular careers, and factor in potential job seekers from Europe, Asia, and Latin America also migrating to locations believed to have jobs, the job market in those destinations become even more challenging to find work in. Politically, those are the times when residents of the destination markets begin to blame one or two cultures for the difficulty of finding opportunities, instead of realizing that the cause is actually the result of a booming and robust economy that will attract job seekers worldwide.

History lovers are aware that a number of wars were started when one country sought to claim the wealth of another country. Throughout history, fresh water has continued to be a reason why people (and their cattle) migrate from one location to another, often causing the inhabitants already dwelling around the water hole, to fight to protect their valuable water resource. Then you begin to see increased discriminatory practices against the refugees, immigrants, and migrant workers. Political talking points and new laws begin to arise focused on trying to reserve the water hole for the people who arrived before the latest group. This is a similar scenario to when people migrate and move from state to state and across international borders to find income and jobs. We can't continue to believe that the only influence on getting employment is only within the borders of the United States; but instead, we must recognize that world economies also impact employment worldwide. We can't ignore that global events also impact diverse career paths.

Some may not consider when there are large numbers applying for a job, it becomes even more of a challenge for hiring managers to whittle down the large numbers of applicants to one or two candidates. The hiring process becomes less and less a review of one's talent, but more of who you know, who will vouch for you, or who is presenting a convincing defense for why you and no one else, should be selected.

Jobseekers should always expect large numbers of people training for the more popular professions and *"work-for-success"* opportunities. Here are a few in the popular category: a doctor, nurse, medical assistant, lawyer, teacher, secretary, banker, accountant, musician, actor, artist, hair/makeup stylist, office/store manager, website designer, chef/cook/food preparer, cashier, waiter/waitress, salesperson, truck driver, cleaning specialist, security/protective services professional, personal care specialist, social services specialist, customer service representative, hospitality specialist, flight attendant, builder/construction worker, childcare worker, mechanic, or computer business professional.

Obviously, everyone hopes to land a good *"work-for-success"* opportunity which may or may not be a profession where you can build a viable career. But if you are targeting a popular job or profession known for having large numbers of jobseekers lining up for the next opening, you should be aware that there will be all kinds of tactics utilized by some to reach the front of the line. Having good grades, having a friendly personality, being attractive, being the best person for the job, and fully following an application process published by a hiring manager, will often result in heartache and disappointment. Also, placing your trust in politicians claiming they will bring jobs once they are elected is a promise they really have minimal control over when considering there are huge numbers of individuals training for the same popular opportunities. It also can be disappointing when hiring managers actually post positions after they have already selected someone, possibly presented via an approved network of vendors. And while many are training for S.T.E.M.-related careers, and the expectation is that opportunities for those careers will continue to grow, you can expect the battle for prime locations, high salaries, and benefits will be a moving target that will require you to also keep focus on changes within your specific job market.

But, if you would like to find opportunities where the lines are shorter, you might want to turn your attention toward emerging industries. As our population grows and the migration of individuals and families continues, so does the need to grow new careers proportionally along with population growth. As cultures begin to evolve, the needs become more diverse and varied. In addition, more people will choose to create their own businesses, innovate new products and services, and prepare to support future, emerging industries, yet to come. I personally find it refreshing to discover restaurants offering fusion menus that might blend Brazilian and Japanese, or Creole with French, Spanish, and Caribbean. If food can fuse and create new types of offerings, why not other products and services? As our population continues to expand, and more and more individuals train for the same popular careers, at some point, dependent on your geographical location, the open availabilities can become increasingly constrained. People leave small towns and even their country of birth for that exact reason.

It's true that there will be some careers where the growth in population will also demand a proportional increased need for more to enter that profession. But the possibility also exists that the higher numbers entering into a profession will also increase the competition to capture customers within specific markets. Retaining a viable market share gets tougher as more enter, providing customers more choices as a result of the free market system. For example, if you live in a large city and you require the services of a real estate lawyer, my guess is that there will be a large number of lawyers available. There will be some who get more business than others. As our population increases, no doubt there will be a greater need for experienced physicians. Their challenge will be for them to prove they can deliver excellent patient outcomes.

In addition to the perceived potential for success, people may also be motivated to choose one of the more popular professions because of family tradition or there's a limited number of choices in their area (a key motivation for leaving town and for leaving a country). And of course, motivation may develop because of an expected income, lifestyle or associated reputational image.

But for many, another key factor may be the *lack of informative details* that can be used to help them make a decision. If this is the case, you may find later, after you gain more information and learn more about the industry, your earlier choice is not really something you want to do. So, collecting details about a job before you commit is critical to making a viable decision, even though there are some who have found their happy place by making decisions purely on what they feel.

But there is another perspective behind the question of "What's in it for me?" that many may over look. The perspective is: *innovation*. The act of creating something new or fulfilling a need differently than what has been the norm. If you begin to utilize empathy to determine what could enhance your customer's experience when using your product or service, you should find new opportunities to innovate. And if you applied empathy when determining your career opportunities, you should ask "What is it that is missing that could help a company?" or "What could benefit people?" impacted by the industry you are targeting for a career. By using empathy, you can introduce *innovation* to carve out a job market niche where there is less competition to fulfill the needs previously unrealized.

So just for giggles and kicks, how about we drill into how a new career opportunity might emerge, from nothing to something? If I only had "x", I could have been able to do "y", so much easier or better. Or, if only I knew that was available, I would have bought that instead. Now, let's try some real-world examples.

Years ago, I was navigating around on a website and was having all kinds of trouble trying to find where open job opportunities were listed. I thought, if they only had a link at the top of their home page it would be so much easier to find their career section. Someone needs to better organize their website. So, I called them and asked if they might need someone to assist with managing their website. Turns out, they did need some help, and I was hired. Years later, website design has become a popular career, but my thought of what I needed turned out to be something needed by others. Today, there are entrepreneurs and small businesses that have not yet made a decision to invest in a well-designed and managed website. You can find them by simply looking at their website and thinking that if this website only had "x" it would be so much easier for people to do "y." A website designer who can identify ways to make websites easier to navigate might be recognized as an innovator and be able to develop a diverse career path.

If news media outlets invested in hiring a researcher to confirm the source of their stories, they could publish the source along with each story so consumers seeking factual information could have increased confidence in what is being communicated by the news media outlet. Given the increased awareness of propaganda, a public communications content validator role or source verifier role could present a diverse career path within media groups, which you may not see advertised, and as such, there are probably small lines to apply for those roles.

A key obstacle for so many worldwide is having the money to get an education. If only a non-profit or philanthropic organization created free 'foundational-level' Science, Technology, Engineering, and Mathematics (S.T.E.M.) web-based courses, cost would no longer be a hindrance for getting foundational education. The role of a mass communication educator would definitely be a diverse career path, and would fulfill the formula, if only I had "x", it would be so much easier to do "y."

For individuals who find they or a loved one will be hospitalized or need to go into short- or long-term care, it would be beneficial if they could retain someone having knowledge of medical procedures, policies, and pharmacy medication knowledge who can provide daily on-location checks, act as a liaison between the client patient and providers, and review the care plans and treatments. This could help to prevent negligence or abuse on the part of providers responsible for administering care, and where state compliance does little to protect patients. A personal medical governance oversight auditor could become a diverse career path.

With the increasing fear of urban dwellers being shot by stray bullets, it would be beneficial if a manufacturer could develop affordable bullet-proof material that could be used in homes, automobiles, and clothes to provide protection from being fatally wounded by gunshots. An affordable armor designer sounds like a need that could develop into a diverse career path.

When I was in high school and uncertain about which career path would be the most suitable for me, and my school advisers displayed minimal confidence in my viability, it would have been so much easier if there was some type of reliable free mentoring/counseling service available at a library, college, or community organization that could assist me with narrowing down my choices, have current detailed information available on careers, and someone who could continually be available to assist me over time with adjusting my path when my unique goals and aspirations evolved. The need for an objective career mentor could present an opportunity to create a diverse career path.

I believe there's a strong probability that a high number of people would develop a diminished desire to physically hurt others when the other has angered them if mandatory conflict resolution training was taught beginning in grade school as part of their standard curriculum. There is a need for a conflict resolution specialist which also could develop into a diverse career path.

In conclusion, take some time to not just think about what's in it for you, but *what is missing* that would really be beneficial to you and others, if it was only available? And so, what's in it for you, becomes *what is needed by others*.

Is there something you can think of that is not only missing, but a sorely needed product or service?

Could it be a tool that has not been designed? Maybe an expanded or bolt on service that, when coupled with an existing service, will speed things up when you are in a certain situation. When you are feeding you baby, wouldn't it nice if you had something to make it easier or keep you from getting food all over you?

When thinking about pursuing a diverse career path, I believe you should keep in mind there will be needs that are long-term, while others will evolve into something different. For this reason, I would suggest that you first, always monitor market trends and customer needs so that you can adjust, change, diversify or evolve your path. Secondly, I believe you should have more than one career path in development, or running simultaneously. Businesses often implement diversification efforts via new products or services to strengthen their bottom line and protect against losses as customer expectations change. Some corporations tend to introduce new versions of their products every two years. I'm sure you recognize there are some fast food restaurants that seem to introduce a new sandwich every couple of months with the hope of enticing impulsive spenders, the curious buyer and of course, to attract new customers. Diversification is a tactic used to keep corporations out in front of others, but also introduces risk since some new products or services could easily be something customers reject. With that understanding, reaching a decision on more than one career path should not be taken lightly. But your career strategy should take into account the fact that *change is inevitable*.

Your Career Strategy: How Far is Too Far?

Something else to consider, though it's a bit risky, is how far in the future do you want to reach? For example, there are the obvious changes expected in the future, like our method of transportation, personal communication, monetary transactions, and the types of technology used for medical procedures. I think it's also fair to say in the near future, there will be an increasing number of excursions into space, traveling further and further away from Earth. What might people need if they are living on a space ship, traveling years away from Earth or living off Earth in the year 2259? Would there be a need for products focused on comfort, hygiene, emergency escapes, and long-range communications? What about entertainment focused on managing boredom and space traveler security and defense? Do you think there will be a need for food processing, zero gravity physical training and zero gravity surgical procedures? Would all these be areas opportune for developing diverse career paths supporting the emerging space industry? Yes, I think these are possible opportunities to come. But why wait for the position to be posted? I believe these areas may not have huge numbers of applicants, not just yet. So, could you be an early disruptive innovator? Could you innovate without the expectation to participate? Can you start on development now, to be in use at some point in the future?

The Elijah McCoy engine lubricator, Eli Whitney's cotton gin, Granville T. Woods' locomotive proximity indicator and air brakes, and Cyrus McCormick's reaper, were all developed out of the need to support the migration west and growth of industry. The number of people preparing to support the space industry is nothing close to the number of people training for careers in medicine, legal, education, business, or creative fields. To begin training and positioning yourself to support new frontiers will no doubt be a risk since its unknown territory, but it's hard not to believe there are huge opportunities in the wings. Space industry support specialist – a diverse career path.

For the Visionaries, Future Frontier Opportunities Exist Now

Currently, the space and clean energy industries present abundant diverse career path opportunities which I would refer to as frontiers. Both are growth areas similar to what developed during the nineteenth century migration west and the California gold rush. As of the writing of this book, those having a variety of transferable skills and working in either of these industries, working in space, and supporting those who work in space face relatively minimal competition for jobs compared to the competition for more popular careers having documented years of job descriptions, job titles, and career paths.

In addition to the space and clean energy industries, there is a profession which, at this time I will label as the visionary industry, where only visionaries need apply. This industry doesn't have customary recruiters or published open opportunities, but instead the opportunities emerge from the minds of those who have thoughts outside our current temporal sense of reality, and beyond our current contemporary needs. They are fearless, allowing their thoughts to envision probable needs based on assumptions and a preponderance of human tendencies and probabilities.

Well, I've always recognized the visionary gene in myself and I believe that we all have the capability to be visionaries. Maybe some overlook our capability to be visionaries possibly as a result of spending most of our time dealing with what's going on around us, right now, and thoughts on handling the challenges of our own sense of reality, that we don't try to think past our sense of mortality. We don't pause to daydream past what's in front of us. And for some they think of daydreaming as being unfocused as opposed to being able to think beyond their physical self. When we do day-dream, requirements would have new guidelines for creating new opportunities. For jobseekers, I believe that just might turn out to be a good trait to have.

For instance, if for a moment we pondered on lifespans continually lengthening, what kinds of challenges might that present and what might someone whose lifespan has extended to 110, 120, 125, or 150 years require? Depending on their physical health, they definitely would need more savings than someone whose lifespan is seventy. What types of challenges might our atmosphere present at that time? If we were then to create milestones for expected events to occur, say in the next one hundred, two hundred, three hundred years, a visionary could then begin to work toward developing the result, product, or service, now, even though the odds of them personally being there to see the realization may or may not happen. But why should that keep you from developing opportunities, or a new career path, now? A new path that you could benefit from as a full-length, viable profession, and a new diverse career path. Aren't we seeing this process being played out with computers, cell phones, virtual reality, 3-D movies, artificial limbs, etc.?

For visionaries, the opportunities are limited by thoughts. What will people need in the future when it becomes normal to live 150 years? Will there be new needs for living, eating, and for transportation? Visionaries are now working on self-driving cars because they expect humans will become more and more beings of comfort, not really wanting to control the car driving experience, but to be driven, or chauffeured. This belief is carried over with computer personal assistants that through voice commands, can shop for us, sweep floors, protect homes, remind us of upcoming events, and alert us of pending financial issues.

As you can imagine, the number of opportunities increase when you begin to think about your future, and the future of your children and their children.

What might be needed two generations after your own generation? If we consider the concept of life insurance, one could consider a plan that would pay for your funeral service and provide enough for your children to become debt-free, start their own business, or never have a need to build income. When thinking about life insurance, one could think about ensuring that their survivors will not be responsible for burial costs or they could think about ensuring multi-generational wealth, well beyond their current generation.

A good sample of the visionary industry can be seen in sci-fi movies and movies based on events that happen years in the future. In those we see a variety of items and concepts, yet to be realized in our time. There are so many examples here. Most display life existing on other planets, having artificial intelligence as new life forms, being able to travel far into space, beaming, interactions with beings other than humans, and seriously advanced technology that supports everything we do. What a roadmap by which to fill in the gaps, yet to be realized, just waiting for you to define it.

But in areas of future, frontier, diverse career path opportunities, at some point factors which may have not been identified, will be unveiled and will influence change and needs. So, if you choose to take the risk in becoming an innovator, you also could be the one who disrupts the current norm which could also result in huge rewards. Market disrupters like Facebook, Tesla, Amazon, Google, Uber, Airbnb, SpaceX, Dropbox, and biometric pharmaceutical companies, all took a look into the future and recognized something was needed before customers told them what they wanted. After their products and services were unveiled, customers overwhelming responded with their wallets. But stay tuned; each of these early disrupters will have to evolve as the expectations of the customer evolve.

    Ultimately, upon moving along your diverse career path, one of your decisions will be how far down the road (the future you hope for) are you comfortable visualizing, and then dedicating effort to make it happen? Is your comfort zone restricted to your finances, your situation or current location? Or can you transport yourself beyond physical or psychological constraints, and begin plans further out? Possibly by gathering research, learning about current and trending customer expectations, seeking formal training or volunteering within a targeted area, or seeking out a mentor who can share their experiences with you?

    How far away from your safe zone are you willing to explore? Time could be one determining factor. If you encounter a critical roadblock while pursuing one path, will you have enough time to adjust, re-train, recover or diversify? This is a good reason why many take calculated researched risks earlier than later. To give themselves more time to recover from the unexpected. Logic being, if they encounter roadblocks or failures, they will have time to write it off, learn from the experience, and start over with another idea, only this time, having a more hands-on experience. But at some point, one's tolerance for risk diminishes due to personal and external influences.

Are You Ready to Manage Your Own Business?

With all of the previous text raising considerations for diversifying your career paths toward careers that can fulfill new customer and business needs that are emerging on the frontier, or creating new paths spinning off from currently popular careers, I would be negligent if I didn't also bring to your attention the need to have entrepreneur skills, and specifically, training on how to run a business.

Every single time when I've traveled internationally, when it comes to the employment of each country's residents, there's one aspect I consistently observed. The number of individuals having jobs with large, prestigious, high-visibility or central down-town companies requiring business casual or suits, was nowhere close to the high number of individuals running their own small shops, store front boutiques, operating open market booths, being street barkers or involved with direct sales of all types of products and services. The trend of individuals worldwide who have chosen to take the risk and control over their own abilities to provide income for themselves and their families is overwhelming. When taking the time to talk or barter, you find a number of these small business entrepreneurs had businesses passed down from their parents or learned their trade from their parents. And when you take a closer look, in many U.S. locations, you see the same trend being carried out by residents who have international awareness, come from families who were immigrants, or people who have been excluded from the skilled worker job market. The number of people standing in streets selling small quantities of products, running a home-based business, selling products to their friends, working as service providers like wedding planners, event caterers, private drivers, private workout trainers, and in internet services are just some of the areas where individuals are increasingly gravitating toward entrepreneurship. There are also large numbers of individuals who are learning to work in a family business instead of choosing to compete with the large numbers seeking one of those popular jobs. And those individuals, along with those who create their own unique career paths, will surely benefit from building expertise in how to manage their own business.

With creating entrepreneurial diverse career paths also comes the need to understand something about running a business. You'll need some accounting knowledge for keeping the books, pricing, billing, and payroll. You'll need customer service skills, know how to manage employees, how to protect your intellectual properties, how to market your product or service, legal protections and tax responsibilities just to name a few.

I would highly suggest that if available educational institutions in your area have not integrated into their existing curriculums, some type of entrepreneur course of study or elective training courses related to gaining understanding on how to manage a business, then you should seek to find training on your own. This specific type of educational need could also be considered a diverse career path for students training to be educators and looking for a niche area of concentration.

In summary, here are a few thoughts you might consider the next time you hear yourself ask, "What's in it for me?" Would you rather be one of the first to know when there might be an adverse scenario in progress which could impact your job or career? Do you have strong or weak faith? If strong, what are the foundational principles on which your faith is built? How strong is your faith and belief that you will be successful? Do you consider yourself to be a leader or follower? What is the motivation that drives you along your career path? Is it focused on helping others achieve their goals or to help them be successful with their business? If so, it's possible that their strong conviction could reinforce your conviction while their weak conviction could negatively impact your pursuit. Is the motivation that drives you along your career path more self-centered, focused on acquiring things of value, having less value for those who help you or for those you encounter while on your path to reach your goals? Over time, that could leave an extensive profile of scorched earth and burned bridges requiring continuous efforts focused on re-builds, re-orgs, diminishing circles of support, the need to find new partners, and continual damage control to re-build your reputation. Will you choose to follow a career path where the initial competition for getting hired is low, or a path where there's a long line of hopefuls? Becoming an early disruptor like the founders of Facebook, Tesla, Amazon, Google, and Uber allows you to determine your personal marketable value, viability, economic worth, your commitment to social responsibilities you would like to support, and brand reputation.

    I personally believe that there are some key guiding factors one should consider when seeking to achieve psychological and physical success when taking on the risks of navigating a diverse career path: having strong faith, and confidence, being considerate to others, and utilizing positive and fair policies.

Chapter 4: What's the Point?

What's the point? One philosophic point of view might be the challenge of awakening your higher self. The moment when your unrealized potential collides with unsatisfied needs, common sense, and current knowledge. To evolve, or not to evolve; that is your question.

How many times will you hear the recurring revelation, "If only I knew then what I know now?" I, too, have joined the ranks of voicing those same words at different points in time. But, I often wondered how long could that revelation retain its relevance if we had available to us the solutions to the problems others have already solved. Theoretically, that would allow you the ability to focus more of your efforts to solve new problems created by change or innovation, and less on recurring problems. Well, that would require collaboration on a worldwide level, the thought of which shoots down the hope of that actually happening. But there could be the development of think-tanks and organizations which pool their experiences to strengthen like-minded thinkers who are willing to collaborate on sharing the solutions to problems they've solved. Imagine that. A theoretical challenge that you can actually build starting with your immediate family and friends, and continuing outward in concentric circles built with those who choose to share their lessons learned. Maybe a worldwide matrix of lessons learned is a bit too much to believe will ever happen, but what if you were able to build a strong network that you can rely on, consult with, and provide input? Is that too much to consider?

And you ask, "*What's the point?*" Well, I believe you can increase your probability of successfully achieving multiple career goals by exchanging lessons learned within your trusted network as you move along your diverse career path. With each obstacle or decision point, you can have solutions within your grasp, or more than one recommendation for you to consider which ones would provide you the best results.

The idea of a trusted network focused on sharing lessons learned introduces you to a different twist or perspective to an existing tool that you can add into your existing toolset. This would be a network not just of friends and acquaintances, but of those whose goal is to share lessons learned. As you read this book, hopefully it will become clearer that this is a central theme of this guide. I have faith that through the lessons learned that I share, there will be something you will be able to use and build upon so you don't have to re-solve problems already solved. And you will have awareness of what I've already seen. Also, the recommendations included in this guide can be the subject of further discussions for you to amend, personalize, or share with those who are members of your trusted network.

Know that there are always one or more moments in one's life when a glimpse of clarity unveils itself to you and allows you see a part of yourself that may be overlooked or just waiting there under the surface. In addition, there are days when your thoughts are so cluttered with focus on actual expected and imagined problems, that the need to prioritize issues from high-to-low, rank them to decide which ones are the most urgent, and finally figure out a plan on how to eliminate them, can in totality, be overwhelming. When your mind can manage some time to insert a relaxation break, you may be able to use that moment to obtain some clarity on what are your primary motivations, the actual needs for what drives you toward carving out you own unique path that will unveil the wonders you'll recognize only by embracing your special and unique life.

Your thoughts may constantly annoy you with those overpowering needs which rise to the top and can make you turn one way or another. Hopefully, you have started working towards figuring out what are your unique character types that define you. And as a result, you are starting to identify the type of person you want to be, or *don't* want to be. For most of us, it's really easy to set our own values similar to the ones we know, our father, mother, or that one person we walk by every day on our way to a destination. We all experience at least one, but probably more moments of clarity as we think about our present day and future existence. Our hopes and dreams. The runners and sitters. The star gazers and builders. The ones who reach out to retrieve, and the ones who hold their palms up to receive. Each time we open our eyes and begin to acknowledge those unspoken messages already woven deep within our minds or passed along through our blood lines, you'll need to consider what will be the paths that you believe should be highly valued and worthy of a life-long endeavor, and a battle to raise those inner needs and *keep them from falling* into a bucket of dreams deferred, unfulfilled, and lost in the realm of the unrealized needs.

And when you begin to acknowledge the paths taken by your parents and other family members, at some point, you turn around and discover, you too are on a path which will impact those coming up in the next wave, behind you. The kids on the block who are watching you, hoping to get some type of clue for their own direction. The one's trying to stand on your shoulders. I know it can be difficult to look backward when you are working so hard to move forward. What does it really mean that we stand on the shoulders of those who came before us? What is the true impact of those shoulders, to you? And who will stand on your shoulders?

The Endless Circle of Lessons

I remember stories about my relatives and the challenges they faced. And yes, it was those stories which gave me something to think about for my own paths. I watched. I listened, simultaneously while my attention also focused on running through the house and playing games. I thought about the ones who I felt sad about, because of what had happened to them along their paths. But there were others whom I felt very proud due to what they had achieved while moving along their paths. To this day, I enjoy thinking about them all. I have value for the stories of their lives. It's during those moments of clarity when I visualized being able to make the types of decisions that would result in creating stories that others in my family will feel proud of, and hopefully will motivate them to achieve a productive, happy state of their own.

I sometimes wonder, could it possibly be that my thoughts, the stories and lessons learned of those who came before me, have merged to supernaturally influence my decisions and actions, which emerge into desired results for myself and many others to come? What actually emerges as a path for my own life, also somehow becomes a template for others, based on actual lessons learned for a life or lives, yet to come. Lessons learned become a continual communication, from one generation to another. So, if my hypothesis is true, you'd better pay attention because you are in the stream, and what you do could make, or break not only you, but someone needing to stand on your shoulders.

Someone who is watching you right now, as you sink or swim in the river of lessons, learned.

This is your moment. This is your time. Don't mess it up.

So, when I summarize, it is unquestionable there will be something you do or say that will impact somebody. As you might already be aware, there is what is referred to as "Six Degrees of Separation." This chain of relationships will undoubtedly include at least one family member, a friend, co-worker or that person behind the counter who hands you your order after you've paid for it. It's not hard to realize we all are watching each other, learning from each other, and interacting with one another. And it only takes a moment for one person to instill a long-lasting memory, create an influence and stimulate a reaction. But, there's not just one person walking around. We exist in an 'order of magnitude' reinforced by bold complex communication channels that are available for worldwide consumption and utilization. What you say, and do, matters.

Aside from whatever diverse career path you choose to follow for yourself, keep in mind you will touch others. So, no matter how many people who might be working with you, and considering you could choose to select a path where you will be working independently, it may initially seem as though it's all about your success, when in reality, your actual success will be when those benefiting from the industry you are in declare your success, by imitating and re-using what you showed them. When you ask "What's the point?" you should consider the value you provide to your customers, clients, industry, your family and your neighborhood to be a good answer.

When asked what would you like to do in life, or what would you like to do when you grow up, I hope that you will consider including, "providing legendary service in whatever you choose to do" as being a key ingredient of what you want to do. I've encountered so many who never realize the service aspect is how internal and external customers will honestly proclaim how well you helped them with their needs, goals, or helping them manage their problems. Yes, along the way some will falsely rely on other measures unrelated to providing service to the customer; but be not dismayed. So many in the work environment spend their time bouncing between personality conflicts and battles over internal power, and very early in the game, they forget their activities are supposed to be focused on providing service to the customer. Hopefully, you can keep your eye on providing legendary service, and not get side-tracked.

Chapter 5: World Cultures

In preparing to begin my career, I wish I had received some counseling while I was in high school and later while in college, that alerted me about how quickly business needs and expectations fluctuate proportionally with *changes in the market* and are driven by the *needs of consumers in various cultures* and *geographical locations worldwide*. As a result of constant change, the requirements aligned to training needed by employees also change. No matter if your present concentration is focused on finding a job, finding a suitable profession, or focused on figuring out your long-term career goals, everyone at some point will be impacted by external change, influences, and dependencies beyond your control.

What does that mean for you if you're just starting your career or already moving along your career path? It means you probably will not be able to remain in the same job assignment without adding on to your existing skills or adding entirely new skills. In addition, as a result of the increasing amount of external influences and dependencies worldwide, it's becoming *a rare occurrence* to find individuals who have worked their entire careers with the same employer. World conflicts, changing trade agreements, changes with international isolationism politics, cultural lifestyle needs, business decisions, changing economies, and personality conflicts between powerful government and/or wealthy private organizations and individuals, all throw their hats into the ring on a regular basis, resulting in constant change. Either one of which can play a part with impacting your industry, marketplace, and workforce decision makers seeking to pivot and make appropriate moves to compensate for potential risks, new issues which have been realized, and of course, taking advantage of emerging opportunities.

With this understanding, I'm sure you can recognize the training you are receiving, or received in school will not be enough to keep you viable. You'll need to look at your foundational training as the credentials to get you in the door, moving with your career, while holding a glass half-full or empty, but your knowledge gained up to this point, should be considered a living event. I still remember after completing one mentally challenging and strenuous degree program, loudly proclaiming I was done with school. And then months later finding myself signing up for non-degree standalone courses to gain training in specialized areas of concentration, which I deemed when combined with my existing skills and training, would considerably increase my overall marketability and long-term viability.

Science, technology, engineering and math (S.T.E.M.) will continue to have discoveries that cause change. As a result, the fundamentals you learn now, will ultimately need to be updated as new discoveries, processes, and customer expectations evolve. And here's the kicker; changes are occurring worldwide, initiated by people, governments, businesses, and organizations within cultures distinctly different from the ones you are the most familiar.

But for many, countless opportunities will pass through their hands if they don't make a little effort to continuously increase their capabilities and prowess with interacting on the worldwide stage. Becoming deficient in current needs could make one inept with being able to remain current and making strategic adjustments when events occur on the worldwide stage. Interestingly enough, there's absolutely nothing blocking you and nothing in your way, from being able to empower yourself, little by little, with some capabilities that can increase your long-term viability.

Becoming more knowledgeable, perceptive, in-tune, and empathetic with the needs of various world cultures is one way to have better awareness of potential changes in the market and customer expectations. In addition, world culture communication training could provide additional insight into the mannerisms and needs of others.

For instance, knowing what are some key influencers socially, politically and economically in different world cultures may provide early warnings of change. That in turn could enable your ability to provide services, create products, and conduct business across worldwide markets. And of course, being able to converse in multiple languages is a definite advantage, seeing how so many in the United States only speak one language while many who are from other countries can speak two or three languages. Having multiple language skills in combination with having grown up in regions bordering, or having geographic proximity to other countries where there are different customs and where different languages are spoken, can complement their world culture flexibility and increase the opportunities available to them. In addition, if they grew up in countries which have strong education systems, the ability to adjust to change facilitated by worldwide events is heightened.

I do, however, acknowledge there is a constant battle in some countries focused on keeping "the old ways" and traditions, maintaining certain cultural boundaries which define a region, and I see nothing wrong with being a traditionalist. I believe it's important to maintain one's culture. There is a phrase that you can't know where you're going unless you know where you've been. In other words, you should always understand the history of your people and culture to help you know who you are and possibly help to unfold some of your own mannerisms and beliefs.

But, when thinking about increasing one's career opportunities, there is an undeniable truth; the world's population is consistently growing, not decreasing. And as a result of having so many ways to travel, people can easily travel from one country to another, and when people travel, some will discover places they choose to build their families, which is not the home of their birth. Eventually, some regions could develop new blended cultures. With that blending comes changes in lifestyles, communication and language. The introduction of slang terms and mannerisms are often adopted from other cultures.

For traditionalists, the blending is the type of change they will fight against until their last breath. And if you choose to be a traditionalist, the fact is, as the marketplace blends and the needs of blended cultures increase with more desire for new types of products and services, the traditionalist *who has decided not to adjust* in their abilities to communicate and fulfill the needs of a blended culture, will undoubtedly find their market base *limited and decreasing*. With that comes *fewer opportunities*. And if there is a recession, or other negative impacts, they have the potential for suffering the most. They may blame the influx of outsiders as the cause for their loss of opportunities, profits, income, and available jobs. That is somewhat true, but their resistance to adjusting to change and conviction to allowing their traditions impose on their business and careers is probably more the reason for their loss.

The new emerging cultures actually create new business opportunities, new customers, new demands for products and services, and new sources of revenue. All of which, from a business and career perspective are what dreams are made of. Most businesses use marketing techniques focused on increasing their customer base, revenues, piece of the pie or market share. And here it is, smacking them in the face in the emergence of new cultures bringing new needs and desires. Yes, the reality is this world is alive, growing, and evolving. There's nothing wrong with maintaining your own cultural awareness and practices.

With the emergence of new cultures, you have two choices. You can bring a fishing pole and either drop your baited line into a river fully stocked with a variety of fish, or you can drop your line in a river that only has one or two fish swimming upstream, once or twice during the course of the year. It's your choice. But I think you get my point. When looking at a plan where you become increasingly knowledgeable of world cultures and keeping an eye open for emerging cultures, the potential to benefit from a wide pool of career opportunities is great. If you choose to continue conducting business only to customers who speak your language, or adhere only to your cultural beliefs, well do the best you can for as long as you can. But the writing will not only be on the wall, but on the ceiling, floor, outside on the lawn and everyplace you turn. This world is alive and growing. And I don't doubt at some point in the future there could be the emergence of new languages along with new cultures.

So, if you hear someone say "We only speak one language," in this house, store, school, or other public place, you are hearing the voice of someone who is slowing losing out on a growing base of opportunities presented in the form of people moving from country-to-country, state-to-state, town-to-town, building their families in places they feel safe and believe present more opportunities than their former location. If you choose to bet your cards on finding long-term career and/or business opportunities within one culture, it definitely is possible, but highly probable if the cultural group you choose to support has an economic cold or problem, you will too. And that is what I would call a risk, and one of the reasons businesses diversify. This is why companies often expect their employees to continue enhancing their skills, well after they are hired.

If you are currently in school, you may not realize that your early school years are the most opportune times *to stack up a variety of fundamental skills* which could make you more viable when you are actually on your own diverse career path. Knowing what I know now about how quickly requirements change proportionally to changes in the world market, I would have been much more aggressive about stacking up two to five different skills just to get me rolling.

World Influencers

Here are a few examples of world influencers where individual and/or customer market expectations resulted in change.

Example One: Gordon Moore's Law claims the computing clock speed of a computer semiconductor chip will double every eighteen months. But with new innovations, the speed will probably double even faster since the time of Moore's 1965 prediction. As a result, we regularly experience new products claiming to be faster than something you purchased a year ago. And *our current expectation* is that any product utilizing computer logic, must be able to return or respond with real-time results. We now are more accustomed to wanting results now and expecting to get them now, not later.

Example Two: For centuries, the Maasai people of the Serengeti Plains Eastern Africa have been known throughout Africa for their bright red shuka garments, elaborately braided, bright red dyed hair, and the women wearing elongated leather earrings. These cultural practices were eventually adopted by people from other countries as fashionable. I don't know which cultural group was first to integrate the red hair into their culture, but I definitely recall seeing young Japanese women dyeing their hair bright red, pink, and other bright colors. The Maasai practices were also integrated into trendy American cultural groups. When the elaborate African braiding style for hair prominently re-emerged into African-American culture in the seventies, it symbolized a cultural and political movement. For those *resistant to the choices of other cultures*, this style was somehow deemed as offensive. As a result, some women wearing this style were expelled from entering schools or the workplace. But later in the twenty-first century, the braided hair style became accepted by most as just another hair style. Overall, this culture influenced the need for hair stylists, worldwide, to add new skills and capabilities.

I should note there are those in disparate cultures who refuse to be considerate to the practices of other cultures, and still seek to use their influence and bully pulpit to limit how one culture chooses to be happy and express itself. The wearing of a hijab, a scarf worn by some Arab women that covers the head and neck, is another practice that some who are not empathetic to other world cultures continue to show a lack of world culture knowledge and at times, outwardly antagonistic to this practice which some have deemed not to be part of, or having value to their own culture. Just like all music is not written for everyone to like, cultural customs are also not created for everyone. If your culture chooses to wear a large eagle feather in a hat or headdress, someone who is not a member of that culture should not feel the need to go around and disrespect the customs of another culture, and yet it still happens. Loving one's own culture does not require the need to hate other cultures.

Example Three: The customer expectation of "I want it now, anyplace and anytime" has resulted in changes to customer service practices, including 24/7 on-line chat support, the ability to interact via your mobile phone, increasing development of virtual reality communication, live streaming, and on-demand entertainment content. The "I want it now" community is here, and commonplace.

Example Four: The low cost of workers in India, South America, China, and Mexico have influenced U.S. businesses to open offices overseas to benefit from the low cost of labor outside of the U.S., and motivated U.S. businesses to encourage workers from those countries to move on-site and work for the same low wages as if they were still living in the countries having low costs for labor.

Example Five: The growing awareness of successful implementations of nationwide universal healthcare strategies in Germany, Australia, Sweden, France, Canada, and other countries around the world, has created a high demand for nationwide universal healthcare coverage to be implemented in the United States.

Example Six: Let me just say, "The Spice Trade" and the "Silk Road." I thought about this small, possibly forgotten bit of world trade history that proved, hands down, without any refute, the value of having world culture knowledge and acknowledging the right for other cultures to exist and to enjoy all that makes them different. By learning to understand the needs of people who live outside your own communities, you can ultimately develop diverse career paths that incorporate providing products or services worldwide.

More Spice

I thought the mention of "The Spice Trade," which is a pivotal bit of world history, would provide you proof of what was, and is probably the largest successful international trade model that began centuries ago. And the road is still open. I'm not going to try and state when it started, but highlight the spices and products traded facilitated the growth of cooking skills in which distinct spices were used to create distinct flavors in the food of clearly distinct cultures. In addition, there were other goods and products discovered that were then sold along the routes. Over centuries of time, "The Spice Trade" wove its way through major regions of China, India, Pakistan, Japan, Indonesia, the Philippines, Africa, South America, Europe, and North America. The impact of "The Spice Trade" is probably undefinable. But we know the movement and interaction of people from different cultures, and the exchange of innovations, concepts, knowledge, medicine, and entertainment resulted in many nations being enhanced through the benefits exchanged. And yes, on the downside, there were increased conflicts possibly resulting from the perception that some countries had more valuable benefits than others, and there were unbridled obsessive behaviors and coveting of riches, property, and people. It was also inherent that there were traders who had little or no respect for customs, and the people, who were their customers. There were lies, deceit, theft, violence, disrespect for other cultures and families. There was bad customer service in that agreements for services were not honored. Where have we seen these practices and behaviors before? Interesting that we still see some of these predatory business practices today.

And with "The Spice Trade", there is another huge lesson related to the quest for available jobs and career opportunities. Throughout the history of "The Spice Trade" there were countless documented and undocumented skirmishes and wars over the control of trade routes (distribution), established trade areas, open regions (markets), and over who would be allowed to trade (trade agreements). Just like today, there are turf wars between street corner hustlers and battles to dominate market share by countries, international businesses, and organizations.

The street corner hustler will continue to wage war over the control of a few blocks and over who will be allowed to conduct trade within those areas.

Safety, Water, and Jobs

Both the blue-collar and white-collar worker seeking to find employment will continue to battle against the migration of people coming across national borders. They will blame the migration as the cause for their inability to have an *abundance of jobs* in their own area of residency. This excuse will continue to be used as the reason why they can't find jobs quickly and easily. They obviously have no awareness of "The Spice Trade" still in operation and still moving jobs, products and services around like pieces on a chess board. Whether those migrating are authorized or unauthorized, documented or undocumented, legal or illegal, we historically *will continue* to experience people from various countries, whether they are Europeans, Chinese, Mexicans, Cubans, Ukrainians, Syrians, Irish, Haitians, Polish, Asian-Indians, you name it, all finding their way to places they believe will provide *safety* and *jobs*. Whether you like it or not, people will always move to where there is *safety, water, food, and jobs (opportunities to make money)*.

Some people are able to gain official government approvals for leaving their country and entering another. Others are not afforded official approvals, and as such they find creative ways. When it comes to the migration of people, it really doesn't matter which ones had official time-bound Visas and then overstayed, or who once risked their lives as stow-a-ways in the bowels of a ship. There were those who ran across borders in the darkness of night, and those who found someone empathetic to their struggle to get them across by using fake identification.

The bottom line is any location that can instill and reinforce a sense of *safety, has available water and job opportunities*, will always, always attract people, like bees to honey. In addition, the results of one country or region being able to fulfill these basic survival needs will realize continual changes to its demographics as a result of immigrants entering from different countries and from *existing citizens* migrating from region-to-region, state-to-state or town-to-city. Along with the change in demographics comes innovation and the need for residents to increase their skills, performance, and production in order to remain viable within a continual refreshing demographics.

Distribution

Throughout time, and over centuries, history has proven that *nothing* is going to stop the natural need for survival, and that often results in the need to leave where you have been living.

Corporations will continue to battle for their products or services to dominate the markets in their country and to capture a respectable market share from national and international markets. Their continual desire for lowering their operating costs and increasing profits continually focuses on cheap or free labor, which in turn, *increases the flow of immigrants* hungry to find work that pays anything more than zero. The skirmishes documented in "The Spice Trade" are still happening today, but the ability to control trade routes is much more difficult since they have expanded immensely.

It was likely in the days, centuries ago, when the early "Spice Trade" initially began flourishing, one might experience being robbed or killed while traveling on one route. Or maybe traders had to pay varying safe passage fees in order to use specific routes. As a counter, distributors began seeking alternative, and hopefully safer, less expensive routes to transport their goods. They scouted out and then expanded land routes to go through different regions, made agreements with people of different cultures, and they began to seek routes through various waterways.

Today, trade distribution opportunities include moving products not just over land and sea, but now by freight train, air transport, and unlimited electronic transactional routes. While international trade laws do exist, the ability to move products and provide services has been getting easier, even though turf wars, a.k.a. the battles for increased market share, still exist. As a result, the *diverse career opportunities have also increased.*

Where the street corner hustler is obligated to move product hand-to-hand or by land-based vehicles, obviously, their market area is severely limited. As a result, the skirmishes to control turf can be much more violent for them since their limited geographic boundaries are considered to be their *only* source of income. The same may be true for the blue- or white-collar worker resorting to physical violence and hate crimes focused on the groups they believe are the cause of job opportunities not being abundantly available in their town or village.

This should *not be the case* for *those including world market opportunities as a part of their career plans.* If you think more toward the world market and the available diverse career opportunities and trade distribution opportunities, you realize even with participation in a small share of the world market, one could obtain some measure of success with less need to attack other cultures for seeking to achieve similar goals for their families. I sure hope you can begin to see the career opportunities which currently exist and still expanding, as proven by "The Spice Trade," centuries ago.

Cultural Customs

When considering diverse career opportunities, there is an important aspect that I would highly suggest you not overlook or be too naïve about. That is a need to become increasingly aware of important cultural customs as you work to establish career opportunities across cultural boundaries.

So often, individuals overlook or ignore the common courtesy of showing some basic respect for others' customs. If you think about it, not taking into account anything to do with business, but just considering what you already know about courtesies expected when interacting with family and friends. And many have experienced what can be the result when you meet someone and don't know about something they consider to be important. Tension or conflicts can ensue if you say or do the wrong thing, are unaware, or forget to do the right thing. The same can happen if you ignore being considerate to the customs that people hold so dear to their hearts.

For example, do you know anyone who insists you take your shoes off at the front entrance upon entering their home, or standing up and taking your hat off when being introduced to a lady, or saying grace, giving thanks to God before taking the first bite of food, or not talking while a movie is being played in a theater? How about being punctual, tipping for services rendered, not loudly passing gas in public, shaking hands when you first meet someone, maintaining about a two-foot personal space distance when talking with someone, not smacking chewing gum or chewing with your mouth open? Then there is the customary throwing of the flower bouquet by the wedding bride. All of these are customs in the United States, but not necessarily the same in other cultures. We should be cognizant that each culture may have their own distinct customs.

Relationships can be ended, agreements can be withdrawn, families broken up, weddings postponed, fights started, and feelings hurt for years, just because someone was insensitive to another one's customs or beliefs. On top of all of that, there are also unwritten practices, which only trusted conversation can reveal. (E.g.: a friend having a relationship with the friend's "ex" can result in issues.) But when it comes to career opportunities, a missed step here can result in impediments that will need to be undone or could result in a negative impact on the ability to achieve one's career goals. Some will often refer to a level-set conversation to gain understanding, set boundaries, and reach an agreement on how to best proceed in the relationship.

But of course, when it comes to working together, there will always be some who are indifferent to offending others. As businesses increase their delivery of products and services across cultural boundaries, we face the potential of offending neighbors and creating *unnecessary conflicts* just because of being insensitive to customs. Hardliners will be quick to say they don't care, and they would be the same ones who probably will be insensitive to anyone and everyone, including their own family. Those who have no problem being insensitive to another's customs generally are more likely to find their way into conflicts, personal and/or professional, which ultimately could result in a loss of business. But if you want to be able to enjoy career opportunities which span across cultures, you should take the time to understand the customs of the cultures you intend to service, that is, if you want those you seek to provide service, to feel comfortable doing business with you.

Is Mine Yours, or Yours Mine?

It's natural to be so content with your own cultural customs that you might overlook the fact that you are actually conducting business based on adhering to your own cultural customs. That's a good reason for the need to understand the differences and similarities between world customs. There are some cultures where being humble is extremely important, or where you are expected to invite others to participate in discussions *before* they will. There are cultures which if you don't provide specific detailed information or descriptions, the other person will assume you want them to make up their own rules. Almost every distinct culture has their own unique verbal and physical way of greeting each other, acceptable body language, proper ways to introduce a potential business provider to a potential client, appropriate dress for women and men at a given occasion, colors or days of the month that are considered lucky or taboo, or when is it appropriate to speak when elders are present. As you might imagine, even within the borders of one country, there undoubtedly will be customs in place aligned to the distinct cultures around you. The challenge can appear when one decides their own customs are the only customs that need to be respected.

In retrospect, when going back to learn from the history of events that occurred along the spice routes over centuries, we all can gain by understanding the causes of the failures and successes. Obtaining knowledge of world cultures and understanding what are fair trade practices within each distinct culture must be a high priority for achieving successful diverse career paths that include working across cultural boundaries. Consider learning about one or two cultures that you believe could result in a good experience. And, I would caution you: having a belief that you will be able to apply your own values and cultural practices on others, and/or deploying a practice of intrusion on the beliefs or values on others, has consistently resulted in creating serious conflicts.

For those who begin to recognize the vast accomplishments of the ancient Silk Road and spice traders, and choose to proceed with career paths that include working with multiple cultures and limitless geographic boundaries, I think you can find the opportunities are even greater in this day and age since we really don't have to physically travel along physical trade routes, from country-to-country in order to trade or provide services worldwide since we have free, real-time video communications apps, countless capabilities to conduct monetary transactions online, and there are worldwide drop-ship package delivery companies.

I might add, if you choose to develop diverse career plans that focus on interacting across diverse cultures and have a scope that is unbridled by geographic boundaries, I have a strong feeling *you will not be one of those in the crowd* shouting about some new group of people coming across the border and taking your jobs, or making it more difficult for you to quickly find suitable jobs. Why? Because you will be busy crossing world market borders and conducting business across cultures, virtually or physically.

And if and when you determine the need to have serious objective debates about this perplexing concern of many people who happen to be obsessed about other people crossing the borders, migrating into their home towns and country, legally or illegally, I suspect you might discover that the *one* common characteristic across most who are concerned, will be they believe their main opportunities for work *exist only within the close geographic boarders in which they currently reside*. And as you personally begin to recognize *many of the products and services* you currently use *are from people of different cultures* who might also be from different countries, you should also begin to realize increased opportunities actually exist for you when simply contemplating about the history of, and outcomes from "The Spice Trade" that conducted business across borders and with *many different cultures*. Knowledge of "The Spice Trade" can be used as motivation that validates why you just might, and I say might want to avoid developing diverse career plans that are restrictive from working across diverse cultures, and only focus on a limited geographic dimension. (Just a suggestion.)

I would also like for you to consider this puzzle when debating about people coming across borders. First, it's a fact that if a country or region, is able to *fulfill* basic survival needs of safety, water, and jobs, then that country will always attract people. These attractions will result in continual changes to the demographics of a region as a result of immigrants entering from different countries, and also from existing citizens migrating from region-to-region, state-to-state, town-to-city.

Also consider that big cities constantly experience their own residents migrating to locations having *lower costs of living* and deemed to be *safer from crime*. Worldwide refugees are seeking to find locations with clean water, available food sources, and are safe for raising their families away from continual civil wars, terrorism and abusive people in power. Historically, immigrants have been known to seek out locations where they can be safe from being persecuted as a result of their religious or political beliefs. This leaves definitive global destinations of hope, which become desirable choices since they are also associated with an imagery of being shiny cities on a hill.

Now, an interesting puzzle arises, when considering "Why do people migrate?" For discussion purposes, let's focus around *only legal entries* into a country: those who arrive as visitors, seek political asylum, have been commissioned or contracted to work for local businesses, are accepted in as students to better their education, and who seek to be citizens. Now, if individuals fitting any of the above criterion, all found work *within one geographically bound area or metropolitan region*, would they effectively diminish the number of available job opportunities throughout the duration of the time they remained in that geographically bound area or metropolitan region? Could their presence, *which has been approved legally*, place a strain on the available opportunities within the specific geographic area where they worked and utilized infrastructure? And if the legal processes for entry across borders have become acceptable as long-term, continual practices and policies, what impact would you expect these legal practices and policies to have on the residents and citizens already living within the targeted geographically bound area or metropolitan region if those residents rely on employment *only within the targeted region*? What might be a solution for those residents? I hope and trust your solution to the puzzle will provide you with some useful options which can provide viability to your own diverse career path plans.

When considering one notable social responsibility opportunity related to building higher employment numbers in communities, anyone working to develop their own diverse career plans that includes a world culture concept, might consider dedicating some time with *assisting those* who feel their only source of jobs and income exist only within a town, city, state, or country or only focused on conducting business by helping *with increasing their awareness and scope of opportunities.* Maybe you can help them by providing objective suggestions, to at least help them think outside of their box, and begin to think about other options that could help them move beyond their geographical boundaries. After all, it costs nothing to have a conversation.

Hopefully, the examples I provided will motivate a curiosity of world cultures and increase your perspective on how a lack of world culture knowledge can constrict the vast opportunities available to you. If you choose to acknowledge, and increase your awareness of the customs of other cultures, I believe you can continually expand the scope of available diverse career opportunities. You also should expect to find your ability to converse with broader groups will continue to expand, be enhanced, and be valuable.

In addition, I hope you will grow into one who accepts the rights of others to exist, and their right to be able to love their own culture without simultaneously being deemed as being indifferent to your own culture. Loving your own culture *shouldn't also have to mean* that you need to hate other cultures. There's nothing to prohibit you from loving your own culture and being able to enjoy the cultural customs of others. After all, most of us have overcome the challenge of eating the food created by other cultures and can easily name out the names of food and drinks having origins from different cultures. And its recognized that many cultures have a custom of breaking bread, sitting down at a table, or on the ground, eating a meal together, not just to eat, but because the eating of a meal presents the opportunity to get to know one another.

When I think about the continual debate that exists within cultural groups worldwide which focuses on people from distinct cultures and geographic locations migrating across borders into new locations and allegedly taking work from the current residents, we rarely consider the reverse opportunities. Specifically, if the current residents were thinking globally, they could expand their services externally to their proximate job market, beyond their current location, out to other world cultures and geographic locations. Instead of focusing on people arriving and adding stress to the job market you have proximity to, if you considered the global job market and needs of various world markets and cultures, you could effectively participate in expanding into markets around the world.

This is exactly what numerous organizations have been doing by opening global offices to provide their services to the residents within global markets and hire resources from the areas where they have offices. I suggest for those not *thinking globally* when it comes to career plans and available opportunities, you realize that you will be left with trying to protect the benefits, resources and opportunities you believe are limited and finite. In reality when thinking globally, your available opportunities are not limited and finite. As more people enter a location, many incorrectly conclude, possibly the result of a lack of financial awareness related to the cultural life support needs of inhabitants, that you will have less, as opposed to the services needed increasing, thus expanding job opportunities.

In many cases an increase of people actually results in proportional increases in housing and real estate needs, food services, transportation, sales tax base, retail services, and on and on. From a business perspective, this would translate into a bigger pie, a larger market available to capture increased revenues.

But I believe it would be wrong to overlook the fact that there will be increased costs for expanding support. But business plans and strategies are supposed to determine tolerable returns on investments. They are supposed to decide how much they can safely expand into markets considering regular market analysis assessments of the total market size of the expanding market, the percentage of market share they plan to target, their profit margins and investor obligations, and the amount they need to capture based on projected revenue and profit goals.

It also would be wrong to overlook the fact that some industries will realize additional costs and face challenges to recover costs. Notably, municipalities will face increasing use of their public infrastructure, which may result in increases on sales taxes to recoup from migrating residents. The healthcare industry can be impacted if fee-for-service healthcare providers are not paid.

Realistically, both scenarios can take place even in the absence of cultural migration. We continue to witness public infrastructure diminishing as politicians avoid passing legislation to maintain and enhance outdated infrastructure with the latest innovations, which over time should save money. And without effective healthcare cost controls even the national citizenry and permanent local residents often find they can't afford to pay their medical bills because of numerous financial circumstances.

For those working on career strategies, there is no reason why one can't hedge their bets toward increasing your probability of having a successful diverse career path when you are considering world cultures and the market needs for customers throughout the global market.

And it's just my personal opinion that the effort needed to focus on tearing down or prohibiting the practices of one or more cultures in favor of having *just one homogeneous, nationwide culture*, is just a no-win scenario. If you really hope to enjoy the benefits of an increasing level of career opportunities as you move along your diverse career path, I believe it can benefit you to learn to acknowledge, communicate with people of different cultures, and hopefully enjoy the vast richness offered by our world cultures.

For anyone having been astute enough to have studied any of the lessons learned from the trade history related to "The Spice Trade" and the "Silk Road" and then utilized the knowledge gained, I would suspect they will be seriously focused on playing on a worldwide stage. Fully recognizing that the needs of people flow at a high rate of speed, worldwide. And people don't like to wait for service and benefits, so there is the need for a continuous flow. Without continuity, people get cranky, angry, and frustrated. They all want whatever it is that fulfills their needs, now.

Take a good look around you. Your interest should get perked up when realizing you are already swimming in a sea of goods, services, and products provided from around the world. And there are many who recognize the value of "The Spice Trade" in that *they are still using it*. Validation is easy for those who live in proximity to, or have visited a mega-sea port of entry. At any time, visitors will see the impressive sights of huge cargo ships, each carrying 3,500 or more colorful shipping containers stacked high on top of each other. At the cargo ship berths, visitors can also view a seemingly endless number of mammoth seaport cranes being used, non-stop, for unloading the containers onto trucks and trains which when loaded and approved, then drive off toward their intended destinations. In this day and age there are not many roadways where drivers don't see the 18-wheelers driving fully loaded. And there are not many drivers who have not been angered having to wait for a long freight train to pass. Some of the deliveries of foreign products are so massive that U.S. Ports of Call have terminals allocated specifically for unloading the goods from countries that are regularly bringing in large shipments like refrigerated perishables, auto parts, furniture, paper products, toys, and home furnishings. There should be no smoking mirrors when wondering if products and services have been moving worldwide for centuries. By foot, camel, mule, train, ship, plane, rocket and electronic technology. And here's the good part; it's still expanding.

These are fascinating career possibilities, just through how you think about cultures.

World Cultures. Knowledge of which can really be a simple, impactful addition to your career planning approach and an inexpensive concept for increasing opportunities, while broadening your probability for enjoying a successful career.

Where are you, now?

Chapter 6: Know Your Own Core Values and Moral Compass

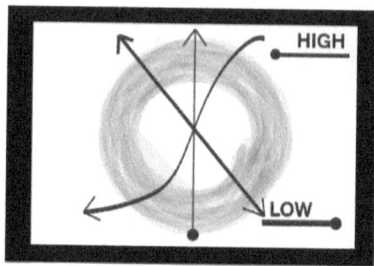

In this day and age, we are clearly in the midst of a communications revolution, where we are no longer subject to messages and propaganda solely delivered by the rich, powerful, government officials or the main stream media. But now, through social media we are witnessing the age of unlimited content channels, wide capacity informational tunnels, capable of delivering high levels of upfront and in your face, unbridled and unfiltered expressions of one's individual beliefs and values, good or bad, and without principles or controls. Truth and lies battling it out on the main stage.

Communication channels now exist for individuals to impose their beliefs and values onto others through workplace environment hierarchy, mega churches, law makers and elected politicians, law enforcers, social action groups, main stream and social media. With money no longer a hurdle, anyone who can use a cell phone can communicate any and every thought that's in their heart, mind, and soul. Unfortunately, the increase in our ability to socialize individual messages, has not yet included ways to easily discern messaging that is untruthful, propaganda, or insinuations.

This new communication era also makes it more challenging to raise children to have positive moral and ethical values and principles. It also creates a challenge with being able to control the types of messages they will hear and might need additional explanations.

We all rely on some level of foundational principles when interacting with others and when making decisions. Even though there will be some who believe there should be a separate set of rules for how you treat your family, friends, work associates, and complete strangers, I suspect at times if relying on conflicting principles the result could become conflicting personalities, which, to my knowledge, has never turned out well psychologically. Ideally, even with so many diverse messages being communicated, I hope you can determine one set of fundamental principles to act as your baseline to work from, no matter what setting you're in. Obviously with any set of guidelines, there will be discriminating circumstances where I expect you will treat someone more favorable than others. But relatively speaking, by having a baseline set of guidelines, you can have a starting place for how you treat people and to make decisions.

You may find your foundational core values and moral compass will initially build out from family experiences as well as from influences or peer pressure related to friends you respect or hang out with. But over time, you should expect to develop additional values to be molded as a result of unique individual experiences, good and bad. Many might be forged as a result of discussions with family members and trusted friends.

When it comes to utilizing your moral compass while working on your career, most employees enter their workplace environments with the assumption that their organization's leaders and their direct managers also follow a moral compass. Employees also tend to trust that business leaders have put competent managers in charge of critical projects and decisions. Who would entertain the thought of someone being put in charge and not being competent? But similar to what we are experiencing with mainstream and social media communication not having implemented ways to discern between messaging that is untruthful, propaganda or insinuations, the same exists in the workplace environment. Fortunately, business leaders will at times inadvertently show signs of their guiding principles, in the ways they manage their work environment. Employees rarely consider they could be working for an organization whose leadership lacks morals or positive values. As such, employees need to remain constantly vigilant and be mindful of this reality.

This is why it's so important for you to establish a moral compass. Since it will be your own personal values which will become your unique filters to discern what might be the values of the leaders guiding the organization. This is also important since your values can be used when vetting an organization that you are interested in joining. It is important to acknowledge that your own set of values may not be aligned with the leaders guiding the organization where you work. As individuals, we should not expect to have the same personal values as others. But extreme distances between values may be the reason you are experiencing frustration and tension in the work environment. For example, if you find employees are constantly treated with disrespect or placed in unfair or unsafe working conditions, the odds are you are seeing a clear indicator of top-down acceptance.

Core Values, Published Versus Actual

For many organizations, leaders identify three to five core values which they communicate to managers and employees to help drive their organization toward strengthening their brand. At times, the way they form their values is influenced by current concerns or challenges they've recently faced. For example, if the organization experienced an event which damaged their reputation, you can probably expect one of their core values will bring focus on compliance, integrity, fairness, and/or quality.

The core values might be centered around areas like integrity, ethics, honesty, openness to diversity of ideas and hiring, welcoming transparency and feedback, focus on diligence with adherence to internal controls, external regulations or growth, personal responsibility, being accountable for their actions, team work, collaboration, implementing effective cost controls, and of course having prudent financial management. But your personal core values can amount to principles that make up who you are as an individual, which ultimately guide your decision process and daily actions. The challenge could materialize when the published business' core values are not actually supported and, as a result, are contrary to your own.

For instance, you could have personal values centered on honesty, integrity, and ethical behavior. But while at work, you experience managers who are regularly dishonest, despite the organization having core values focused on integrity and ethical behavior.

Your Moral Compass and Working Conditions

You will find that it will be to your benefit to always vet an organization the best you can before choosing to pursue or accept any offers. To help you in the vetting process to decide whether or not to accept a job offer, I would highly suggest you begin to visualize your idea work environment and build a list of what might be your deal breakers.

Below are some high-level thoughts to get you thinking:

- Do you have at least five words that describe how you would like to be treated by managers and peers in your workplace?
- What types of people skills would you expect to see in managers?
- Do you believe you have a high, medium, or low tolerance-level that needs to be met before you would speak out after observing or experiencing some type of unethical behavior?
- Have you thought about ways you can maintain a positive reputation if you are required to work with individuals who make you angry or uncomfortable?
- How would you feel working with someone whose values are extremely contrary to your own?

Knowing your *core values* will provide you key directional points of reference on your *moral compass*, and can be a basis when making decisions. It will be continually helpful with understanding why you might become happy or unhappy within a personal or work environment.

If you were to jot down a list of your likes and dislikes, it could help you paint a picture of various paths you could consider pursuing when formulating strategies for your diverse career paths as well as professions which you might excel.

Who you are as a person will probably set a tone for how you interact with others in a work environment and will influence the decisions you make throughout your career. If you felt the need to help someone you saw being unfairly treated in a public place, you should feel the same need to help someone you saw being unfairly treated in your work environment. In contrast, if you are anti-social, have values that focus on taking advantage of people, or just happen for some reason to be a mean-spirited person, you should not be surprised if you regularly have conflicts with others. In that case, you might consider careers *that don't require team-work* when planning your diverse career path.

Here are seventeen actual scenarios to help you gauge your own core values. Under each scenario I have provided four generic responses to the scenario given. Select the one that best matches your values. And please select some or all to discuss with others so you can hear different perspectives. Don't be surprised when your answers and values change over time.

Scenario 1:
As part of your interview process you spoke individually to a couple of current employees. Unknown to the other, they both warned you that the manager you will be reporting to was known to bully people and be verbally abusive. How would you feel about working with that manager?

Select one response:
- A. A deal breaker
- B. Make you uncomfortable to work with him/her
- C. Would prefer not to have to collaborate
- D. Could collaborate but will have little or no respect for him/her

Scenario 2:
If you became aware that your manager was convicted of spousal abuse, how would you feel about working with that manager? Would it make a difference if that manager was male or female?

Select one response:
   A. A deal breaker
   B. Make you uncomfortable to work with him/her
   C. Would prefer not to have to collaborate
   D. Could collaborate but will have little or no respect for him/her

Scenario 3:

If your manager was known to lack integrity, be a pathological liar, or displayed sociopathic behavior, how would you feel about working with that manager?

Select one response:
   A. A deal breaker
   B. Make you uncomfortable to work with him/her
   C. Would prefer not to have to collaborate
   D. Could collaborate but will have little or no respect for him/her

Scenario 4:

If during your interview process you spoke to a current employee who warned you that the manager you will be reporting to is known for not taking responsibility for their own actions, how would you feel about working with that manager who always blames others?

Select one response:
   A. A deal breaker
   B. Make you uncomfortable to work with him/her
   C. Would prefer not to have to collaborate
   D. Could collaborate but will have little or no respect for him/her

Scenario 5:

If you were aware that your manager practiced non-traditional, extreme political or religious views, how would you feel about working with that manager?

Select one response:
    A. A deal breaker
    B. Make you uncomfortable to work with him/her
    C. Would prefer not to have to collaborate
    D. Could collaborate but will have little or no respect for him/her

Scenario 6:

If you were aware that your manager was a convicted violent crime felon, how would you feel about working with that manager? Would it make a difference if that same manager was male or female, Hispanic, African-American or of European descent?

Select one response:
    A. A deal breaker
    B. Make you uncomfortable to work with him/her
    C. Would prefer not to have to collaborate
    D. Could collaborate but will have little or no respect for him/her

Scenario 7:

As a result of a company re-org, you become aware that your new manager is discriminatory toward people of your specific race or religion, but is protected due to a friendship with a powerful executive. How would you feel about working with that manager?

Select one response:
    A. A deal breaker

B. Make you uncomfortable to work with him/her
C. Would prefer not to have to collaborate
D. Could collaborate but will have little or no respect for him/her

Scenario 8:

Your manager regularly has a tendency of responding weeks after receiving emails from you and customers regarding urgent issues, showing comfort with being inconsiderate to others. How would you feel about working with that manager?

Select one response:
A. A deal breaker
B. Make you uncomfortable to work with him/her
C. Would prefer not to have to collaborate
D. Could collaborate but will have little or no respect for him/her

Scenario 9:

You become aware that your manager works part-time in the adult entertainment industry, how would you feel about working with that manager? Would it make a difference if your manager was male of female?

Select one response:
A. A deal breaker
B. Make you uncomfortable to work with him/her
C. Would prefer not to have to collaborate
D. Could collaborate but will have little or no respect for him/her

Scenario 10:

Your manager has a tendency to make decisions without considering your input, and the decisions continually result in making you and others appear incompetent, but the manager takes no ownership in their actions. How would you feel about working with that manager?

Select one response:
- A. A deal breaker
- B. Make you uncomfortable to work with him/her
- C. Would prefer not to have to collaborate
- D. Could collaborate but will have little or no respect for him/her

Scenario 11:
Each time a member of your team experiences personal issues resulting in their need to arrive late to work or take off from work, your manager notes that it will be counted as a mark against getting a raise. Employees are then afraid to miss work even when they are ill. Your manager displays little if any compassion for others. How would you feel about working with that manager?

Select one response:
- A. A deal breaker
- B. Make you uncomfortable to work with him/her
- C. Would prefer not to have to collaborate
- D. Could collaborate but will have little or no respect for him/her

Scenario 12:
You notice that every instance when there is a conflict between two coworkers, your manager shows little concern for fairness and justice, and only reprimands those who have not brown-nosed to gain favor. How would you feel about working with that manager?

Select one response:
- A. A deal breaker

B. Make you uncomfortable to work with him/her
  C. Would prefer not to have to collaborate
  D. Could collaborate but will have little or no respect for him/her

Scenario 13:

You work with a manager who is always talking about themselves, always hoarding free handouts, never shares with others, and is overall selfish and extremely egotistical. How would you feel about working with that manager?

Select one response:
  A. A deal breaker
  B. Make you uncomfortable to work with him/her
  C. Would prefer not to have to collaborate
  D. Could collaborate but will have little or no respect for him/her

Scenario 14:

Every time you speak with your manager about getting an increase in salary he/she tells that you your raise will be in your check the following month, but it never appears. After three-months, you conclude that your manager is not trustworthy. How would you feel about working with that manager?

Select one response:
  A. A deal breaker
  B. Make you uncomfortable to work with him/her
  C. Would prefer not to have to collaborate
  D. Could collaborate but will have little or no respect for him/her

Scenario 15:

You work with a manager who always talks over other people when they are speaking, showing no courtesy for their coworker's opinion. How would you feel about working with that manager?

Select one response:
- A. A deal breaker
- B. Make you uncomfortable to work with him/her
- C. Would prefer not to have to collaborate
- D. Could collaborate but will have little or no respect for him/her

Scenario 16:

You work with a manager who you discover is consistently taking credit for your work. How would you feel about working with that manager?

Select one response:
- A. A deal breaker
- B. Make you uncomfortable to work with him/her
- C. Would prefer not to have to collaborate
- D. Could collaborate but will have little or no respect for him/her

Scenario 17:

Over two-years you have been successfully completing assignments, and those who benefited from your efforts have been complimenting your work, but your manager gives you no recognition at all. How would you feel about working with that manager?

Select one response:
- A. A deal breaker
- B. Make you uncomfortable to work with him/her
- C. Would prefer not to have to collaborate

D. Could collaborate but will have little or no respect for him/her

In retrospect, over the course of your career, I'm certain there will be a majority who will face situations that will require them to make decisions in which they will rely on their foundational core values. And your decision could place your employment at risk, or if you remain, result in your political capital negatively impacted. This is the risk you might face if you don't show allegiance to a manager who can impact your ability to advance. There are many other scenarios like the following: you may choose to go against your personal values for fear of losing your job, and as such, compromising your personal and financial obligations. You have a family to support, and a car loan or house mortgage to pay so you don't want to lose your property. You might find, one day, that you face a decision of needing to support an unethical business decision, and if not, potentially risk losing your job. Or it could come in the form of having to tolerate sexual harassment or psychological abusive behavior from managers or peers because the organization's compliance process turns a blind eye.

I often wonder what might have been the circumstances and pressure employees faced when they decided to compromise their own values in favor of supporting a criminal activity, unethical activity or immoral activity. Unfortunately, the events leading up to employees being compromised are rarely publicized until the activity has become a public scandal.

Below are some notable events where the reputations of employees and/or business leaders were impacted by their moral or ethical decisions.

1. A number of media channels, clergy, and public officials were tolerant and/or completely silent when some political candidates focused on bullying those who didn't agree with their ideas. Many were silent, even knowing morally and ethically that bullying is a recognized abusive behavior that psychologists, public service announcements, and the socially responsible public have focused on encouraging against such language or actions for fear results could psychologically damage the victim in a variety of negative ways, including suicide. Business and individual decisions were made to allow this to happen.
2. A number of media outlets, hoping to increase their ratings and their number of viewers, are allowing political candidates, private organizations and individuals to use their channels to disseminate known lies and propaganda, which actually misleads the public. A business decision was made to allow this to happen.
3. Government and financial oversight professionals ignored the activities of a number of financial institutions that developed sub-prime mortgage products designed to make available mortgage loans for borrowers with poor credit histories. These products created unfair disadvantages and introduced an extremely high level of risk for borrowers since financial institutions already knew, based on the borrower's credit history, they would be unable to keep up with their payments once the financial institutions increased interest rates; yet they approved the loans anyway. Between 2007 and 2010, these products resulted in a worldwide financial crisis with thousands of property foreclosures and total losses of property as individuals from all walks of life, living in urban, rural, suburban, and affluent areas were unable to keep up with the increasing high interest rates. Some borrowers were forced to liquidate their

entire savings resulting in an expansion of poverty levels in urban, rural, suburbs, and affluent areas. Thousands lost their jobs as businesses were forced to lay off employees since they too, were caught up in purchasing sub-prime loans.

4. A number of politicians hastily accepted, without verification, misleading and unsubstantiated "Weapons of Mass Destruction" presentations delivered by members of a presidential staff, which focused on a false rationale and justification as to why the United States needed to initiate military actions against Iraq in 2003. The misleading and unsubstantiated statements that alleged the existence of an active program in Iraq focused on creating weapons of mass destruction, resulted in thousands of men and women losing their lives, for a program that was not confirmed.

5. Potentially there were members of the support staffs of U.S. Presidents and other elected officials, which may have collaborated to keep the knowledge of their extra-marital sexual activities hidden from public view. History has documented details that were used against a U.S. president as part of his impeachment hearings.

6. As part of the Iran (Nicaragua) Contra scandal in 1986, there were a number of cover-ups to hide what was allegedly a secret sale of U.S. weapons to Iran in exchange for the release of U.S. hostages. Allegedly some of the proceeds from the arms sales were used to covertly support the anti-socialist Contra fighters in their civil war against the socialist Sandinista in Nicaragua. A National Security Council aide liaison and U.S. Marine Corps Lieutenant Colonel, allegedly misappropriated public funds by moving some proceeds of the arms sale into a secret private account slush fund. The Lieutenant Colonel was charged with conspiring to defraud the United States by channeling the profits

from U.S. arms sales to the Contra fighters in Nicaragua, altering and shredding government documents, accepting a bribe by illegally accepting the gift of a security system for his home, and aiding in obstructing a congressional investigation by seeking to keep the truth from Congress, all of which he was later pardoned for.

7. In the United States Watergate political scandal of the 1970s, there were a number of collaborators supporting the cover-up of a break-in at an opposing political party's headquarters. An investigation resulted in charges like criminal burglary, conspiracy, illegal wiretapping and obstruction of justice. The investigation culminated with a U.S. president resigning from office in 1972.

Since each of these events required collaborative efforts to plan, carry out either an unethical, criminal, or immoral activity, and then hide the details, individuals involved needed to make the decision to participate in the events, or refuse to be involved. Since we are only aware of the ones who were exposed, I wonder how many chose not to be involved, and as a result were ostracized. This aspect of the ones who said no, is rarely discussed. In the Watergate political scandal, although a number of the key players went on to gain benefits through book deals, speaking engagements and other profitable activities as a result of their involvement, Frank Wills, the security guard whose alertness exposed the break-in that took down a presidency, never was afforded accolades, as though he did something wrong. You might think that he would have been promoted and rewarded by his employer, and a book publisher might have offered him a deal.

What's Your Move When Asked to do Some Dirt?

Are you prepared for a decision-based challenge of your personal values? What would you do if faced with the choice of potentially losing your job or participating in efforts that could get you fined, put in jail, or result in people being injured or killed?

I hope with this chapter, you will do some soul searching. And I hope you will do all that you can to try and remain in a position where you will not be compromised by doing something against your values or beliefs.

No matter what your core values might be, I can guarantee that they will become the moral compass for how you interact with others, how others interact with you, and whether or not you will respect those you interact with. And although your core values are private, personal, and can be unspoken, it's really interesting how so many people have internal sensory and kinetic perceptions which allow them to uncover what someone else may hope will remain hidden by denials.

The risk of being compromised or discovering you are currently in a compromising position are some of the most challenging situations you will face over the course of your career. Do what you can to guard yourself; it's not an easy task, but be vigilant. Vigilance begins with knowing your own core values and moral compass.

Chapter 7: Your Value, Salary, and Income

One of the key influences many will wrestle with when deciding on a profession and career path to pursue, is how much income one hopes to make. If obtaining a respectable salary is not a major decision factor or influence, you may fall into the group whose members have already accepted that their career choices may not provide much economic rewards, or a group which hasn't taken time to research what their career choice pays, or they have chosen a career where they are more focused on service and enjoyment in what they do, not money.

Which Way to Go: High Salary, Your Passion or Both

There will be those who will choose a profession because they have a passion for the work involved, while others will select a career path strictly because they expect to make a high income which will facilitate achieving a certain economic status and lifestyle. For the group that has little concern for making a high annual salary, hopefully every level of success achieved will be a welcomed surprise that will hopefully bring joy, comfort and personal satisfaction.

However, I believe on a much larger scale, some of the greatest influences and on-going distractions many will face, or have faced when formulating, or revising one's career path, are the influences from society and the constantly changing, publicly defined values that so many rely upon as their yardstick for measuring success. As a direct result of these societal influences many tend to lean toward, and possibly fully rely on these influences when determining what they need to achieve before they can be considered as being successful.

Of course, there are many whose decisions are not influenced at all by a quest for high incomes, but a vast majority perceives the quest for high income as essential when formulating their career paths, and the aspirational motivation which drives them throughout their careers.

For both groups, you'll want to remain aware that your decision process will probably be quite different than others since the measure used to determine success is often not the same measure others use as their measure, because *unique individuals will have unique aspirations*. In many cases, the dominant measure that so many rely upon is based on some totally arbitrary monetary value, social image, or stereotypes.

Personal Value-based Perceptions

What type of person do you think of if you are told someone makes $15 an hour, $50,000 per year, six figures per year, a million-dollars a year or has a billion-dollar net worth? In thinking about each person, do you suspect each one has a different set of values, personal character traits, or principles by which they live? Would you think of the billionaire as being snooty, privileged, arrogant, not caring for the little guy, or the recipient of a huge inheritance? Would you think of the one making $15 an hour as young, poor, having limited education, and maybe grew up in a rural or urban area? Would you expect the person making $15 an hour could also be the actual same person and same personality as the one having a billion-dollar net worth? Could their incomes actually represent snapshots of the same individual taken at different points during their diverse career paths with only time being the difference? In reality, each scenario actually could be for the same person, at different points of their career paths. This person could easily be someone in their early twenties who was not thinking about making millions of dollars, but just thought of something that would be fun and helpful to people, and behold; it resulted in the creation of an innovative product or service. And along the way, this innovator maintained their same principles, values, and character.

No matter if you choose to pursue a career based on the expected income, or one where you're not influenced by the salary, we still have our opinions, possibly false opinions on how money aligns to or is associated with one's character and perceived value. There are countless innovators who have no idea of the long-term value, but only thought of something they believed would be fun or helpful. The value became realized after the customer market set the value. In other words, people liked the idea, and believed they would benefit by having it, so they relinquished their money for it.

Do you have a set amount in your mind on how much do you need to have in order to feel as though you are successful or have earned the right to proclaim you are a member of a certain class of people? And do you think money will change the person you are? It's possible.

Despite Your True Character, You Will Be Reviewed and Perceived

There's a good chance, and I might add a high probability, that as you achieve more personal success, others will begin to define you based on their personal measures of how they define success. As they notice you've obtained fruit from higher branches of the tree, further from their own reach, they deem you as being more successful, despite your own measures of success. As such, those close to you and who know you from way back when, will hopefully try to reinforce your need to "keep it real," "stay 100," and not forget where you came from. They see you evolve, but also continue to remind you in various ways, not to lose yourself.

I remember the time when I first became aware of public perceptions being in play that could influence how people measure your success. As a member of a college marching band, which performed regularly during the half-time periods of football games, I never considered that my participation as *one of many* members in a college marching band, would increase my popularity, specifically in how people began treating me as someone deserving special treatment and privileges. It was almost as though being around me somehow enhanced their image through proximity. At times, I wondered if the spotlight on me, equated to shared success for them, which they somehow could share in each time the band performed on the field. I experienced receiving free access to private campus parties where I didn't know the event organizers, and as such, whomever they were, had not conducted any vetting to know anything about my personality or character before allowing me to enter. Maybe by being a member of the marching band, we all had favorable public images, celebrity status, and as members, people believed an aura of happiness engulfed locations wherever we were. We were believed to be carrying good college fun everywhere we treaded. We were fun embodied.

    I also recall one pleasantly warm fall Saturday afternoon in Nashville Tennessee, where, as customary after the marching band finished their half-time performance, I and my drum line would stroll proudly up from the field, up the stadium stairs, and then make our way through the crowd, back to the reserved block of seats where the full band would sit. Along the way, we would banter, laugh, and re-live the on-field experience. During our stroll, we were usually so hyped up from the rush of our recent performance that we were often pretty immune to the crowd who were shouting as we walked through the crowd, all types of praises confirming their approval of our performance. But these were our classmates, and we never realized that some lived through us and participated in our expertise, the results of our daily practice, culminating in the execution of routines often at a higher emotional level than how we had practiced all week. And when it came to half-time on Saturday game day, we were them, and they were us. The crowd emoted with us. And when we came off the field, still hyped, they were too. Funny thing was, we seemed to forget we were wearing uniforms which made us stand out from our classmates in front of the entire university, on TV, and in front of public crowds. We never realized by being a member of the marching band, and putting on the uniform, we had somehow magically increased our value and worth to them, without them knowing one thing about our individual values, principles, beliefs, or character. In their eyes, we had increased our stock, moved up steps of social status, and were in fact, viewed by the crowd as special, campus celebrities.

And then for me, there was that one Saturday I won't forget. While we were heading back to the band's reserved seating area, I heard a young lady in the crowd shout out boldly to me, clearly over all the buzzing of crowd noise "I love you!" I had no idea who she was, and was unable to see in the crowd who she was, but the guys had a field day, because we all stumbled and kind of tripped over each other, and they began ask what I had done to encourage some lady to call out at me like that. And there it was; I had just realized fame and adornment that others were embracing us all along, but I never realized it until it was such a bold exclamation, a wake-up call which made me pay more attention to how the public often has measures of success that can influence in untold ways.

Years later, I was once again surprised. I clearly remember walking along a neighborhood street, heading to a metro bus station to go to work, when I noticed a young character in my path who in retrospect, appeared to be managing a street corner position like a military general, watching his troops pass in review. People were rushing hurriedly past him, coming and going to catch their bus or train, which like clockwork were whisking them away from the hub out towards all directions of the city. As I approached his street corner perch, I looked him in the eyes and gave a quick nod, showing proper street etiquette, without which could result in conflict that day, or some other day in the future. I made sure to exude confidence that I was not to be messed with, just in case he was trying to decide if he would be successful in a shake down attempt. He returned the nod. And as I passed his perch, almost immediately after the nods, I hear the words, "Whad up, money?" And I thought to myself, *Me? Money? Are you kidding? I'm riding public transportation, not a limo.* I chose not to respond, but instead to keep steppin'. Be cold. Leave him hangin' without any response and leaving him unsure if I might snap the next time we cross paths. But now, after boarding a train and headed downtown to work, I sat in my seat a bit puzzled and concerned by having received a label from a street corner hustler as "'money."

Once again, just like after my half-time experiences, I'm wondering what was the value measure that led a street corner hustler to believe it's appropriate to paint me with the "money" label. Was he just greeting me with a popular urban phrase of respect, or was it how he greeted every man who appeared strong, confident, with an attitude like having somewhere to be and didn't have time to banter. Was it my clean clothes? Probably. But there it was. He had a measure that he used to assess my value, maybe worth, determined who he would give respect and possibly was attempting to size up my character. And although he really had no real idea of my economic position, character, values, mission, or beliefs, or if I might be dressed to adhere with some type of employment dress code policy, his measure concluded, and so he shouted, "Whad up, money?"

After that, I became a bit more conscious of how my public image, or business casual uniform re-defined my public image, simply by what I was wearing. Even though I was the same person after getting home and changing into my soft, well-worn jeans and faded T-shirt.

The Monetary Measures in You

When using monetary measures for defining success, you may find that you focus on answering questions like, how much will you make, will you be able to live the lifestyle you want, how exclusive is it, or how unique is it? Will this make others envious of you because you have something they don't have? Will you feel the need to tell people you live in an exclusive community or the "good" or trendy part of town (which means you've decided what is the "bad" part of town)? Do you feel the need to proclaim that you have a luxury car or you're a member of an invitation only club? Will you be able to create some sense of security that makes you feel you are safe within your home boundaries, and where you travel.

And then there's the standard conversation starter when someone you just met, asks what do you do for a living, which is a slick way of conducting a value judgment or getting an idea as to how much money you make. I always find this to be a fun conversation exchange, which can be considered inappropriate to raise with someone you just met, but can be countered by just citing the industry and maybe area of interest as opposed to providing job titles. But the conversation can be treated as an entertaining game, by trying to find out their own value measures, or what might be their cut-off income threshold requirement for rejecting suitors. If someone says you don't make much, or your job must be challenging, a fun response could be, "In comparison to what?" For instance, if you have an annual income of $60,000, that's a good salary when compared to someone making $15 an hour, and a good salary for someone who doesn't carry much debt. But if you have amassed $100,000 in debt and make the same $60,000 per year, you undoubtedly will feel you don't make enough. Also, if you aspire to have a lifestyle which requires large amounts of discretionary funds, making $60,000 per year will definitely not be enough. I would suspect if someone interested in you is bringing in $60,000 per year but you aspire a lifestyle that includes a home worth $1-million plus and you want to regularly travel world-wide or own homes in various locations, you might decide that the person interested in you doesn't make enough money. And if you are already in a relationship and one decides to spend with the goal of achieving aspirations beyond your combined incomes, well now, you will face a crossroad decision based on if you need to change careers, add on additional sources of income or sever the relationship. In the case of money, you probably have a specific number in mind as what you need to meet your own measure for what is success, or what amount will facilitate you being in a certain lifestyle, or be able to help manage current debt.

    Unfortunately, these types of personal value assessments of others are a common occurrence that can result in one person humiliating the other and/or evolving into an increased level of tension centered around financial challenges and individual aspirations.

    Hopefully you can see why it's so important to determine your specific basic and psychological needs and aspirations so that you can determine a plan, have acknowledgment of your potential given your career plans, and if you are in a relationship, be able to communicate with your partner, and develop a mutually acceptable plan and timeline to achieve your pie in the sky, which may be quite different to the needs of your partner.

This is why when someone asks how much you make, you should recognize their question is focused on attempting to make a value assessment using a distinct amount or profession *they might have in mind.* And the conversation should include what are their aspirations, and the associated monetary amount.

So, in reality, if you are making your career plans or adjusting them based on your passion without much regard for how much income you'll make, or if you are making career plans based on an expectation of making a high income, or you aspire to achieve or maintain an expensive lifestyle, you really can't get away from determining what exactly is your personal measure for success and aspirations.

Pyramid of Needs

When considering Maslow's pyramid of needs as one way to begin to assess the needs for yourself and those you impact, it becomes a bit easier to have conversations about what level you are currently, and what would you like to achieve over a set period of time. For many, after fulfilling basic needs, they will be happy and satisfied just to live in a safe community where they can feel comfortable taking walks and leaving their doors unlocked. But if that person is partnered with someone who needs to fulfill self-esteem needs, that person may need to aspire to a profession that facilitates the ability to obtain high visibility or highly paid roles.

I would, however, caution you that if you choose to make your career choices based on *how you might appear to others* and less on what you really enjoy doing, or have a passion to do, you may be targeting a goal that overlooks *what you really would like to achieve.* I also would add, many often work to please their parents, while parents are often pleased to see their kids being able to leave the nest, sustain themselves, and stop asking them for money. So, I would ask you: in the absence of trying to choose career options to please someone else, what might be the considerations for your career plans?

Unfortunately, for some, there could be a down side in that a learned lesson will often be realized, after the cold slap of truth hits you in the face. That is, after you've fought so hard and long to obtain *something that someone else has*, or you've worked so hard to be in a class or caste you sought to be a part of, or seek to mimic the achievements of your peer, many may find they have short-term happiness or gratification from their perceived achievements. A Pyrrhic victory. But then again, there will be those who lavish in their economic achievements, and if that floats your boat, then be all you can be.

For others, you could face a steep let down when considering the amount of effort, you've dedicated, sacrifices you've made, which could amount to years of charging after goals which don't result in fulfilling your inner passion. Result: dreams deferred and misdirected. Go back twenty (or more) spaces, and do not pass go. (Sorry, that game reference just seemed to perfectly fit here.)

But behold, there's candy for all. There are clearly some professions which are not known for paying high salaries, while there are others that are assumed will guarantee a certain economic plateau.

Recommendation:
It may be to your benefit to periodically re-assess your psychological and emotional needs so you can tweak your career plans along the way and avoid needing to make a hard stop.

Recommendation:
If income is your motivation, I highly recommend you should review available salary surveys on the profession or career path you're interested so you can get some idea as to what is the expected salary.

More importantly, since salaries vary by location, and can change over time, you'll want to confirm if your career choice currently pays the amount you are expecting, in the specific geographic area where you reside. For example, a physician practicing in a rural area may not expect to make the same as a physician practicing in a large metropolitan hospital system, despite having similar expertise.

Are You Seeking a Character Makeover? Consider Your Pyramid

You should also be cautious if you are choosing a profession that pays out a certain salary because you hope your choice will build upon your self-esteem, or allow you to be able to establish some level of acceptance by your peers. You may be disappointed since the amount of money you make and the profession you are in, does not automatically create or enhance the character of a person. Salary is not going to resolve emotional or psychological needs.

Please look-up Maslow's hierarchy of needs. I found this pyramid interesting in identifying what might be motivating you. If something stands out here, especially if they are deficiency needs, you should keep in mind that the decisions you make in formulating your career plans *could potentially change as your needs are met.* You'll want to think about this soon and work toward achieving your full potential. Hopefully at some point, you come to realize that you won't be able to hide behind a job title or salary, since you'll still be you, no matter what your salary or job title, even though some may think specific job titles comes with entitlement.

When I think about the hierarchy of needs, there are three true stories that come to mind; they're different, but all centered around bullying. I recall one acquaintance who was bullied throughout their formative years, another who was battered in an adult personal relationship, and another who enjoyed bullying and controlling others on a regular basis. All three had different psychological motivating needs, experiences, and perspectives related to bullying, and all three chose to pursue careers in law enforcement.

Driven by Passion

Income and net economic worth are not true measures of assessing the value or character of a person, and definitely not cure all answers for fulfilling psychological and self-fulfillment needs.

Many religious leaders may not command high salaries (although some do), but who would be so bold as to proclaim that men and women choosing to pursue a faith-based profession don't generally seek to provide value and worth to their communities? How could you place a monetary amount on the value of their contribution to the communities they serve?

I've had the opportunity to interact with individuals working in the medical policy and medical care professions who command high salaries but their personal character was such you might have difficulty placing your trust in them for medical advice or care. Conversely, I've had the opportunity to interact with some in the same professions which I feel comfortable relying on their medical and personal consul.

Teachers are also not known for being paid high salaries, but when considering that they are the ones who nurture knowledge growth from early through advance levels, it would be hard not to acknowledge the value of teachers who provide critical thinking and training to so many around the world. And yet individuals who choose to go into the teaching profession are so often treated as though they are not valued or have worth. Often, they have to go on strike to fight for benefits or respect to obtain adequate investments in books, programs, and conducive work environments so they will be empowered with the tools and support needed to be effective teachers.

I've also had the opportunity to interact with members of the legal profession. In one recollection, the firm didn't have the common courtesy to return my call after leaving multiple voice messages when I was seeking help. Others were so professional that they would provide extensive support focused on providing general consul to help you decide on whether or not it would be to your advantage to move forward with a legal claim.

I've also had the opportunity to interact with individuals working in customer service. Some seemed as though they hated talking to people in general, while others made sure you had information to help you and then provided additional contact information in the event you still needed additional support.

So, what I'm saying is the amount of income does not align to the measure of the character of the individual. Salary definitely does not equate to the character or perceived value of a person where worth is intrinsic and not economic.

When looking back on my own income growth trends, my early income journey began below minimum wage. Over the course of my career, I added on additional skills, increased my network of connections, focused on having integrity, provided reliable service, maintained a collaborative attitude, set S.M.A.R.T. goals, which included implementing an innovative plan to change roles and responsibilities within a predetermined timeframe, and building a results-oriented brand image among other things. The result of working on intrinsic value along with increasing my tangible skills has been a consistent rise in salary. For those who showed little support for me when I was struggling on minimum wage, they had no idea of my long-term growth potential, faith, confidence, conviction, and resolve.

When making any type of plans, it's normal to identify achievable goals and also estimate the amount of time needed (time-bound) to facilitate a focused drive to achieve the goals. For those where a high salary is a key consideration for selecting a profession or career path, I would ask you to consider, how much money is your goal and how much time will you place in your plan to achieve your goal? If you make a salary of $100,000, and your neighbor makes $150,000, will you feel you are not successful or feel motivated to match, or one-up your neighbor? Do you feel you have achieved success only after you have acquired a specific high-end sports car? Will you consider you are successful after you have assisted fifty under-privileged individuals graduate from college? Or will you consider yourself successful after you've helped one hundred people who were falsely charged with a crime, get released from jail?

Point being, I would suggest as part of your decision with choosing a profession or career path that you set your success criteria so you *will know when you are successful by your own measure*. Else, there could be periodic influences that could cause you to constantly change your plans to accommodate the most recent influence, and that could become a plan with unachievable goals, having a moving, ever changing finish line, that is hard to obtain.

Peer Pressure from Family and Friends

Another aspect that can greatly influence how one formulates or revises their career plans is from family and peer pressure. Some parents will be quick to encourage choices they believe will result in a happy life for their children. But, they are often likely to suggest professions and career paths based on their own personal experiences and beliefs, while not taking into consideration what are *their offspring's own measures* for what they might consider to be success, their personality, true character traits, and passion that drives them. And although one's passion could lead you on a path that will not result in the ability to acquire items like their neighbors or what society deems to be signs of success, it should be up to each individual to follow their path, hopefully having a clear understanding of the trials and tribulations they could face. With any decision, you will hopefully receive support and objective consultation from your family, friends, and peers. Although the decision should be yours, it would be a mistake to think your decision will not impact those around you.

Those close to you will most certainly have their own measures of success that may not align with your own measures and value system. This is where peer pressure can turn into verbal, psychological, and potentially physical abuse, which can become challenges for you to achieve the success you aspire to achieve.

For example, one might strongly suggest that if you can't provide an expected level of comfort and benefits, it's because you are not really a smart or strong individual. In some cultures, the concept of wealth succession relies on the family business eventually being turned over to other family members. *Being unable to meet the expectations* of the elder or dominant family member could lead to being dismissed or expelled in some way.

When a family member, significant other, or close friend has a different measure for how they define success than yours, it's not unusual for them to display anger, disrespect, meanness, lack of support, lack of considerateness, or develop less restraint with publicly humiliating the other because of a lack of belief in one's potential to achieve the success they want to see. Wives might be heard claiming that their husbands are not much of a man since their salary is less than the woman's salary. Husbands might claim that their wives don't meet their needs, and that provides them an excuse for infidelity or divorce. In each case, they are both measuring the worth of the other based on subjective values, and not on the character of the person or because they love how they feel when they are together. Husbands might be heard demeaning their wives because their wives have less education or their salary is only enough to cover the smallest bills. You might also experience one proclaiming that the partner who makes the highest income has the right to make decisions for both. Again, these examples of abusive psychological and verbal language are fueled by one person having different measures for what they believe is needed to obtain success.

Unfortunately, make no mistake about it, individuals finding they are in any of these situations will experience increasing levels of humiliation which could result in: 1) the need to change one's career path to something not aligned to one's passion, and thus resulting in dreams deferred; 2) increasing levels of abusive behavior from one person to another; 3) a growing apart or total separation initiated by the abuser or the one being abused; or 4) the deterioration of one's former personality into a demur personality, created by what is communicated by the abuser and a lack of support. Although we all hope and expect our families, friends, and peers will fully support the career path we chose, it can be difficult if your choice is far from the views they perceive to be normalcy or how each individual uses as a measure for success.

Ultimately, every individual situation is unique, and hopefully everyone will receive support from their family, friends, and peers, even if only in conversation alone. Given that some career paths will be a struggle, it's to your advantage to work toward openly encouraging your family, friends, and peer to lend you moral support to at least see if you can get to the top of your hill or fulfill some of your goals.

Often, it's through struggle before some can truly define what is value for them, and through that realization, they gain better understanding that happiness and success are concepts each of us must determine on our own, as unique individuals. Although those societal influences on values and worth will continue to change from generation to generation, for the most part, it's one's individual perceptions that lead people to aspire to have what those acknowledged as being rich, famous and respected possess, not actually taking into account their individual character, value, or morals as being measures for success. I believe by having awareness of both the strong hypnotic influences associated with monetary-based aspirations, and having awareness of your non-monetary aspirations, can help you during critical decision making to determine what is the best career direction for you based on your needs, and the needs of those close to you. Ultimately, we all face battles with seeking to achieve our true passion in life. And we all, at some point, may seek to reach the goals of being debt free, having the resources to travel at will, being able to purchase what we want, enjoy luxury, and enjoy a safe and comfortable living environment.

So, I encourage you not to rely on what your peers or society deems to be successful, but take some time to *think about what you desire to achieve*. Take time to encourage moral support from your family, friends, and peers no matter what might be the income associated with your profession or career choice.

Takeaways To Be Considered

In retrospect, here are a few thoughts for you to take-away:

- Many people inadvertently believe the amount of salary one makes is the measure by which to judge a person's character or worth instead of the person's actual character and principles for which they stand.
- If someone chooses a career path that is not expected to result in a high salary or upward move in social status, they should encourage their family, friends, and peers to continue to respect them as a person, not because of their economic status. Friends should remember why they are considered to be friends. Hopefully their support group will choose to provide moral support, if not financial, as they strive to achieve *their own goals*, not the goals of their family, friends, or peers.
- Humiliation is an abusive tactic and form of psychological abuse, often used without malice, by some when they have strong concerns that the income of a family member, significant other, or friend will not be sufficient to meet the goals they personally have in mind for the one being humiliated. In this case, humiliation could be an overt

indicator of the need to have constructive conversations to re-visit, align, and agree on mutual goals.

- Upon making the decision to choose a profession not known for paying a high salary, or if you haven't assessed what is the income associated to the same profession or career, the choice may result in personal sacrifices. This path could result in times when the lack of discretionary funds makes it difficult to provide tangible signs of appreciation, affection, and support to your significant other, immediate family member, and friends. However, this path, when unbeholden to monetary gain or profit, can nurture organizational goals focused on care, service, innovation, achieving better health outcomes and practices, scientific discoveries, new product research and development, expanded educational pedagogy, increased personal assistance, developing better public policies and other humanistic results. Individuals following this path are often known for work that delivers tremendous gratification, help to the underserved, and social improvements not motivated by profit. Ultimately, this group often accounts for contributing immeasurable impacts to how we live, interact, and evolve, while simultaneously being the target of negative feedback because of the reliance on discretionary funding, monetary contributions, and low take-home pay for individuals.

- Making the decision to pursue a profession without concern for income often is the decision made by someone having an *extreme passion* for the profession or career of choice. It's important for the person having the passion to have a trusted support group of family members or friends who can provide objective input since your passion can impair your decision process. For the members of the trusted support group, keep in mind the person whose passion is driving them along their career path could be following an honorable path, an innovative path, a creative path, a game-changing path. As a result of an unrecognizable or proven path, it may be difficult for many to recognize their long-term potential. But moral support costs you nothing, but could mean so much for the confidence of the person being driven by passion. Just think about all of the "thank-you" speeches where Mom, Dad, and a significant other were acknowledged: "...for without you, I would have never made it!" Key point being, "Never made it!" But of course, there is another perspective. Everything is not always blue skies and caramel popcorn. If I'm going to keep it real, there were the ones who made it *without any support* from their mom's, dad's or significant others. And well, that missing and did I mention, "free," moral support, resulted in..., Well I'll let you think about what they got.

- Your psychological needs should be considered when formulating your diverse career path plans.
- No matter the influences, motivations or needs that will be considered as part of the process you use to make a decision on which profession or career path you plan to pursue, it will be prudent for you to have some idea of the income potential associated with your choice. There are numerous free salary surveys available. By having some general idea, you can be cognizant of the lifestyle your income will be able to support, and when you deem it necessary, you can level-set with anyone who relies on you, or are in partnership with you, to help them achieve their goals or lifestyle. This will be especially important to be able to level-set with your immediate family members especially if they are expecting or

assuming you will be helping them achieve their own personal goals or lifestyle. If your child is expecting help with higher education, they should know. If you are in a relationship, and your partner has a certain lifestyle they expect to experience, they should know how much you can contribute, and come to acceptance.

Chapter 8:
Career Market Indicators

The early morning sun was gentling beginning to shine through the café-style, sheer curtains that framed the small, rectangular windows over the kitchen sink. At that time, Kozi, a young student, with an extreme passion for astronomy, was sunk in the comfort of his bed, deep within the boundaries of one of his exotic dream journeys. This time, his dream placed him sitting on the side of a hill, overlooking a small yellowish-tinged village in a slightly wooded area on a distant planet, while looking up at twin moons and being sprinkled by a warm mint-scented mist sprayed from a nearby waterfall. In reality, he so eagerly hoped to actually visit a planet like this one day. But just like other mornings, his dream was suddenly interrupted by the voice of his mom shouting from the kitchen, "Kozi! Are you woke?"

His mom's shout startled him, and her question rolled into focus as Kozi slowly awakened from his dream. He knew, not only was she urging him to wake up, get out of bed, and start getting ready to start another new day, but simultaneously, he also knew she used the term "woke" as a dual meaning, just for him. It was their own language used, to keep him motivated through a daily encouragement ritual, focused on his need to dedicate time, every single day, with keeping on track with his efforts that are part of his diverse career path strategy. This second meaning, kept him focused on the thought that if he ever was going to achieve his goals and realize his dream of having a successful future career in astronomy and space exploration, he needed to be woke (aware), mentally of what actions he needed to work on this day, and every day, to help him move forward towards achieving his goals, which he and his mom had initially mapped out in his diverse career path strategy. He needs to be woke (aware) of what he was going to do to remain current with changes taking place around him. Since he had identified his curious character type and others that lead him toward innovation, exploration, and being a visionary, he knew he will need to stay aware of on-going developments taking place in the space industry. He needed to remain aware of what's going on globally as financiers and investors made their moves to capture space-related contracts. He would need to know what's going on with international politics as various countries worked toward implementing space industry policies. He knew he needed to increase his cultural awareness, language skills, conflict resolution skills, and S.T.E.M. studies. And of course, he will need to stay aware of various personal obstacles and challenges he'll need to address to ensure he is trained and ready for his next *"work-for-success"* opportunity.

For Kozi, the profession and career opportunities available to him will extend far beyond the town which he currently lives, and into the stars. As a result of the extremely large scope of opportunities spanning beyond his regional area, his *awareness and concern* for refugees, immigrants or the migration of people moving from one city to another and taking jobs in the region where he lives, is not adversarial, but empathetic. His studies will be focused on future opportunities, some of which have yet to be developed. In addition, his scope will not only include worldwide needs, but also the world's perspective on the space industry and impacts occurring within the realm of outer space.

I provided this fictional journey around Kozi to help alert you of what we all should be considering, which is the fact that when planning a career path, we need to look at what is being developed for future endeavors and doing all we can to have a *mindset of preparing* for changes yet to be developed. We should consider not only opportunities that are available within the region where we live, but as a result of technology, we can pursue opportunities across borders, including interplanetary.

As I looked back on challenges I personally faced while moving along my diverse career path, I recognized there were events which took place nationally and globally which created a need for me to tweak my plans. For instance, the sub-prime mortgage crisis of 2007 through 2009 turned into a national recession that impacted world markets and economies, and created the need for many to find alternative means of income, or new jobs. The scope of this crisis spanned across international borders, and impacted thousands of individuals and businesses. I personally made adjustments, including adding new skills, cutting back on expenses, and seeking opportunities that focused more on some of my basic skill sets, and less on the goals I intended to reach. Dreams deferred, but not stopped. For many, this man-made sub-prime crisis was brewing before being realized. Later after symptoms had surfaced, the cards cascaded and fell, resulting in many, many dreams deferred for wage earners and investors around the world.

Who Was Watching When the House Fell Down?

Who would have seen the sub-prime mortgage crisis coming? But wait; there actually were signs. Preceding up to the crisis, there was the dot-com tech industry bubble that popped, in which overpriced stocks were eventually deemed as overvalued, and eventually the bottom fell out, taking investors with them. Also, the September 11, 2001 terrorist attack created instability as countless and sometimes unbridled military actions took to the front stage. Worldwide banks turned their focus on stimulating the economy anyway they could. Plus, there was a political culture that focused attention around financial deregulation policies. If you see similar signs of instability, you just might want to make sure you have put some safeguards in place.

Unfortunately, when the symptoms of a crisis were unveiling themselves through a number of impactful events, families continued to focus on achieving their dream of owning a home, all while ignoring the house they were in, and the neighborhood around them was falling down. And so, the demand for consumer mortgage loans increased, even in light of the shaky economy. Mortgage loan lenders found it an opportune moment to take advantage of the increasing demand and make some quick cash. They responded to market demand and began creating products focused on issuing loans to individuals having poor credit. Despite all of these indicators, so many continued as though there would be no real impact on the job market and their ability to pay their debts. National debt continued to increase and lenders kept lending. All these symptoms were clear indicators of problems.

In all of my efforts to learn about strategies for identifying and then obtaining a suitable career that matches my skills and aligns to my goals, *no one ever alerted me* or even suggested that in addition to national events, *there are worldwide influences* that are constantly in play and ever changing *that could impact my current* as well as future opportunities. There are a number of indicators accessible to you that you can and should periodically monitor.

Since there are numerous events and indicators taking place worldwide, I don't propose that you try to keep up with every indicator, since that would be quite a challenge, but you could program your computer assistant device to alert you when specific indicators hit a predetermined threshold. It's interesting that financial accounts now offer alert features for their customers. Your balance gets too low, you get a text or email alert. I wonder what influenced them to do that. (Hmm.) But when thinking about the industry you are focusing on for your career, maybe only include as part of your career path plans to periodically check various indicators and try to be aware (woke) to identify events that could influence your profession, job markets, and your specific career. A good example might be pivotal changes to federal or municipal regulatory policies, or the introduction of new tax structures, which, depending on whether there's an increase or reduction, could either attract new businesses or influence flight.

If you include a mindful strategy for monitoring changes within your career market or industry as part of your plans for developing and managing your diverse career path, over time you could become increasingly knowledgeable of influential industry-specific events, and also create an opportunity to help others with your knowledge. And since some events or indicators may not be so apparent until after impacts begin to materialize, you'll need to keep watch and be vigilant. The hope is that you will become more skilled with identifying events and assessing changes of key indicators that might give you early warnings of probable needs to make adjustments or add protections to handle approaching influences that may impact the job market and potentially impact you.

To help you, I've started a partial sample list of items you may want to periodically check. Knowing that over time, indicators, markets, and customer expectations will change, I urge you to start your own list, revise it, adapt it to your own specific areas of concentration, and then continue to determine new list actions over the course of navigating your diverse career path. Without doubt, there will be career specific indicators that track to your specific industry.

Starter List of Indicators That Could Alert You of Change

Here ya' go. Please keep in mind that web content owners change over time so the names I've provided below, may change in the future and require the need to conduct new searches for the information you need.

- State unemployment statistics
    - Bureau of Labor Statistics.
- Become familiar with migration patterns in the United States and worldwide.
    - Pew Trust
    - Pew Social Trends
    - Atlas Van lines
    - United Nations
    - World Bank
    - Organization for Economic Co-operation and Development
    - International Organization for Migration
- National Debt Clock for national debt; per citizen, taxpayer, median income, etc.
- Consumer Confidence
    - The Conference Board
    - Organization for Economic Cooperation and Development
- Check changes to the Gross National Product worldwide
    - International Monetary Fund
    - United Nations
    - KNOEMA
    - The Economist

- The World Bank
- Statistic Times
- Check changes in census
  - National Census Bureau
- Find out what are the current areas of growth and growth rates
  - United States Census Bureau
  - Forbes
  - Trading Economics
- Track the top products and services companies
  - INC
  - Forbes
- World Conflicts and turmoil
  - Global Conflict Maps
  - Council on Foreign Relations - Global Conflict Tracker
  - Conflict Map
- Terrorism Watch
  - Terrorism Watch
  - Homeland Security.
- International Trade Policies
  - World Trade Organization
  - Department of State
  - International Trade Administration
  - Economy Watch
- Cost of crude oil / petroleum dollars per barrel
  - OPEC
  - Index Mundi

- o   United States Energy Administration
- World Poverty / National Poverty
    - o   World Hunger
    - o   Global Issues
    - o   World Bank
- World Health / Pandemics / Epidemics
    - o   World Health Organization
    - o   Health Map
    - o   Outbreak News
- Global Warming
    - o   NOAA
    - o   Global Change
    - o   EPA
    - o   NASA Climate
- Travel Trends
    - o   United States Travel Association
    - o   Travel Trends
    - o   AARP
- Consumer Spending trends
    - o   United States Department of Commerce
    - o   Bureau of Economic Analysis
    - o   Gallup
    - o   The Balance
    - o   Selig Center Terry College of Business
- Follow new discoveries
    - o   World Economic Forum
    - o   MIT Technology Review
    - o   Live Science

- o Popular Science
- o NASA
- o Jet Propulsion Laboratory / California Institute of Technology
- Follow emerging business process trends
  - o BPM Institute
  - o ECM Connection
- Identify your local and national government representatives, check their sites for legislation created and/or passed. This could provide you a glimpse of something politicians are aware of or concerned with regarding employment or specific job markets.
- Check foreign newspapers for political, economic or conflicts that could result in their residents beginning to migrate to other countries
  - o InkDrop
  - o OnlineNewspapers
  - o World-Newspapers
  - o Refdesk
  - o HeadlineSpot
  - o The Assignment Editor
- Find specific indicators that track your area of interest, profession or industry. For example: The Healthcare Industry; Manufacturing jobs; Research Funding; Corporate Expansion; Infrastructure Investments; Consumer Protectionism; the Travel and Leisure Industry.

Hopefully this list can act as a sample guide for creating your own industry-specific list of indicators relating to your area of focus.

Chapter 9: Search Approaches for Finding a Job

First of all, I want to start out with some realities associated with searching for a job:

1. There is no single approach or method that always works, just some that tend to work better than others for various individuals. For example, my customized approach tends to get me results but that same approach may not work for your unique character and personality.
2. Over time, you can expect that the current practices being used by hiring associates to onboard new hires will change due to company decisions or external influences outside the control of company management. This presents an opportunity for you to develop creative approaches that might return successful results for you and/or increase the adoption of new approaches by hiring associates. So, I would suggest that you always consider being innovative and creative with your search approach.
3. Every organization has a unique set of dynamics, policies, processes, and individuals working behind their doors. This means that one résumé will not fit everyone, and I personally believe that it becomes a hit or miss exercise for anyone to attempt to craft customized résumés until you understand the preferred communication style of the hiring manager, actual end user, or consumer. For example, some may prefer summaries with bullet points, others may prefer descriptive summaries, others may only want executive level summaries citing how you were involved with notable projects, while another may want to see measurable metrics. The options never end, so before you customize a résumé, I would

suggest that you attempt to learn about the hiring manager and then present whatever makes you look interesting and capable of helping in some way. I consider a résumé to be your marketing document that is focused on capturing the attention of a decision maker.

4. I believe one of the easiest and most casual opportunities to meet someone who could potentially become a champion in assisting you with obtaining *"work-for-success"* opportunities, to learn about what it would be like working at their company, or find out about the current direction of the company, is to identify and then attend community events where employees of your targeted companies are scheduled to attend. Having a face-to-face conversation is considered to be one of the most preferred methods to market yourself, even though many will just say networking and getting referrals from your trusted acquaintances are the best ways to get hired. In addition, the face-to-face conversation is often the way people talk their way into a role that hasn't been created as yet. On the downside, this approach doesn't work for everyone, especially those who are not too good pitching their abilities. If you are in that category you may need a tactic in which someone pitches for you. And that's alright too.

Accountability

The sooner you embrace accountability, the easier it will hopefully become. Specifically, when seeking to obtain a *"work-for-success"* opportunity, you and only you will be accountable for making it happen. Others can, and will assist you, but you are the one who will need to stay focused and aggressive with working to get results. If you get depressed with the level of effort needed, or the lack of results, you can be assured not to achieve your expected outcomes unless you persist. Keep in mind there is no rule on how long it might take since there are so many influences in play. Accountability is what you must remember is on you, and is your challenge alone. People find opportunities because they don't give up, they are creative, or they have built a strong network that they can rely on over time to obtain some level of favor. But you are the one accountable for making sound career decisions, even if you relinquish or delegate your authority to someone you believe is more knowledgeable, which is more probable early on in your initial career planning phase. But at some point, you will take over the reins, and begin to own all key decisions. Also, your approach may need to adjust over time when needing to fit a specific opportunity you are targeting. In any case, you'll need to accept that you will be the innovator of each new approach and need to decide on the best way to present yourself.

Be not afraid, because in reality, you are the product and hopefully, if not now, at some point you will become the best expert to market your product. That means being able to convince hiring associates that you have value and/or potential. This also means, if they are cognizant of the fast-changing job marketplace, they need to be open to creative approaches, be prepared to evolve, adapt, and be willing to change their current onboarding processes. That means your approach has the potential of becoming recognized as an improvement to their existing process. So, don't be so locked into standardized application processes. I can assure you, I've seen people get hired by circumventing the hiring process completely. I personally have been contacted directly by a hiring manager, asking if I was interested in an open role, that at the time, I was unaware was available. So, by blindly accepting standardized processes as the only channel in, your search approach can be harder for you to stand out from others.

More and More Search Tools

There are some jobseekers who sadly enough, will rely on the effortless approach of applying for jobs found while trolling websites. Since there's no cost associated with this approach, there's no reason why jobseekers can't continue to use it to assist in their job search. Of course, there are so many who enjoy this approach, you are going up against quite a large number of applicants. I'm actually surprised these job sites actually still exist, knowing that in many cases, the short-list of candidates is more often built from candidates who have been *referred* by internal employees, managers, or someone who has some type of business or personal relationship in place. After the short-list has been created, in some instances, the actual job opening is then publicly posted online for a couple of weeks, to make it appear as though there was no discriminatory hiring practice in play, even though in reality, a non-public selection process has already initiated and potentially completed.

I like to utilize the career sections of targeted organizations for the purposes of self-marketing by creating an online profile that includes my current résumé, reviewing the messaging they are putting out, and looking for signs of attrition or growth. Uploading your résumé to targeted organizations allows you to get it into their database far in advance of future opportunities being actually posted. In other words, this is more of a long-term self-marketing tactic. Some companies have a process where hiring managers must fill out a job description (JD) form, which the HR department might use to run a search for internal employees and non-employees whose résumés are in their database, to find any which are the closest to matching the newly created job description. When a role is posted at some point in the future, having your résumé in their database may get you some unexpected attention. The HR associate will also ask the hiring manager if there is anyone in their department who would be a good match for the new role. If so, they only have to follow an internal promotion or resource transfer process to fill the open role, which cuts you out of the picture for that role. In some cases, the internal employee is promoted before external candidates are considered. It's just too easy and much cheaper to promote internally, even though the opportunity to find the so-called "best person for the job" is circumvented.

Another benefit of using their career sections is you often have the opportunity to "follow" the company and create job search agents that emails you when there are new postings matching your search criteria. If they maintain a current list of open postings, or are beginning an upward trend of hiring, you may catch signs of expansion or growth areas.

However, *if you keep seeing the same job* or postings where the job description is just a bit different when compared to others, you might be seeing the results of something happening internally that should raise concerns. I like to think of these approaches as good *preliminary vetting* that you might want to consider, or develop other vetting plans, that you implement well in advance of actually triggering your network to begin pursuing connections that can introduce you for a role that matches your diverse career path plans. These are the type of tactics you can initiate while you are currently in a role, but casually looking for something new.

For example, if you are interested in pursuing a career in the advertising profession, you might want to create a job search agent that will email you postings at least once a week, or use a social network or the company's own career site to "follow" ten or more advertising agencies, two to four months (or more) before actually seeking a role. I can tell you that I have found some companies posting the same role over and over again, letting you know they are just collecting résumés, or they might be having difficulty getting someone to accept their offer. This may also speak to their credibility if they actually don't have a job they are seeking to fill, but have one posted. You may tend to overlook this as a usable *assessment* indicator, but this policy of posting *without actually having a role* they need to fill, lets you know that they are okay with having a process that works for them while not telling the public the truth about actual availabilities. When vetting potential businesses that you are considering working with, you should ask yourself if you are okay with a company openly showing a lack of integrity. Maybe they actually consider their process as just being a little white lie that hurts no one. But this could be a glimpse through a window that is concealing something bigger, like other similar policies and practices.

      For me, this would be the first check mark in the pass or skip this one column. A weight placed on the negative side of the balance scale. And not knowing why they chose to post to the public what appears to be an open position, I would begin to look for other signs that might ultimately lead me to deciding, this is not an organization I should dedicate time pursuing employment. And then I can cross them off my target list of desirable organizations.

Start-ups Hire Too
      Another search tactic you might consider is to target start-ups and organizations seeking to expand their existing business. By checking angel investors, venture capital, or start-up funding sites where you might find new organizations seeking seed money to get started, or ones that are expanding, you might locate businesses seeking to service areas you are interested in providing support. You could also become aware of businesses which are seeking to expand their existing organization.

Once they reach their funding goals, you can expect them to need to build staff. You also might have the opportunity to reach out to the founders to offer your services before they have obtained their funding goals.

Keep in mind that when focusing your diverse career planning toward start-ups, there is some risk in that opportunities could either be short-term (five years or less), or deliver substantial growth opportunities as a result of getting in on the ground level as the business grows. This is also fertile ground for having a face-to-face conversation that results in a role being created based on your unique abilities.

But regardless of your approach, nowadays people often get jobs through a trusted channel. This could be through a referral from someone trusted, community organizations, or staffing firms that have already developed a relationship, or have an internal preferred vendor status. In these channels, hiring managers expect the potential candidates have been vetted before they are submitted for consideration by the hiring manager.

Vetting Should Always Be Done

I can recall soon after graduating from college, my career plan at that time focused on targeting one, and only one area of focus related to my degree. I made a list of companies in my metropolitan area, and then began going directly to each office location, initiating a face-to-face, inquiring about their hiring process, which I was already aware but was facilitating information gathering, and if possible, filling out an application right there on the spot. I expected after leaving there was some fifty-fifty odds it would either be circular filed, or hand delivered to an appropriate manager. At the time, I had not realized the value of vetting a company before bothering to make an unscheduled face-to-face visit. It takes a little more effort, but can save you some pain in avoiding unsavory businesses by conducting online searches, asking counselors at your school, or inquiring a few individuals within your network.

For me the result of not doing thorough vetting was, in some instances, finding businesses who needed someone to fill an immediate staffing need, right then and there. In those rare instances, when I discovered a company which was seeking to fill a role, a manager would come out, introduce themselves to me, have a quick chat, and ask, when can I start. But the roles they needed to fill really had nothing to do with my own career goals. And other times, after accepting an offer based solely on the notoriety of the brand name, I soon experienced the cold, figuratively back-hand face slap of an adverse work environment and culture where I had to question, how did I get into this mess, why did I take this job, how did their brand name get such a good reputation, and how do I get out?

Vetting should focus on helping you to see past that prestigious brand name of a company that has dedicated effort and a good amount of time, building their brand recognition and street 'cred' (reputation). In some cases, vetting will unveil an organization's efforts to cover up an evil cabal. Yes, unfortunately, businesses like that do exist.

Of course, there are many businesses whose brand names are respectable and are known for bona fide legendary service and customer care. But then, there are the others, which are not, let alone some of their employees.

Fast forward to now. There are so many challenges with identifying a suitable company to work with. The odds are high that you could end up needing to reverse negative results, after you joined the team. I might add that even if you are contacted as a result of a referral, before jumping up and down celebrating with joy, I would highly suggest you ask around and run some internet searches to gather any details related to events associated with the company contacting you. Fortunately, more people are realizing after the fact, there are adverse working conditions and work environments. As a result, job seekers are learning to conduct searches to avoid feeling like they received a blunt kick in the head for not heeding this warning. Conduct your search first. Always conduct vetting.

But every now and then, you may find people would rather learn from their own mistakes instead of considering the advice of someone who has experienced a situation and now want to help others avoid similar issues. Do you recall one of your parents warning you not to touch a hot stove, and maybe you did it anyway? There's also a phrase about not drinking the juice (possibly in reference to the drink used in the 1978 Jonestown Guyana mass suicide). These are both legendary examples of someone trying to keep you from experiencing pain or discomfort. But, many have to feel the pain for themselves instead of heeding the warning. I can add there was an instance when my haste to get a job and my lack of vetting resulted in working, unknown to me at the time, for a shady, unscrupulous business owner which after quitting, I was concerned about the business having my social security number, home address, and worried that someone might show up at my home to rob me. Imagine that.

I also found companies that had just fired, or laid-off a number of employees, later only to realize they let go too many, and then realized they could no longer provide adequate customer service. Unfortunately for me, I initially looked at this type of scenario to be an opportunity, not thinking that those employees left over and still working, were emotionally impacted by seeing their co-workers and friends let go. And now you find yourself a new employee having to work in a hostile work environment. I can tell you, it's not a happy feeling to work in that type of environment. That can speak to the inability of leadership, their inability to conduct accurate analysis, or they were just insensitive to what's happening within their organization. Odds are, those leaders are still there when they probably should have been let go with the previous group.

Here are a couple of memories to motivate and encourage you:

- At one point, there existed actual video stores that rented video tape movies. Where are those stores now? The market changed, those stores are gone, and so are the employees.
- At one point, getting in a line to speak with a bank teller so you can conduct banking transactions like depositing your paycheck, getting money out of your account, or paying bills was the primary method for interacting with your banker. At some point, banks were convinced to change their focus toward mobile and online transactions. As a result, there is an increasing trend for those who are computer savvy to conduct transactions using their phones, online banking, and ATMs.

I highlight these two examples to help you realize that you should really conduct vetting before accepting what you think are opportunities. Bank teller jobs dwindled and were replaced with technology. Video store clerks were replaced with technology. I can imagine there was a point when individuals in those jobs began getting out but the organization needed to hire someone before the budget was pulled completely for those roles.

In Closing

Everyone has potential and each day new opportunities are created. You'll have to stay alert as trends, politics, the environment, society, people, cultures, morality, governance regulations, and influential group dynamics change. Overall as the signs of the times change, we change. What does that mean for search approaches? They will change, and someone will influence those changes. Is there any reason you can think of as to why you shouldn't be the one who comes up with the best tactic for finding opportunities and then marketing your abilities?

Chapter 10: Adversaries in the Shadows

Early in my career, I began to realize that I generally view people through a lens of objectivity, in that when I first meet someone, I generally like to start from a positive place, taking on a perspective that *most* people are friendly and not predators, have somewhat good values and want some sense of happiness and safety for themselves and their family. But as I moved along my career path, I increasingly realized my youthful vision of a kinder, friendlier world made me a bit gullible when considering it was extremely hopeful of me to believe most would fit into, or practice a 'world peace' point of view. It's also unrealistic not to acknowledge in addition to a basic concept of most wanting some sense of happiness and safety, there are in fact, people who include in their world view, the need to obtain their happiness by taking various things from others, who feed on a need for conflict, conquest, or obtaining power as essential elements they hold dearly to compose the fabric of their personality. There is also a number of people who grow up only knowing turmoil, despair, battling to stay alive in their neighborhoods, taught by loved and respected elders, to hate specific groups of people, and to develop a cold heart toward anyone in their path. When working to achieve one's desire for health and safety, many will go as far as to impose their beliefs and values on others as opposed to taking a 'live and let live' point of view. And those who enjoy implementing authoritarian control over others, or having a "take no prisoner hostage" perspective when it comes to the viability of others, be very aware, their presence in the workplace will certainly increase the probability that they could introduce obstacles at some point along your career path. My early view of the world really didn't account for the antagonists, who actually exist, some of whom were sitting within a close proximity to my workspace.

Discrimination is one of the tools used to interrupt your journey along your career path, but upon learning of the various masks worn by antagonists, discriminatory practices can become apparent and can be managed to some degree.

So, for me, upon entering the work environment, it didn't take long for me to realize, as I moved along my own career path, in addition to focusing on achieving my goals, I recognized the need to remain vigilant of individuals within the work environment whose personality traits include and require their need to insert control, focus on conquest and/or obtaining power at the sake of attacking the reputation and efforts of others. And then there are those who, for whatever reason, have decided who should have a hall pass to be in their own self-proclaimed space. These two types of individuals have the propensity to hinder, or temporarily disrupt the speed in which you achieve your goals.

For individuals who are currently working toward formulating their career strategies and getting on the path leading toward fulfilling their career goals, you should be on guard that the work environment presents a philosophic construct to become a daily playground, battlefield, and a constantly varying opportunity to display and impose one's values. And it can provide some level of fulfillment for individuals whose roles potentially span across all levels of job titles, as well as bona fide or usurped responsibilities. And that includes individuals whose actions congeal into disruptive plans against others. On a more complex level, a substantial number of challenging scenarios exist in that there are disruptive plans being implemented, unveiling like the plot in an espionage novel, since some people prefer to express and impose their values through the utilization of indirect (as opposed to direct, face-to-face), covert, closed door and behind the scene actions, which, if exposed, could result in embarrassment, rejection by others or even physical confrontations by those who may not be versed in non-violent conflict resolution techniques. And so, you will always have some who implement their tactics *behind doors, in the shadows.*

And for those who need to contest the existence of control freaks, it's easy to confirm the existence of these 'control' personality traits by reviewing a few world history books that have previously, and continue to document countless numbers of individuals and national leaders who have aligned to these values. History documents many controllers as impactful. Often there is less documentation of those they hurt or destroyed while moving along their own path. But let's keep it real. You will definitely discover that these individuals are sprinkled throughout many work environments, so don't be surprised when you see the signs of their presence. Many of whom love to work in darkness, and hope to remain undetected. But there will be a few who actually don't care if you discover who they are, almost as if they want you to believe they are invincible. They are the ones who, at times, almost seem to dare you to thwart their disruptions. And although tactics and methods will change, there are some easily recognizable signs. When assessing whether or not to consider a job offer, always ask why is the job available, and conduct your own search for published feedback from former employees. If there are signs of high employee turnover, attrition, constant re-orgs, lack of engagement by groups of employees, and signs of unhappy employees, run.

During the early stages while on my career path, I assumed if someone had an issue with you, there would be some type of direct confrontation. I never considered there are some who find gratification with setting you up for failure. Or interfering with your path to acknowledgment, rewards, or benefits. And it's also difficult to believe that some actually dedicate their time to focus on implementing character assassination tactics with the goal of making it a challenge to collaborate with others, gain critical information and support, all while lurking in the shadows, trying to maintain their anonymity to any repercussions if exposed. Who would have thought these antagonistic elements exist within the workplace environment? Well, they do, so try not to dwell on the negative, but plan ways to remain vigilant and to protect yourself.

Early on, from my perspective, I was bright-eyed, happy to have landed a job where I would be getting paid every two weeks, looking forward to being able to acquire things and travel wherever and whenever, without having to successfully deliver a "value-added" presentation to my parents to convince them to invest their money to support my pitch. In those early years, going to work and getting paid was still sunshine with no rainy days. I no longer was just peering through the looking glass, but now going forward to achieve the dream, collecting notable items that I saw all those years while peering through the glass, as tangible mementoes that reinforced each goal I achieved. I should note for me the looking glass was actually more like looking through a telescope since I always seem to enjoy far-reaching sets of creative visualizations. Needless to say, as a result, I was highly motivated to be exceptional because of tangible aspirations and visions of goals that required me to get a car, a passport, some clothes to reinforce my style and class, plus more. And I believed I could get things done because I was lucky to have been told that I could achieve anything, and I believed those words wrapped in confidence delivered by parents, relatives, and a few mentors. Those *words of reinforcement*, once received, *will be tucked safely away in your pocket* so you can carry them with you as you march along your career path.

It was only natural that my focus each day upon crossing a work environment threshold, was directed on being exceptional so that I can achieve my goals. I was focused on my goals and never really thought about the idea of adversaries, even though I knew the definition. And actually, I found the words antagonist and protagonist to be interesting words that flow off the lips and somehow stuck in my mind, possibly the result of some homework assignment. And although I had ample exposure to the experience of discrimination, I never really expected my real-world experiences would also flow into my workplace experiences. I initially expected when coworkers saw the good, hard work and dedication, how could they possibly decide to take part in any discriminatory practices. I was wrong. In a similar fashion as the words of reinforcement I received from people who cared about me, I found that *those who discriminate* will *tuck discriminatory practices in their pocket* and carry them everywhere as they slither along their paths.

I was unsuspecting and unprepared for attacks from co-workers who were clandestinely targeting my reputation or seeking to derail my positivity. I really had not spent time contemplating why do people attack others *who haven't done anything to offend or disrespect them*. I was never taught the ways of hate, never raised that way. Never once imagined when you are hired, there might also exist a sub-story that could present obstacles that could impact your ability to advance. Demanding that you dial up some battle capabilities, specifically the defense mechanism in your brain, which also triggers your offensive game mode of seek, destroy, or disable. I never suspected or was told there might be employees who actually dedicate time to spread disinformation about coworkers, work to undermine the work of others, discredit the accomplishments of targeted employees, or to gain allegiance from others to join in their plan to diminish individual reputations. I never considered that people contemplate the ways of war, just for fun, or have a quest for power which can drive their need to make others look bad, or incompetent to managers. For me the work environment provided validation of good and bad characters which, previous to entering the workforce, were just on television.

Yes, adversarial practices are negative. For those preparing to enter the workforce and were not taught the ways of hate, you should know that adversarial practices actually exist. Keep in mind that you can't rely on television to validate the character of each individual you meet since everyone is different, and requires individual assessments in order to avoid generalizations.

I feel sad each time the news reports someone losing their life, and it's mentioned that they were a kind person who didn't deserve what was done to them. I think of my younger self and the times I was attacked by a coworker or manager, and I had no idea, why. In my more gullible stage, while I focused on achieving the visions I saw while peering through my telescope, I never felt the urge to or value in dedicating time to plan how I could smack, hurt, blame, shame, or belittle someone else in order to make me feel good about myself. That's not what I saw in my telescope. That's not the person I am deep down inside. But when some felt the need to play, many found out, *I'm not the one* they should test. They found I can bring it when I need to, since evidently, my parents wisely provided various opportunities for me to learn tactical skills to use in multiple game modes, and they do come in handy.

At a higher level, this sub-story can evolve into a battle of wits for an esteemed role, or being assigned a high-profile assignment. Who would have thought that there are individuals who posture within workplace environments, similar to politicking for a political office, seeking to recruit servant-like minions, to join their cause of targeting various individuals who they have determined will participate in their war game in which honor, integrity, or reputation is on the table. In this game, the first challenge may be that you are totally unaware that you have been targeted for the role of the unsuspecting opponent, and unaware the game has begun, and the adversary in the shadows has already made a number of moves to feel good about themselves. Well, in reality, it's not really a game when you realize you've been targeted. And the group size of adversaries within a work environment may not really reach a point where there are many minions, but more likely two to four individuals who have lunch, or go out for drinks together. Often, I discovered there was only one leader, or instigator, while the others were more like supportive friends or acquaintances of the instigator.

Slime Undercover

Their clandestine activities could be fueled by their personal beliefs, a long-seeded need to bully others, un-happy childhoods or failed relationships. They might have a fear of being around individuals not like them, never learning as a kid how to play with other kids, or have concerns that your presence may result in their loss of currently perceived favor, power, rewards, advancement, or attention. Or, it could just be as simple as a few mean individuals that at some point were hired by a mean Mr. Grinch or Mr. Scrooge-type hiring manager, who saw those mean individuals, just like him or her. Ahh, recruits to build a power base. But, regardless of the motivation, you should be aware there is a very high probability that there is someone in the work environment who will be engaged in plans to damage reputations of targeted employees. And you should remain vigilant for unexplained actions or changes to your responsibilities, statements made about your character, or points of view that are clearly not accurate. When you become aware, you possibly could have caught wind of the work of *an adversary working in the shadows.*

Guard Your Character

It is extremely important to combat attempts to assassinate your character, reputation, and integrity since years later you may find questions arise that will require detailed explanation or defensive evidence. I once heard a psychologist state the human brain doesn't develop with the ability for one to be able to discern what might be the result of one's actions, until some point after they reach mid to late twenties. Summed up, you could potentially but unknowingly, do things that are damaging to your character between twelve to twenty-six years of age. So, sexting, taking nude photos to make some quick cash, live streaming something that incriminates you, or taking photos while you and friends are binge drinking or involved with illegal activities, could all make it difficult for you later when you are seeking a major opportunity. When it comes to reputation and integrity, I can say there are some managers I've worked with that I would never want to work with again. In addition, there are a few companies that continue to lack integrity and so they are regularly engaged in aggressive and sometimes deceptive practices to attract new customers as current customers drop them. Over time, these companies re-appear in news stories focused on alerting the public of regulatory fines being issued or lawsuits being filed against them. For some reason, these organizations just keep reappearing with similar issues. That often will mean there is a culture that reinforces similar misdeeds.

Inexperienced, But On Guard

In retrospect, I believe you should take extra heed in realizing that during your growth and career formulation period, when you are most vulnerable, there could be times, when you are still increasing your awareness, formulating your career goals, and lack a well-tested 'due diligence' discernment vetting process for filtering out bad people and bad job offers. Your lack of having these tools at your discretion could result in pitfalls or challenges rising up later in time, that could be difficult to overcome. And for individuals who are well along on their career path, it's also not unusual that you might pay more attention to your current needs and urgency as opposed to taking time to really learn about the manager and organization you are considering to working with. It's not uncommon that during one's career that the process you'll use to decide whether or not to accept a job offer, will lack much vetting of the reputation, beliefs, integrity, and personal values of the hiring manager or the company seeking to fill a job opening. You'll want to conduct a search to determine if the job opening became available as a result of the hiring manager's or company's adverse reputation, beliefs, integrity and personal values? Unfortunately, many focus on the perceived immediate gratification and benefits like the pay offer, location, office aesthetics, apparent ease of the responsibilities or prestige associated with the role.

Keep Your Eyes Open for These

Here are a few examples that if you knew about a manager or company before deciding to accept the job, you probably would have concerns about accepting the job offer:

1. During the hiring stage, you are told you will receive a specific hourly or annual pay, but after being hired your paychecks are consistently less than what was promised. I actually experienced this early in my career. I kept reminding them every payday that there must have been an accounting error since my check was not what I was told it would be during the hiring discussions. After no resolution, I realized I was working for an organization whose company leaders did not have integrity. I should had begun looking for a new job after the first year. But I remained additional years, partially motivated by the fact that my salary was a substantial increase from my previous role, the work location was in a prominent area, I was working in a field I actually had trained, and I hoped the company would eventually treat me with respect once they realized I was committed to doing exceptional work. But I was wrong, and really should have begun an exit strategy immediately. My lessons learned here were to always request a written offer letter before accepting a new job, and after being hired, always keep your eyes open for signs of how leaders adhere, or don't adhere to the corporate values they publish. At that time, I was unaware that the core values are actually the windows into the business's soul. Business leaders will either prove that their published core values are important, display tactics focused on public deceptions, or display clues into how they actually conduct business. For me, this experience was a case of dreams deferred, but not stopped. I did overcome, I did diversify my skill set while putting together my exit plan, and never experienced that 'bait and switch' again. (See also the Dead-In Job Blues chapter.)

Recommendation: After you reach a point when there is a firm offer by someone or a company for utilizing your skills, *always request* some type of *written offer letter, employment agreement* or a simple statement that spells out expected responsibilities and the agreed upon compensation (hourly, annually, or by specific effort of work).

2. On expected pay days, you are told your check will be provided on a later day, different from what was initially stated. A clear sign of financial problems.
3. You are told to lie or misrepresent information you provide to customers or coworkers which results in their individual harm or puts their safety at risk.
4. After being hired, you are told that as part of your job you will need to participate in activities which are against your own beliefs and values, and could damage your reputation and integrity.
5. After being hired, you are told to do something that could result in you being included in a criminal investigation.
6. While employed you witness your manager verbally abusing and/or physically bullying or abusing others, all while company leaders look the other way, which allows the acts to continue.
7. You become aware of a manager threatening a coworker with being fired unless they perform sexual favors.
8. You are told your career will benefit if you participate in non-work-related activities like running personal errands, attending parties, or working as unpaid labor that benefits a manager or clients.
9. Your manager enters false statements or inaccurate details in your annual performance review report which results in you not receiving a bonus, raise or promotion.

10. A manager regularly undermines your ability to successfully complete your work or assignments, and then unfairly accuses you of poor performance. You're being set up for failure, and your manager is possibly building a case to get you fired from your job.

Although it can be a challenge to conduct a reputational or value-based review of a hiring manager or a company, you can however request to speak with members of their team, conduct searches on social media and search engines, request their HR recruiter to provide 'masked' feedback from employees or request recommendations previously sent from clients.

In addition, if your action items you'll need to complete after accepting a job offer includes moving to a new location you should consider a no-harm exit agreement with a specified review period of time, which will allow you to re-coup some moving costs if things don't go well and you may not be able to return to your former job.

If you want to be successful achieving your career goals, you will need to remain aware of your environment as it changes around you, as new employees enter the work environment, as current employees change responsibilities, or if there is a re-organization of reporting structures.

In closing out this chapter, it's actually sad to have to talk about the negative things. Some will probably conclude there must be an excuse for me writing about and exposing these dark aspects of the work environment. But, in reality, once you enter the work environment, I would bet the majority of those you interact, *will not talk about the dark and negative aspects for fear* management will catch wind, and label those talking, as ones to banish, eliminate, or be placed at the top of the list if and when there is a re-org or layoff. This is why I felt it was important so that through awareness, you may be able to diminish any impacts that could materialize from having direct experiences with any of these dark and negative aspects of the work environment.

My career has advanced as a result of overcoming negative experiences, by becoming aware, and then making positive adjustments, executing damage control where possible, and putting safeguards and risk mitigation plans in place, to avoid being impacted by the same or similar negative experiences in the future. I'd like for you to be able to do the same, and overcome the negative experiences, or at least be prepared should they find you.

I also wanted to take a small amount of time to help those just starting out on their career path, as well as those well into their path, to bring awareness to what I would call shadow adversaries. These shadow adversaries can be in many forms, but often spread misinformation behind closed doors, initiate actions in secret without you knowing they have targeted you, and regularly linger along one's career paths.

I've witnessed these negative aspects happen to people across cultures and gender. I was never really informed of the existence of these shadow adversaries but became aware of them only after they had initiated their attacks on me. It is my hope to help you to identify them, so you are not surprised if you encounter them.

I remember being very naïve early in my career and at times, didn't conclude the need to remain alert until I was far along the path. Mainly because I was so heavily focused on doing my job by completing the responsibilities assigned to me and completing assigned goals. I went into the workforce with the belief that if I kept the terms of the job description and responsibilities communicated during the hiring process, I would have no issues, receive role promotions, higher income, and experience no problems. But I quickly found that sometimes it may not work out that way, especially if there is an adversary working in the shadows, focused on working against you or possibly conducting misinformation campaigns against you, without your knowledge.

As a defense mechanism, I would highly recommend you always initiate an on-going public image campaign, like having a damage control effort running *all of the time*, to counter any negative misinformation dispersed without your knowledge. Also, work to develop a risk mitigation strategy to protect yourself from an adverse work environment. That plan should include having more than one independent income stream. And finally, if you begin to *sense* a situation you feel is doing you harm, you should consider there are *at least two potential reasons*. Either someone is trying to teach or prepare you for something you aren't currently aware of that will be beneficial to you later, possibly by using 'tough love,' or you could be under attack from an antagonist. If you determine it is the latter, you need to determine how best to protect yourself, or get out of the situation. But you must act.

Chapter 11: Be Good to Yourself, Along the Way to Success

If you were to predict your chances of reaching your planned objectives that you created as part of your long-term career planning strategy, it might be safe to predict for those who have marketable skills and fortitude, they will have at least a fifty-fifty chance of achieving some level of success. One might also assume they will *not* have total control over all of the events they will face along their career paths and some unexpected obstacles could impact the level of success they achieve.

But one aspect you can be assured to have considerable control over during the course of your career, is being able to dedicate time to *be good to yourself*.

No matter the types of challenges or difficulties you face, you can always schedule some time in your calendar for R and R. That's right: rest and relaxation.

People often overlook the need to *regularly* and *consistently* manage stress, which over time, can negatively impact your physical and psychological health. Rising levels of stress could also impact your ability to figure out effective ways to handle daily issues or to develop the best tactics for navigating the obstacles you encounter along your career path. In addition, your inability to handle stress could impact your overall endurance and longevity.

Unfortunately, there are many people who attach a monetary amount to being able to enjoy rest and relaxation. Rest and relaxation is actually not cost prohibited unless you create scenarios where you can only chill when you have a certain amount of discretionary money available. Yes, you need money to take a trip that you can put in your scrap book, but there are also short trips that only require some form of transportation, and that includes walking. Attaching money to whether or not you can enjoy R and R would be your self-imposed requirement that could prohibit you from something as simple as meeting up with some friends and maybe carrying along a few folding lawn chairs to enjoy a free concert at a local park. Or if you don't like the outdoors, going to a local university for a free indoor concert, movie, book club event, or informational discussion.

Can Work Stress You Out?

Believe it or not, it's not unusual to find employees so wound up, they skip their allotted lunch breaks and eat their lunch at their desk while simultaneously continuing to work on their assignments. I've witnessed employees having the belief that if they don't work every single second, they will not be able to complete their assignments. And since there has been an increasing trend in which senior and mid-level managers seeming reluctant to own their responsibility of managing resource demand and capacity planning, resources are unfortunately left having to guess how much capacity they have to take on new assignments while concurrently working on on-going efforts, which often include impromptu, as soon as possible requests, also known as ASAP requests.

And of course, without managers knowing when their employees are over-allocated or how much capacity is available at any point in time, it's not unusual to have unrealistic completion goals for resources to complete their assignments. Along with the practice of some managers loading up the amount of daily assignments, almost as though they suspect their employees will not return the next day, this too can create unnecessary work-related stress. I recall a manager always coming up with some last-minute assignments for the team right around the time when people normally headed home from work. And the assignments were always ones that actually didn't need to be completed until days or weeks later. Eventually, people learned to leave earlier or just provide some type of 'family matter' excuse.

You should stay alert, if managers tend to rely on unrealistic completion timelines that consistently result in resources needing to work into their off hours, and at times, through their weekends, this may be an indicator of someone having little courtesy or concern for their resources' personal time, and their work-to-life balance. A reliance on the phrase "It shouldn't take that long," can over time result in unnecessary stress for you, all due to a practice of not conducting realistic estimations of efforts, and *you*, actually becoming the solution for managers not having any idea as to how much time will be needed to get an assignment done. Although having estimation skills is a normal management prerequisite, I should note, it is often a normal practice within many organizations, for managers to rely on their resources just putting in the time, no matter what it takes to get the job done in the time set. Without utilizing estimation skills, managers are known for setting project completion timelines that are way off from reality. Unfortunately, the only way they find out is when their resources miss the set due date, even after putting in extensive hours.

This *normal and accepted business practice* is why it's so important for resources to make plans to relax *each week* instead of holding out for vacation time scheduled some point in the future. Managers who are not effective estimators can easily be identified as the ones whose teams are consistently overallocated and working long hours at work, which then carry over to working at home. Beware: if you are regularly working without realistic planning, this can result in *high levels of stress* and *adverse health issues*. As such I highly recommend that you plan regular rest and relaxation as preventive stress measures and for managing your overall health.

A Real Manifestation of Stress

I've actually experienced a day when a coworker had a heart attack at work. He was one who believed in the need to eat lunch at his desk and work every single second, only taking bathroom breaks, and the time it took to walk to the cafeteria, purchase lunch, and return to his desk. In fact, our entire team was constantly under constant pressure as a result of being overallocated with assignments. We were in this routine for at least seven-months. And when that coworker was laying on a gurney being rolled out by paramedics, the risk of how stress can impact your health turned out to be really real. That was the only lesson I needed to validate that you are the main person who must guard your health, and that I needed to begin paying much more attention to my work-to-life balance. Seeing my coworker being rolled away was a sight I won't forget.

After that experience whenever I was job searching and saw in the job description any expectation like "You may be expected to work hours in addition to normal hours," I avoided those completely. I think it's not unusual, that in an emergency, working long hours should be expected. But when a hiring manager needs to spell that out, like a legal disclaimer, I now think, in the event you should happen to have a heart attack, don't get mad or blame them since you were warned up front, of their expectation that you will regularly be expected to work long days, hours after leaving work, and probably weekends.

At some point, if working beyond a standard work day becomes the norm, and managers appear to pay little attention to effective project estimation, resource capacity and demand planning, you should consider negotiating something additional to compensate for taking that type of health risk and sacrifice in making yourself available 24/7.

Recommendation: I would suggest if you choose to accept a role with a poor work-to-life balance, please consider negotiating in writing, additional benefits like more vacation days, ability to work from home, or anything that can help you maintain your health.

Recommendation: Experienced managers recognize that effective project estimation requires a clear understanding of the project requirements, a determination what is the validated solution to fulfill the requirements, an awareness of how many resources will be available to work, and what is the resources' current capacity to work on an effort, keeping in mind that resources normally work on other assignments simultaneously. In addition, less experienced managers should use the S.M.A.R.T. best practice definition as a guide for setting goals, where S means specific in that you understand the goal requirements or details and what will be needed for the solution. M means measurable, in which you determine values that let you know if the goal was successfully achieved. A means achievable, R means realistic, and T means time-bound, where an achievable and realistic amount of time is estimated as being needed to complete the goal when considering all known dependencies.

For those of you who don't have regular conversations with your manager or use a project planning tool where your available weekly capacity is determined, you might want to initiate the conversation and try to encourage your manager to provide individuals a report on their estimated capacity which can be verified during one-on-one conversations. There are project management and methodology tools that allow resources to enter the efforts they are working on and the estimated time needed. The tool will then calculate when resources are overallocated.

You also might want to put more value in your lunch time as being personal health time needed for you to relax, take a walk, and get out to get some fresh air. Just realize that it's *for your health*, and it should not be missed.

Another way to protect your health is by finding some healthy practices that you like and can continue for a lifetime. I do acknowledge that no one can predict one's lifespan, but I prefer to consider the "what if" scenario where you consider, "What if I am fortunate to experience a long lifespan?" If that blessing is destined for me, I want to do as much as I can to have physical, mental, and spiritual capabilities that I can rely on and that provide me benefits as long as possible.

With that "what if" scenario in mind, I began to search for solutions that could hopefully help me now, and in the future. That is my philosophical response for those naysayers who say, "Why should I try to stay healthy when I have no idea how long I will be alive?" But what if you end up having long life? You are going to need funds. You are going to want to be able-bodied and physically strong. You are going to need a strong immune system. These are some of the requirements, and of course, there is more you should consider adding as part of your risk management planning.

Below are a few health-conscious considerations that may help you figure out what might be enjoyable for you. And if you can meet your requirement for what's enjoyable, at some point, you should begin to recognize benefits. I'm one who believes if you find at least one activity that you like, you'll be more likely to continue doing it, maybe not consistently, but periodically over a longer period of time than if you tried to maintain a full body exercise routine.

- Go to an outdoor art fair, farmer's market or open-air concert. There are also walking groups. All of these activities allow you to walk at your own pace and have fun doing it.
- Purchase an inexpensive stationary bike. This can be used year-round, for years, and allow you to exercise any time without cost after the initial purchase.
- Learn Yoga. This can be used for years, once trained, there's no cost, it can be done at home or when traveling, can help manage stress, provide strength training, and increase and maintain your mental focus.
- Learn meditation techniques to help manage stress and help achieve relaxation.
- Read books and/or magazines to help you unclutter all of those thoughts and worries rolling around in your mind.
- Learn about nutrition. Over time with new discoveries, there will be food choices that can provide value, help fight off diseases, and maintain a strong immune system.
- Adopt a food intake practice that supports healthy living. With practice, the techniques you're currently using can be continually tweaked over time to achieve better and better results.
- Go to a swimming pool, throw a beach ball, float on or in a circular tube (or ring) and paddle kick, take a water aerobics

session (which is a very low impact way to exercise), stretch, relax your muscles, and lower stress. Check neighborhood pools for low cost or free class offerings.

- Find a low-cost, "pay-as-you-go" health club or gym membership. Being around others can help to motivate you, whereas working out at home may require strong self-motivation. Also, some health clubs try to keep up with the latest equipment and new innovations that may make it easier to stay in shape.
- Learn how to create a healthy meal, dessert, or fitness shake that you can enjoy over and over.
- Find something that makes you laugh and smile.
- Join a group that supports individuals with similar interests.
- Find and then periodically visit local museums, college events, theaters, music, dance, poetry, or sports event, art exhibits, and free events.
- If you have discretionary cash, travel to a location of interest.
- Get out of your house or apartment, and go to a new restaurant in town. Some will be great experiences, and others will stimulate conversations on what was not so great, but you can look at this as entertainment that you can laugh about with your friends. And laughing is healthy.

I can add, that my personal health-conscious approach has continually benefited me up to this point. There have been numerous times when having access to a swimming pool or a whirl pool helped to reduce stress, including tight, achy muscles. When I had colds, the benefits of being able to use a hot steam room or dry sauna to clear them out is immeasurable. The result of regularly riding my bike has increased my overall endurance, flexibility and relaxation. And I can say that having body strength definitely has been a benefit when having to handle an extended day of efforts.

Recommendation: Take all allowed time off and sabbaticals if available. Try not to miss out on opportunities to smile, laugh, stretch out, smell the roses, watch a sunset, or experience a moment you can mentally re-live over and over again. Having fond memories and pictures can help you to re-visit experiences even when you're down. I was fortunate to find out early in my career that rest and relaxation is definitely a beneficial part of your diverse career path, and you totally own this.

And if I haven't said it somewhere before, please promise yourself to enjoy life throughout your career path journey. It is your journey, the history of you, and every journey will unveil some unexpected challenges and jewels. The challenges you can learn from, and the jewels you can enjoy. So, enjoy, look around, help everyone you can, and just be happy as you spread your wonder. Every moment is yours to marvel.

Chapter 12:
The Dead-End Job Blues

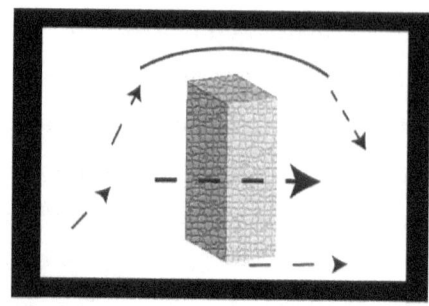

There is a possibility that at some point, you could find that you are in what is commonly referred to as a Dead-End job. This situation could occur through no fault of your own, or as a lack of due diligence on your part. In reality, there are all types of dynamics in motion, where one day you could get hired by a fantastic company, be in a role in which you're very comfortable and happy, and then the next day, you come to work and there's an emergency town hall meeting in which there is an announcement about a change in leadership, impacting the reporting structures, or the company has been acquired by another company. Yes, a change can happen just that quickly. In each case, these types of changes could result in a totally different experience from what you have been accustomed to, and then the walls start coming down around you. But there could also be changes that hit closer to home. For instance, your direct manager or a key knowledgeable resource suddenly decides to leave for one reason or another. Next you are re-assigned to another manager, need to find a replacement, or you are merged into a new team of people with whom you now need to bond. In this day and age, rapid changes and business re-orgs are becoming a regular occurrence every year as a result of emotional decisions, panic, or political or market influences. In addition, decision makers often rely on real-time analytical tools, key performance indicators (KPIs), and dash boards which can provide them a daily snapshot of how their business is operating, and alert them of pending risks, issues, or impacts that need to be addressed or face potentially serious impacts. There could be influences that indicate the business direction needs to be changed, or there is a merger or acquisition that will create a competitive threat.

But there is also the possibility you're in a Dead-End job simply because you didn't conduct adequate due diligence by thoroughly vetting a company before joining. Or possibly, the job you accepted didn't turn out to be what you were told, or expected. Imagine that. Yes, bait and switch does happen in the hiring process.

I caution you to be diligent in obtaining a clear explanation, in writing, of the responsibilities you will be expected to fulfill, since business needs can unexpectedly change, and there is also a practice very similar to a bait and switch marketing practice, where they may not want to tell you everything about the job for fear that you will ask for more money, or choose not to accept the initial offer. I would expect those companies may not consider their process as being a bait and switch, since they would probably just say business needs constantly change, and in your case, they just happened to change after the point when the agreement was negotiated. Hmm.

But from the perspective of the individual being hired, he or she may feel cheated if their negotiations were based on a communicated set of responsibilities which later turned out to be quite a bit different than what was communicated, before negotiations completed, before an offer was accepted, and before you left your current job to begin the new job.

As a protective measure to encourage fairness, the potential candidate should initiate a discussion around this concern during the negotiation phase, and request a statement to be included in their offer letter for a "make whole" negotiation if there have been any major adjustments to the job responsibilities shortly after the start date. Obviously, it's expected your role could change as business needs change at some point after being hired, but it shouldn't change within a few weeks after starting a new job. If that actually happens, the newly hired may feel as though they were not provided all of the details of the role, which would allow them to make an informed decision on whether they should accept the offer. That awareness could taint the hiring experience as lacking integrity, ultimately impacting how the candidate might feel about the organization as a whole.

No matter how you choose to define it, from the hiring perspective or the new hire perspective, we all want the opportunity to make critical decisions from an informed perspective. When hiring managers are reluctant to fully communicate the full scope of responsibilities for some type of fear that full disclosure could impact the signing on of good candidates, managers should keep in mind the organization could begin to build up negative social media feedback if candidates feel they are being baited. I currently know of some organizations that continue having difficulty recruiting because of their street reputation. As a result, they are left with pursuing less experienced candidates.

Also, for you the job-seeker, you want to be on guard for companies who publish a job description that seems to be a standardized description like one you've seen published by other companies. In this case, you should ask for specific details related to the level of effort expected. Ask why the role was created, and inquire about the current capacity of the existing team. You also want to find out if they are at full capacity, needing to cover for each other, or if they are working in their assigned roles. If they are overallocated, it's not unusual for people in one role to be asked to assist in or take on entirely different roles where they don't have much experience, but as a result of the circumstance, will need to work in dual roles. At some point, you should want to be compensated for fulfilling a dual or multiple role capacity. If this happens within three-months after being hired, and now the job description you initially believed was consummate with your career goals and expectations, has now changed *to one that is not*, this should let you know the manager was aware of the need at the time of your negotiation, or has poor planning skills and unable to foresee work needs one to three months in advance. And if your role has changed such that the level of work now appears to be two or more additional roles, I would guess you might feel cheated in the salary you accepted. This is the bait and switch from the new hire's perspective and introduces questions about the integrity of the hiring manager.

However, on a positive note, the increased responsibilities should be one of your key points of focus during your annual review and become a defense for a promotion and salary increase. In this case, you should use your initial job description as a baseline, and document all of the efforts that went beyond what you agreed. If you are not acknowledged or rewarded for helping the team, your manager and the company mitigate the overallocation issues, you should begin to direct your focus toward other options available for obtaining your career goals. Definitely don't delay with expediting your plans to extricate yourself from your current position.

The Benefits May Not be Available to Pay for the Immediate Needs

At times hiring managers will need to hire staff without being provided a suitable budget to obtain top candidates. In this scenario, during their discussions with potential candidates, managers can choose to provide a full disclosure of the level of work, or choose to hold back the full scope of their need, fully knowing you will find out after joining the organization.

Here's a description of their potential budgetary challenge. The team manager submits a convincing request to budgetary decision makers stating the existing team doesn't have the capacity to take on the project(s) the business needs completed. In addition, new assignments will impede their ability to successfully complete existing assignments as originally planned. The budget decision makers then approve a specific budget to hire resources. Based on the budget approved, the team manager and HR department reconcile how the salary range aligns with their existing list of job titles. A problem can now materialize in that the actual work needed to be covered to relieve stress for the existing team, may actually require more resources than the budget allows, or there may be a need for a more senior level person whose salary request is beyond the amount approved by the budgetary decision makers. Both of these scenarios motivate the HR representative and later the hiring manager, to try and negotiate an agreement to get the additional resources. This may be a reason not to discuss the full scope of the job because in doing so, the more experienced candidate, realizing the amount of work, might be concerned with a probable adverse work-to-life balance, and as such will choose not to pursue the opportunity, or request a higher salary. The bait and switch approach is one approach, while other managers will return to the budgetary decision makers to request additional funds be approved, and possibly create a new job title.

Recommendation:

After a company has given you a firm job offer in writing, I think as part of your initial counter offer, you should also attempt to negotiate a "make whole" agreement focused on encouraging the hiring company to lock in and keep the terms of the initial job description, responsibilities and expectations over a pre-determined period of time. Obviously, over a longer period of time employees should expect the needs of a company to change and evolve, and with those changes, their role and expectations will undoubtedly change. But, you shouldn't expect your role or responsibilities to change drastically shortly after being hired. That would fall into a bait and switch sales or marketing tactic focused on benefiting those implementing the tactic. Hopefully, there will be no need to execute a "make whole" agreement of this type, but think about how would you feel, if you left your current company to join the new one based on the presented job description and expectations, and in doing so, there were moving costs, or other costs you incurred as a result of believing the promises made by the hiring company would be maintained over a determined length of time, and for some reason your role changed into a totally new role from what was initially presented? I think most would agree it would be fair to make some type of adjustment to compensate for the differences between what was negotiated and what actually resulted. A make good agreement could include a confirmed bonus, a change in title, agreed increase in salary, or a severance type payment if you decide to exit totally.

This scenario is more probable if you negotiated your role, responsibilities, and compensation with a hiring manager, and then either there was a major event in which something negotiated was not kept, or the hiring manager, who was aware of what was in the job description, really didn't include all of the responsibilities of the role and the expectations. Also, maybe that same manager left or changed roles, there was a merger, the company was acquired, or there were other impacting changes of events that had you been aware of this situation, you would have not decided to leave your previous role. In this case, damages to you were incurred. A "make whole" agreement should also motivate the hiring company to make good on keeping promises made during the hiring process, at least for what could be defined in the "make whole" agreement as a probationary period. Also, a new manager may not feel obligated to keep the agreement negotiated by the previous hiring manager unless you have the "make whole" agreement in writing.

Keeping in the spirit of situations that could be deemed to be similar to a bait and switch, here are a few actual experiences of unrealized expectations where I would have made a different decision if only I had known.

- During the final negotiation for a new job, I was promised a salary that actually made the role more desirable than the one in which I was currently employed. After receiving my first payroll check, I discovered that it was lower than agreed upon. (I brought attention to this in the Adversaries in the Shadows chapter.)
- I experienced completing an interview process with a hiring manager that I believed would be trustworthy, would provide a good opportunity for me to increase my experience, and be someone with whom I would have a good working partnership. After accepting the offer and being hired, I received a communication notifying me the initial hiring manager had accepted a new opportunity and as such I would be reporting to a totally different manager, yet to be determined. This created a concern since now I had

not had an opportunity to assess the manager with whom I would be working. For me, vetting the person you will be working with is extremely important for determining if you believe you can get along with and have a positive working partnership. In this case, I had no idea if that would be the case.

- While already working as an employee for an organization, I was asked if I would be interested in joining a newly created team, which was pitched as an opportunity to work with a group of "rock star" team members who had established notoriety as being highly successful. I made the mistake of accepting the new role without meeting with the hiring manager so I could get an idea of the work environment I would be going into. It turned out the manager was a loner-type who rarely spoke to anyone, consistently had her head down typing at the computer, and was anti-social to everyone on the team. I don't recall the sound of her voice since she rarely spoke. The team never received any guidance or direction, but as a result of their experience, was self-managed. This created a challenge for me as a new team member needing to learn the team dynamics already in place and understood by the existing team members. Without the guidance from the manager, I was challenged with overcoming process impediments without any assistance. I did eventually, which made me a "rock star," but one with scarring from climbing over so many process obstacles and impediments without any assistance.

- I experienced signing up and paying for a course with a renowned educator. Before my first class, he fell seriously ill. I hoped that he would get better before the semester ended, but that didn't happen, and school administrators decided to keep his name listed with the course even though he was critically ill. In this case, I specifically signed up as a result of this educator's reputation but the school allowed students to believe he would be teaching the course.

So now what? Well, I can tell you from first-hand experience that if you find you are in a Dead-End job and do nothing, you could, as I did, experience sadness that could eventually lead to you becoming a depressed individual. And who really would ask for that?

So far, I have never met a person in a Dead-End job who said they are happy. Imagine that. Dead-End jobs can impact you emotionally if you remain in them too long without some type of resolution.

So, you should highly consider taking actions to get out of a Dead-End job as soon as you can, and hopefully with minimum impact. If you wait too long, you may find that you just need to take any job offer you can just for a change of pace or a temporary break from the situation. And that may not be good, but should be looked at as a *temporary remedy*.

I can recall a time where the situation was so bad that I quit the job without having another one to pay bills. At the time, I determined the choice of not knowing how I was going to pay bills was a better choice than remaining in a psychologically damaging situation which could have resulted in serious damage to my mental health, or others, or diminish my ability to continue building upon my future. There is that leap of faith.

But you should remember, you and only you own the finish line, to be you. And everyone, has some type of potential. Each day you see sunlight is another day to create opportunities, no matter how small. If you believe in yourself and a higher power has your back, you will take that leap of faith, without fear of failure. Make that Phoenix rise out of the flames. It may not be quick, but don't give up the fight. Overcoming challenges often results in a good feeling, hopefully makes you stronger, and most definitely will reinforce the need to *always plan for your next role*. I appeal to you, please don't allow yourself to remain in the position where others are determining your fate, especially when their plan is foul.

Chapter 13: The Rules of Discrimination

You may not believe this, but no one escapes the grips of discrimination. Unfortunately, it's only human nature to discriminate against others and to be the target of others who discriminate. As you might imagine, this clearly establishes itself as one of the highest hurdles everyone will face along their career path.

I'm sure most people are aware there are unlimited types of discrimination targeting gender, weight, culture, religion, ethnicity, age, the physically challenged, popularity, light-skin versus dark-skin, good hair, level of education, place of education, having a criminal record, and geographic areas of residence.

In addition, there are a whole set of unfair practices related to your health. In this case, there are Federal HIPAA laws that will issue punitive damages to businesses who are found not to be HIPAA-compliant. HIPAA regulations focus on protecting the privacy of your personal medical history. For example, some women will face discrimination once managers become aware of a pending pregnancy. A discussion might take place behind closed doors around whether or not their female employee will return to work after delivery. As a result of this discriminatory discussion, there are high probabilities that pregnant women won't get promotions leading up to a maternity leave, even if managers previously considered it *before learning of the pregnancy.*

There are also some who choose not to be around individuals with certain disease states and psychological challenges. Others choose not to employ individuals who have been involved with substance abuse recovery programs. What about those who have or are recovering from cancer? What might happen if you need to take off increasing amounts of time if you are a caregiver for an elderly parent, or have a child that requires special attention? Could your employer seek to eliminate you by citing poor performance on your annual review? I actually experienced a manager who stated because I had to take a short-term disability leave due to an accident, he discounted my annual review based on having taken some time off even though I had completed a number of critical projects over the full course of the year, some of which were managed remotely. This same reasoning could be used against every woman who takes off for maternity leave. These are examples why 'return on investment' along with the amount of time utilized should be considered as part of performance reviews.

As you can imagine, it's extremely important that an individual's medical history be kept protected to avoid others using their history against them.

Bottom line, when you encounter discrimination, the probability of getting hired, getting promoted or being deemed as having value can potentially be temporarily obstructed. But be it known, those who discriminate, cannot stop you in the big scheme of your plans. So, let's take a deeper look into you, and discrimination. Afterwards, we can talk about options to minimize discrimination.

Which one of these have you heard? *I don't think* he knows what he's doing. She's a *dumb blonde*. He just *doesn't get it*. She's *from the west side* (or bad side of town). *I just think* you need more experience. *I don't think he fits in* to our culture here. I can hardly understand what they are saying. I *don't like to be around people who* smoke. I *don't like spinach* (or another food). *She's not like us. She's not one of us.* They are *so un-American.* That's *not patriotic.* He's *fresh off the boat.* You *don't belong here.* That's *so ghetto.* She's *a schizo or so ditzy.*

One of the unfortunate conclusions I've reached was the sad awareness that at some point, *we all will face some type of discrimination.* Yes, I said it; *we all will experience discrimination.* It doesn't matter if you are European, African, Asian, some type of Indigenous person, Hispanic, or a non-Earthling (we already have space garbage floating around). And although some people *only* associate *the word* discrimination *with minorities,* the truth is discrimination *has no rules of exclusion.* Whether it's gender, religion, race, nationality, lifestyle, age, nepotism, language, financial history, caste system, or job title. Whether its political association, blue collar or white collar, rural, urban, suburban, level of education, specific college prestige, fraternity or sorority, your close friends or your known workplace associates, no one escapes discrimination. Yes, at some point, you will experience the cold, back-hand slap from someone who actively discriminates against you openly, covertly, or cowardly behind your back.

For those who continue to believe discrimination is only for minorities, when it hits other unsuspecting individuals, it could be a harsh, slap of reality in your face, upfront and personal. Not having any clue as to why something negative and unfair happened. This can be disorientating. And I have to ask: what exactly is *reverse discrimination* when *we all face discrimination?* One day you may ponder, why did your loan application get turned down? Why did you not get a promotion after successfully completing so many projects while the person who received a promotion, hasn't achieved half of what you've done? Why did your date stand you up? Why did you not get hired? Why did you receive food that wasn't fresh or cooked properly? Why did they think it was okay to seat you by a drafty door? Why did the counter service person skip over you when you were first in line? Why is the waiter taking so long to take your order? Why did you not get the actual price that was advertised? Why is your child not getting the same attention from the teacher that other students are getting?

So, yes, one key obstacle pretty much everyone will encounter is discrimination in public places, the workplace, and while working along your career path. And although many are in denial, the reality is *ALL humans discriminate*, because it's in our nature.

Here are a few examples for all of the naysayers.

- Limited hiring of individuals whose age is close to a mandatory retirement age, except in the case of executive and board member roles, of course.
- Protection of the reputation of only specific groups, people and communities.
- Reluctance to alert you about benefits that are available to many, in order to control and limit who actually gets them. Maybe block specific groups from access to ensure benefits will be available for those you believe actually deserve them (in your opinion).
- Reluctance to hire anyone having an arrest record without considering the circumstance. (E.g.: treating someone caught stealing candy when they were a teenager, or someone arrested for talking back to a police officer, in a similar way as someone convicted of murder).

- Hiring of people recommended by favored recruiters, or current former employees, despite the applicant not meeting the required capabilities.
- Hiring of candidates having MBAs directly into lead management roles despite not having experience leading projects or managing people.
- Preferential hiring of candidates who have graduated from more prestigious universities.
- Avoidance of hiring candidates from lessor known colleges.
- Reluctance of hiring and promoting women and non-Euro's into senior and executive leadership roles.
- Reluctance to support diverse hiring practices. (E.g.: some media, advertising, film studio production houses and consultant companies are reluctant to hire non-Euro candidates into management roles.)
- Exclusion due to marital status. (E.g.: U.S. presidents are expected to be married. Only two single men – James Buchanan in 1857; Grover Cleveland in 1886, have been elected president of the United States)
- Inclusions and exclusions due to known associations, residency in a certain part of town, religion or lack of religion, culture, or country of origin.
- Changing of role responsibilities captured in hiring agreements soon after the candidate begins the new role.
- High profile assignments, recognitions, and promotions given more to those who are considered friends of influencers.
- Only those having friendships with managers being included in the pool of potential recipients to receive bonuses, despite having questionable work practices and accomplishments.

And if you still haven't had enough, here are a couple of experiences I recall where I was a bystander who later found myself consoling the employees impacted.

True event 1: One European-American male manager lied about the performance of another European-American male employee. The composite review resulted in an adverse determination in which the employee did not receive his expected annual bonus. The dispute was reviewed by a European-American woman, and resulted in one escaping any disciplinary actions and the other without his bonus.

True event 2: A European-American woman was verbally demeaned by an Asian-Indian American male. After she used some very choice words in standing up for herself and rightfully defending herself by letting him know that she would not tolerate disrespectful language, others, including European-American women and men, began discriminating against her by avoiding commissioning her for available projects. She was unfairly labeled as someone who let her emotions interfere with her need to effectively collaborate with others.

I could go on, but I selected these two incidents with the hope that you should recognize that, discrimination can happen to various types of individuals, and in some unexpected situations.

Being Mindful of Your Political Capital in the Workplace

It's my belief that you should be aware that upon going into work environments, you could be entering a dysfunctional environment or a war zone where at some point you might find yourself in the midst of personal conflicts where you may have to defend yourself. In addition, you may be impacted emotionally and psychologically, which could then transfer over to your non-work, life relationships. Normally when discussing workplace challenges, people will avoid discussing examples of unexpected personality exchanges like the one in which an Asian-Indian American male belittles a European-American woman. In this case, I suspect it was the result of the political capital, or lack thereof, that influenced the European-American women and men *choosing to overlook the demeaning behavior* against the impacted European-American woman. Without having this type of awareness concerning the state of your political capital, you could find yourself in the midst of an unexpected exchange between your peers or managers within the workplace. Without an adequate level of political capital, you may be treated unfairly.

In my experiences, many of the individuals I've interacted with were not so concerned with building their political capital or brown-nosing to obtain favor, promotions, high-visibility assignments or respectable increases in salary. Similar to my recollections of my grade school experiences, I recall only a small percentage of students regularly working to gain the teacher's favor that also came along with a not so coveted "teacher's pet" label from the classmates. Brown-nosing does exist in the workplace, just as it did in grade school. I do, however, believe the building of political capital can be done while maintaining respect among managers and your peers. Of course, every work environment will have its own unique dynamics, so methods need to take that into account to distinguish between brown-nosing and building political capital.

Examples for Building Political Capital in the Workplace

- Work at becoming a subject-matter expert in specific areas.

- Periodically present knowledge training sessions during team meetings.
- Regularly participate in conferences or conventions to expand your network and industry/profession knowledge.
- Get involved with innovation and development projects.
- Seek to learn about future business directions, goals, and deficiencies needing to be mitigated.
- Continue to increase your skills.
- Consider formulating a plan that focuses on gradually adding onto your current set of responsibilities.
- Have fun and learn to play with others.

Recommendation:

I hope you will be mindful of your political capital or lack thereof. Whatever your choice, your decision to engage or not engage in building political capital could impact the amount of opportunities available for achieving your career goals, and speed at which they become available. But, I don't believe having a limited amount can block your success, just potentially impede it. So, be aware, it exists and will be used by others to accomplish their gains, possibly at your expense.

Some Are Not Ashamed of the Things They Do

What should be some options for you if you were offered an opportunity to work for a company where your preliminary search on various media outlets revealed former and/or current employees making claims of widespread discriminatory practices? I would predict if you raise this concern *during the interview process* and before receiving an offer, the company will probably pass on making you an offer.

But after you have completed the interview process and received an offer, now might be a more opportune time, before accepting the offer, to bring up your concerns for what is being said in media about the widespread discriminatory practices. Now would be the time to ask what protections are in place to ensure you will not be working in a *hostile environment*. Now would be the time to ask *what concrete actions have been implemented* to change the culture, and *what recourse would you have* should you join the company and then find the culture still supports discriminatory practices.

Maybe you could suggest *a time-bound written cash payout agreement* to be paid out if you have experienced and documented discriminatory practices, and have attempted to get them resolved by presenting your concerns to appropriate governance stewards, and no resolution was reached within a pre-determined period of time. After all, your concern should be focused on why should you want to work with people *who feel comfortable abusing other people,* and where *leaders accept the practice of their employees being abused.* Business leaders should be concerned with actively implementing processes that ensure their *employees can do their work in a comfortable work environment* and reinforcing that people managers comply with policies and practices. If you get weak answers, or it appears their response tries to deflect, or they really don't have clear policies they can speak of that reassures you will be in a work environment, which allows you to feel comfortable, those should be the types of indicators which you should consider to be *deal breakers.* That would be the time to really consider turning down the offer and continue looking for a company that is more socially responsive with protecting the rights of its employees.

I would strongly advise you to avoid trying to ascertain the truthful reason as to why someone is discriminating against you, since there is a propensity for most people not to admit they are discriminating. This means they will probably give you a lie instead of admitting they are discriminating.

I would, however, suggest you utilize conflict resolution techniques to achieve some type of resolution to stop the conflict, or reach a decision to bring in objective mediators internally, or externally.

Every employee should have the right to work in a *non-hostile environment* and not have to leave a role they enjoy.

After you've begun visualizing a couple of career paths, you will want to think about what you can do to strengthen your probability of success when you encounter obstacles that disrupt your forward movement along your career path. Many will face emotional stress. Some woman and men could encounter inappropriate behavior. Minorities could encounter racial discrimination, and LGBTQ could encounter lack of inclusion. So even though many would prefer to avoid these realities, we can't ignore the fact that diversity influences how individuals determine who they choose to associate with. Diversity is what makes us all unique and can potentially present challenges. But you can plan on how you will overcome and continue along your career path.

The odds are some of those who engage in discrimination, do so as a result of their learned values, psychological dysfunction, beliefs, or jealousy of something they see in you that they don't have. It could also be an internal belief that their attacks on you will make them feel better about their own psychological issues. Regardless of the reason, keep in mind their actions probably have nothing to do with any adverse action you did against them, *unless you actually did something to them*. And, in the profound words of a many young siblings, "You started it!"

It is my hope that once you add solutions for managing discrimination, you learn to acknowledge it, and with awareness and understanding, now hopefully it has less impact. You should also begin preparing what-if workarounds so you can be prepared to immediately move around, through, and over discriminatory practices.

For instance, before applying for a loan, you can also identify multiple other options available from other financial institutions. Don't just rely on one.

If you are seeking a promotion, you can also simultaneously be working on finding external opportunities away from your current position. You also become less emotional about allocating time for trying to determine why someone felt the need to discriminate and what you can do to change their mind.

You should always utilize your conflict resolution skills to address any discrimination. While the discriminating individual is lavishing over having discriminated against you, you on the other hand will have moved on to implement your other options, received what you needed, and continued moving along your path.

You should also keep in mind that no matter who you are, or your background or personality, you have a right, just like anyone else, to be able to work, *without feeling uncomfortable or threatened*. You should not be forced to leave a job, but may choose to if you believe there are other options that present more advantages or benefits. And for you, the victory makes you stronger, empowered, and more confident in what you can achieve.

You are a survivor! Discrimination is just another pest on the road to be dealt with. So, keep your fly swatter handy, and deal with it.

Chapter 14: A Look into Being a Team Player

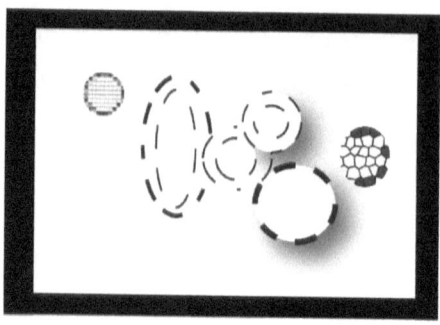

When seeking to hire new employees, why do so many employers include being a "team player" as one of the expectations they communicate as a general requirement? In addition, this expectation is often included within the text of job descriptions. What is the actual meaning behind generic catch phrases and talking points like, we need *you* to be able to hit the ground running, we need *you* (not us) to figure things out, or we need *you* to be available to put in whatever hours are needed to get the job done?

Your first impression might be these phrases sound like warnings to let you know you may not like working with the organization offering the job, or on the positive side, only you will be responsible for handling the problems they need solved. It may also be interpreted as the manager encouraging you to run away, and avoid pursuing getting hired. Any one of these considerations could be true. If it is important to be a "team player," what if you are someone who prefers to work independently as opposed to working on a team? And if you need to hit the ground running, will there be anyone to let you know which direction you should be running? Specifically, will there be someone to provide knowledge transfers so you can understand the organization's internal proprietary processes, practices, and procedures? Will there be someone who will provide any domain knowledge, the names of the people you'll need to engage and information related to intellectual property that only internal managers and existing employees would know? Or are they saying *no one will be assigned to help you*, and as such, you will come on board and just start running around in endless directions, seeking to find out how the organization runs? And how does the "team player" requirement, which implies collaboration, fit into you working alone to find out things on your own?

If this is something you are experiencing, right away from the very beginning, you are forced to wrestle with a need for clarity due to potential contradictions within the messaging of the manager, and possibly the organization you are considering going into an agreement with. Please re-read that last sentence, especially grasp the part about wrestling with contradictions. But before shutting the door on this potential opportunity, and running away as far as you can, I would first suggest for you to put on your detective hat, and attempt to gain better understanding of the organization's core values, the hiring manager's management style, and find out more about the organizational workplace culture from every accessible person who might be able to shed additional light, by providing their interpretations of the meanings behind any and all catch phrases and talking points communicated. One place to start is by checking the organization's website to look for the organization's core values, goals, or mission statements. And you can request any available documentation from the HR representative.

Since many managers might not communicate these talking points as part of standard job requirements, you might have to entice them by acknowledging you understand the basic expectations, and then let them know that you really want to be clear on how their expectations, are related to the specific role they are seeking to fill.

What I've found as a candidate and later an existing employee, the explanation for these types of internal organizational talking points, vary because they could either be driven from a higher senior leader level, or be derivatives created by mid-level managers. If you are a candidate or existing employee, and the actions of the manager don't seem to align to the organization's core values, you may be looking at a renegade, imposing what they want, over what the organization actually wants. Ideally, the organization's core values and how it defines its culture should be the governing influences for how each individual should respond to each of those well used talking points. And when speaking with mid-level and corporate leaders, it might be quite revealing to compare how they define corporate values and culture.

A key indicator for assessing the measure of an organization's leadership is their level of commitment to their organizational core values that ultimately mold the parameters of the organization's culture. This is a key way to measure leadership and the managers who are expected to align to them. Leaders who are not supporting their organization's core values, should be a concern for all who are expected to be "team players" working to help the organization achieve goals. For example, if core values focus on ensuring better customer service but in reality, you are not seeing dedication to upholding that value, the actual culture in place may also be contrary to your expectations and/or impact your ability to be successful in that specific work environment and culture.

Recommendation: I highly recommend that you keep your eyes wide open for signs of how leaders support their organization's values that they customarily order to be published by the communications resources responsible for socializing the voice of the business leaders. Many unknowingly are unaware the core values are *the windows into the business's soul.* Either they will be clues into why they believe in their business, or they could be a set of published deceptions. The communicated core values can expose the leaders who are committed or not. Their actions to support, or not support, will unveil if they truly believe in the published values, which together compose the overall organization's culture.

And although people rarely acknowledge there are in fact, some businesses whose unpublished core values actually expose their comfort with having minimal concern for customer safety, or comfort conducting business using discriminatory, dishonest, deceptive or illegal practices. There are some which can be predatory, manipulative and leave out just a few critical details or information regarding their products. They may use small print or rely on legal loopholes which lawmakers have not yet updated to protect or meet contemporary needs. The potential risk is upon joining them, you might find your own personal values and relationships impacted if you adopt the unsavory core values of a business who has commissioned your services.

Can Core Values Be in Conflict with Social Responsibility?

How would you feel if you found out you were working for an organization that is focused on hurting your community? Is this a real possibility? Yes. You could find that you are employed by a group that is using their influences, monetary contributions, products, or services in ways that might impact your community's health, economic opportunities, property values, or blockade the ability for the public to receive fair services and employment opportunities. It's not unusual to learn about organizations which support adverse political legislation, candidates and against consumer protective measures. Or simply become a hindrance against some social actions you believe in. Whoa is you, are you okay with being paid pieces of silver or blood money, allowing someone to use your skills against your own beliefs or values, all while helping a beast? If you had a choice, what would you really want to do? Yet, so many pay little attention to value statements normally dispensed to new employees, found on customer facing web sites and numerous internally posted locations. And although we naively believe an organization's core values are created to provide the type of positive messaging that help *you to believe* they are a reputable organization, they also use messaging to entice investors, customers and experienced resources. By making a simple comparison of what other organizations publish as their core values and mission statements, one might begin to see similar statements, as though they all went to the same core value 'template' store. And yet, as customers, consumers, investors, and employees, we don't see the same level of service, customer, or employee experience. Yes, there are, in fact, distinct differences in how each business engages their markets and employees.

To What Degree are you a Team Player?

Well here's a scenario for you to consider, which I hope will help you have a better understanding of being a team player.

Imagine you are traveling on a space ship that is carrying a large crew with family members including children, along with precious medical and food supplies for a colony of humans now inhabiting a distant planet. The ship is light-years away from Earth when suddenly the ship's sensors detect an unknown anomaly about to overtake the ship in less than thirty minutes but too large to steer away from it. What would be your course of action? 1) Gather everyone available who might have an ideal on what to do? 2) Gather only those in a close-knit circle who are the ones *you trust* and are comfortable with? 3) Would you be the one who goes to a computer and start working on finding some type of solution, *on your own?*

Now, if you were a family member, *and not* one of the crew working on a solution, would you feel more comfortable *accepting a course of action* if it:

1. Came from *those collaborating in the room* where there are a large number of people trying to figure out what to do,
2. Came from the room where *there are only people who feel comfortable working together* within their close-knit circle, or
3. Came from the *one person* working alone on their computer?

Well, you should know these are all *true to life scenarios on how decisions are made in an organization.* There are the organizations that solicit input from a wider group with the *hope of capturing all possible solutions* which also contributes to a wider buy-in and acceptance of the results, good or bad. There are those who keep others out of the loop and tend to make decisions within a room where *only a few select employees* are invited and could be often like-minded, not introducing many challenges to the alpha leader. And then there are micro-managers, who believe they need to take charge and make the decisions without considering the input from others, who actually have more experience and knowledge than the micro-manager.

How would you feel if the one person working alone on a computer, came up with a solution that resulted in the entire crew, family members, and children losing their lives? If this scenario happened in the comfort of Earth, the solution may not result in the loss of lives due to a wrong decision, *but could result in lay-offs*, loss of business, diminished business reputation, and undetermined difficulties, which could result in negative employee attitudes, less concern for delivering quality, added personal conflicts with friends and family, an increase of risky behavior, criminal activities or suicides. Ultimately, a quick or slow, lingering demise, depending on if you are in space, or on Earth.

So, it's important to know whether or not you are a team player, in reality, *or just when politically correct* to say so, or when, as a result of the audience, it's what you'd better say. If you were out in space, would you feel comfortable accepting the risk associated with the decision from a micro-manager making the decisions for the entire crew, family, and those waiting on a distant planet, or would you prefer a team collaborating together, to come up with the best solution by using all of their collective experiences? The answer supports why computers are so ingrained into almost everything we do, since computers can take into account a huge amount of knowledge, experiences, and varied scenarios to provide the best solution, targeted programming, or a course of action based on a *varied* set of outcomes and levels of impact.

And when it comes to building the confidence of a team and collective intellectual growth, it often comes through *collaborative efforts with solving problems*, which is a team effort, not isolated circles or one person relying only on their own unique experiences and individual knowledge. However, the genius scenario does emerge on occasion, but they will be known by spectacular outcomes, not just by their self-proclamations.

I think it's important to point out you will find business leaders, managers, and coworkers who really emphasize a culture in which employees and customers are respected. And when you encounter them along your career path, I highly suggest you keep in touch with them as well as other positive mentors over the course of your career. They can be trusted advisers as you face various challenges and roadblocks, or need someone who can provide objective input when you have a difficult decision to make. In addition, they can be foundational in building a trusted network that can alert you of new opportunities.

During the course of my career, I can attest to leaders, managers, and mentors who were instrumental in helping me be successful, gain better insight, into how others may perceive my abilities, achieve goals, increase my capabilities, remain employed, and increase my marketability. These are the character types related to having openness to collaboration, team building, and helping others. I might add, these helpful managers displayed character types far different from the character types displayed by those who would expect you to hit the ground running, trying to learn about the inner workings of an organization without assistance from those who have the knowledge.

The Proof is in The Pudding

It is absolutely critical that upon considering and later joining any organization, you assess the overall governing and oversight in place used by leaders to reinforce the expected core values and culture throughout their organization. Their actions and insistence on relying on core values should result in you being able to see the results manifested throughout their organization.

The business culture can influence the character of their customer service practices, how employees are treated, the level of openness for change and acceptance of new ideas from diverse sources, and how success is shared with stock holders and employees. It can ultimately result in added value passed on to customers. An organization's culture can influence the level of integrity, ethics, and value system. But without enforcement, the published core values are merely words on a sheet of paper, or website.

Culture should be mandated and reinforced from the top down. But often without governance, testing and verifications by leaders responsible for insuring a culture is maintained throughout the organization, mid-level managers can use their power over their kingdoms or decentralized teams to implement their own culture. As a result, it's not unusual to hear of talented employees *leaving because of their managers, not because of the organization* itself. This is a clear failure on the part of leaders responsible for maintaining the culture as defined.

So, for employees, it will not be difficult to determine how dedicated and serious leaders are with insisting that their defined cultural visions are actually being maintained.

I worked with one organization where a chief officer once sent a communication to the entire enterprise stating, "For those who don't comply with the cultural changes being implemented, there will be disciplinary actions *up to and including dismissal* from the company." Once you recognize managers are not dedicated to upholding positive corporate values and culture, you should be concerned. And furthermore, if *managers are not being held accountable* for maintaining positive cultural values like ethical behavior, diversity, integrity, fair customer service, transparency of leadership goals, having honest and open communication, having fair promotion practices, respect for employees, and having a healthy work-to-life balance, you probably shouldn't expect many good experiences.

And although I have experienced very positive leaders, I also have witnessed numerous situations where management displayed little respect for employees and/or their customers.

Some Positive Culture Experiences

Here are some examples of actual positive culture experiences where managers displayed sensitivity for developing a culture of customer-centric team, nurturing individual growth, team collaboration, and overall respect.

1. I was impacted by an acquisition. Unknown to many, it is a customary practice that the employees of the acquired business are normally not retained by the new parent company, especially if the merger results in a duplication of existing roles. But fortunately, the business selling off its business segment included in the negotiation that all employees will be retained for a minimum of six months. This allowed what some refer to as a "decent interval" for employees and the new parent company to assess the value of the relationship, and have time to make transitional changes.
2. I worked for a corporation that decided one of their remote office locations would be shut down, ultimately impacting at least one hundred employees. Even with this disruption to so many employees, the parent company continued its practice of showing respect of its employees by supporting a series of internal career fairs to help employees find new

employment before the office closed, setting up outplacement services for six months which included mentoring, networking events and classes, and worked to place employees at other existing offices. In addition, they allowed options to receive lump sum or partial dispersing of severance benefits.

3. I worked for a company in which a senior director regularly, and in front of others, verbally abused employees, had little concern for telling the truth, and regularly changed established processes without warning, resulting in weekly disruption of business continuity. And in case you didn't know, legally, there is nothing in an employment agreement which allows, or makes it acceptable for a manager to verbally or physically abuse you. One would think this type of behavior would be enough for separation from the company. But instead, disciplinary actions came in the form of a promotion being announced in which this manager was re-assigned to a remote "Siberia" location, effectively removing him from the team, protecting his future job interviews, and also providing him a "decent interval" to give him time to find another job away from the current company, all while avoiding the need for the company to award severance and unemployment benefits. His transfer resolved the abusive behavior imposed on the team, but may have transferred it to another team. I don't know, but it was good riddance for those he formerly needed to engage.

4. I was on a team where a couple of managers decided they could get away with promoting their less experienced friends over a group of employees having more experience, accomplishments, and team leader responsibilities. When existing team members began requesting transfers off the

team, and the remaining employees began challenging managers by asking, what is the point of putting in hard work if managers choose to promote junior employees having less experience over senior employees? Senior leaders somehow became aware of the actions of these managers, and as a result, implemented a detailed senior-level review and approval process for all promotions, re-assigned the two offending managers to other teams, and issued immediate promotions to the employees who had been unfairly skipped over.

5. I experienced a couple of managers who made a firm commitment to meet with me every week to discuss any challenges, and more importantly, assign me tasks focused on increasing my capabilities. They were not just scheduling regular meeting with me to be in compliance with their manager's goals for them to hold regular one-on-one meetings with their direct reports, but these managers were invested in working to prepare me for promotion into more challenging roles. Making suggestions on classes to take, assigning me development projects aside from my normal responsibilities, and providing regular feedback to allow me to make on-going adjustments throughout the year instead of waiting until the end of the year to receive feedback on expectations as part of the annual performance review process. These managers clearly were proactive with investing in, and managing their direct reports to ensure they were successful. They took the attitude that it was their personal managerial failure if any of their direct reports did not consistently receive an "exceeds expectations" performance review. If an employee received an annual review of "improvement needed," the question would be,

what did they do as a manager over an entire year to correct their actions which they should have been aware through weekly one-on-one meetings.

As a manager who had low performing members on their team, they would need to provide a very good reason, if they knew a member of their team was repeatedly doing something wrong, not performing responsibilities, or not completing assignments in a timely fashion. The question would be, why would they let them do that *all year* before they said something? Where was their thirty-, sixty-, ninety-day mitigation plan focused on corrective measures? Would they actually let an entire year go by, allowing their employee repeatedly underperform, while wasting company money? I caution you to beware of manager's who don't provide or recommend S.M.A.R.T. (Specific; Measurable; Achievable; Relevant; Time-bound) goals and suggestions throughout the year on how you can improve your performance and value. I also caution you to beware of managers who wait until the end of the year and then unload a list of negative things which, if you had been alerted, you could have addressed, but now they have given you a poor performance review, possibly impacting the size of your annual raise. I often say, a *manager's responsibility is to manage.* And your manager, should have a manager, that makes sure they do just that. If not, need I say more about the culture you are in.

6. I was on a team in which the team culture, as opposed to the business culture, imposed a work-to-life balance that regularly disregarded our weekends off, resulting in the need to work *every weekend.* This was a result of poor weekly and last-minute Friday afternoon planning on the part of our managers. At one point, there came a moment when a new

employee was added to our team. After two-weeks, one of the managers gave the new employee a gift card, citing it was a consolation for him having to work two weekends in a row. Well as you might imagine, the rest of the team was outraged since they were working *every weekend for months,* and had never received any acknowledgment or gift certificate. In this case, the outraged team demanded weekly process improvement meetings in which pizza would be provided as a team acknowledgment for all of the team members instead of just one person being recognized. Senior management accepted the proposal along with the expense to purchase pizza as a means to lower the anger level towards the manager and avoid a possible team implosion.

7. I was working for a company, and as a result of a holiday, a number of employees needed to be on duty to support a special event spanning the entire weekend. The event was one where our company was one of the corporate sponsors so many employees were needed. In taking into account that I had worked through my entire weekend, my manager told me to take off two-days as a make good for working through the weekend. This action was not cleared through HR, but was something my manager did to let me know I was appreciated, and when working on the weekend I should have those days re-cooped. Many managers do not make any adjustments for their employees working over their expected hours per week.

So, although it can be difficult to ensure people managers exhibit ethical behavior and, respect for employees and customers, these are all examples where business leaders and managers *displayed their sensitivity and value for a culture of respect for employees,* which ultimately impacted their customer's experiences. In today's work environment, these individuals may be rare, so when you encounter them, *be sure to acknowledge them*, and make sure they are part of your trusted network.

A Bit More About "Hit the Ground Running"

"Hit the ground running." This phrase potentially lets you know that the hiring manager feels so over-allocated with their own responsibilities that they are not very open to helping you on-board into the company or team. This ultimately means that this manager, not necessarily on behalf of the entire organization, is communicating a disclaimer of an accepted practice in place, in which the hiring manager, will be relying on you to figure out what to do, who you should speak to for critical direction, where is the bathroom, break room, cafeteria, and possibly what tools or system access you'll need to handle your responsibilities. I suggest you be very on guard when you hear the words, "hit the ground running" because this is often stated by those who are not team players by choice, or necessity. Or they could be only willing to help certain individuals, but not dedicated to working to ensure everyone on their team is aware of company policies, practices, domain knowledge, or who are the key people their team needs to engage. They generally expect you to arrive and figure out everything on your own. Again, this is not the traits of a team player, who, as a manager, should be dedicated to mentoring, providing guidance, leadership, and focused on making sure their team will be successful with all of their assignments. And yet, organizational mission statements often speak about helping their clients be successful with achieving goals or receiving the services needed that will meet their needs. But when new hires are brought on-board within a hit the ground practice, it will be very difficult for those employees to provide clients legendary service during the time when they are trying to figure out what to do. During that period of time, there is a high probability, internal and external customers will not get great service. In addition, you are immediately set up for failure, if you can't unravel workplace related puzzles. Sadly, this process rarely comes without emotional stress and anguish. And if you are familiar with the 'hazing' practices of pledgees' working to be admitted into a college fraternity or sorority, the policy of not helping the new hire can be very similar to being hazed.

Is the Hiring Manager a Team Player?

Candidates often overlook the need to determine if the hiring manager is actually a team player or just someone who uses the phrase to filter out potential candidates. Just think how you would feel if the hiring manager told you, outright, I have no intention of helping you fit in, or helping you to be successful while working for me. And yet, one of the most depressing discoveries will be finding that is true, after you accepted a job offer. Yes, there are managers and employers that have no commitment to helping you fit in or helping you to be successful, move up the ladder and build upon your career goals. But there are those who will mentor you, help you mitigate road blocks and work to prepare you for a promotion.

The Self-Managed Turtle in a Shell

I once was transferred to a new team where the manager sat at a desk across from me and never spoke to anyone. She just kept her head down while working continuously on her computer. I still have no clue what she did for all of those reporting to her. She held no meetings, provided no guidance or updates. Pretty much no communications, verbally, or by email. She was clearly no team player, but clearly had achieved a manager's title by following a path of working independently as opposed to working as a team player. She enjoyed working alone, and fortunately, the work culture supported resources who preferred to work alone and independently.

I soon realized I was on a team of individuals who *knew enough to be able to self-manage* themselves. I later found those having the label of being able to self-manage, was in some cases, a gold star. They didn't require a manager, but one was assigned only as part of a procedural reporting structure. They used their personal connections, plugged into the information data flow, spoke digitally via instant messaging and email to socialize updates and direction to each other. This silent conversation made it challenging to identify who were friends or foes. Since I had previously survived the 'hazing' like pledging a fraternity, roughly a year before transferring to this team, I was well versed in "hitting the ground running" speak. I began my investigations and discovery plan, only to find the team was not really a team, but a group of self-managed individuals working independently on separate assignments that were needed as a whole to complete a project. The true team player was not an individual, but a symbiotic group of people working independently, without much collaboration, to deliver a set of goals, every three months. Once your piece of the puzzle was complete, it would fall into place, and you then moved on to start working on the next piece of the puzzle.

One day, one of those reporting to this manager alerted me of a status meeting that was going to begin in a few minutes. I was excited about the possibility of hearing what is going on with this team. While comfortably seated at the conference room table, I listened as various individuals spoke about tasks they were independently working on. And then I heard my name, followed by, "How are you doing with YOUR project?" I almost choked since no one had communicated that I had a project. And in a second, I recognized that someone in that room had probably communicated my assignment, digitally, not verbally, but chose not to alert me, the new guy, about how they communicated. In that moment it hit me, of their digital speak. I avoided falling into the pit of shame and embarrassment by acknowledging I had no issues, and my wit kicked in, allowing me to respond with something like, "I'm just getting started, and will be meeting with my manager to make sure I'm on the right track." This allowed me to avoid attacking my manager who sat with her head stuck in her computer all day and was not in attendance of this status meeting. I also avoided a conflict with her back-up who was actually in the meeting and was smiling upon hearing my quick recovery, knowing that no one had told me of any assignment. This is part of hitting the ground running, and I was running through the maze like a mouse searching for Gouda cheese.

Recommendation: Stay alert for new players entering the game (new hires, re-assignments, re-orgs) who will be either a protagonist, antagonist, or seek to be neutral.

One More Hit the Ground Running Story

I once did an interview for a new opportunity, and while conducting preliminary preparation for the interview, I gained some feedback that the hiring manager *was far from being a team player*, and was boldly proclaiming she was seeking candidates who could hit the ground running. In fact, the feedback sounded as though this hiring manager was of a nature in which you would not be provided any help if you asked for project details after you are assigned. In other words, this manager would give you an assignment but not tell you details related to who is the project sponsor, what are the expected goals needed to be achieved, or who needs to approve actions you need to take. So, in my interview I intentionally asked some polite questions around this subject. The response was more like, "I expect you to figure things out," and

"I'm looking for someone who does not need to come to me with a lot of questions." A lot of questions, hmm. Why would someone new need to ask any questions? What do you think? A team player, or not a team player? I ran out of that interview, and never looked back.

Chapter 15: Social Responsibility

I believe it's unfortunate that so many people miss or avoid opportunities to get to know individuals who live outside of their own neighborhood and their tight-knit circle of friends. As a result, they can miss opportunities to gain better understanding, learn about or expand on existing perspectives beyond their own, have the opportunity to reason together, agree or disagree, or just enjoy having respectful but challenging conversations with each other.

As a result of choosing to follow a practice of avoidance and separation, those same people potentially *decrease* the probability of having opportunities to gain exposure to the *specific needs* of various clients and customers who happen to live in different communities. As businesses or employees tasked with providing a product or service to disparate communities, they could potentially never become aware of the evolving needs of those communities and targeted markets which ultimately should benefit from the business or employees responsible for delivering a product or service to disparate targeted markets over the course of their individual tenures. If your goal is to have a successful career providing a service and supporting a specific market, you could face continual challenges with building your individual or corporate brand past an initial product or service offering. Being viable, and avoiding being just a fad, could become a challenge if you are not able to remain tuned to the needs of the market, clients, and customers, as they change over time. Remember, big box stores and large shopping malls had a strong run for a period of time, but customer shopping needs are moving away from that experience in favor of online shopping and delivery.

Just think how special a product or service could be if they accounted for the specific changes and needs of the communities within their targeted markets. What could be the potential if a product or service was able to closely track to the needs of the target market consumers as they change?

A Walk Through the Market

Well, today businesses are validating their desire to keep up with market and customer change by implementing strategies focused on collecting analytics to track market and customer trends, using technology to understand customer movement within or in the vicinity of stores, use of tools for tracking online searches, their use of phone signal tracking in stores, and by using loyalty rewards programs. In addition, they are involved with face-to-face community events marketing. These are all strategies to gain real-time data feedback.

And for those who are creating career strategies, or in the midst of revising their existing plans, the *inclusion of strategies focused on remaining current on business and customer expectations, trends, and changes*, can reveal a wide range of opportunities for you to develop viable career paths or craft a variance to an existing profession or path. Face-to-face community affairs events are one of the easiest ways to begin leveraging a career opportunity since they present a casual environment to meet employees and learn more about the company and current needs. Through the implementation of such strategies, you can gain understanding of the various needs to be socially *responsible* and equally important, what is socially *irresponsible*. You should be aware that some of the strategies to gather customer trends could be considered by some to be an invasion of privacy, so it pays to understand current privacy boundaries. And yet, we continue to see the emergence of customer monitoring services, which could face backlash. Obviously, in these cases it would appear that someone is not in-tune to the specific strategies that allow customers to feel comfortable. This is where face-to-face engagement with individuals will continue to provide benefits.

As mentioned earlier, opportunities to meet people who live outside of their own neighborhood and tight-knit circle of friends can result in opportunities to gain better understanding, learn about perspectives other than your own, have the opportunity to reason together, agree or disagree, or just enjoy having respectful but challenging conversations with each other.

As for organizations, this presents the opportunity to diversify existing products or services, and possibly develop new items to market.

And Stars Will Fall
During one's career you unquestionably will witness the demise of businesses that lose track of how to be responsible to their customers. For those resistant to change, and determined to continue marketing the same product or services just as their founders did 130 years ago, or continue marketing in the same form as when they initially entered the market, the slow burn from within often brings internal turmoil as the debate for change increases between legacy and more contemporary leaders.

And before their demise, they will slowdown in their ability to retain a respectable market share, and possibly display an insensitivity for adjusting when customer's needs change. Eventually, businesses just fall out from view, left on the side of the road while newcomers, innovators, market disruptors and visionaries, continue to re-fuel and navigate around them. For those managing career paths, the same can hold true for you if you are resistant to change as consumer and market needs and demands change. I would ask, in planning your own career strategy, which business would you prefer to be aligned? Organizations comfortable with remaining aligned to the needs of disparate communities and changes to the market are the types of indicators you should keep an eye on when vetting potential organizations to include in your career planning. And this might be an excellent point of focus when information gathering.

For those building and navigating a career path, when you consider the example of failing businesses not keeping up with changing expectations and expected social responsibilities of their customers as some of the reasons why businesses fall by the side of the road, maybe you should consider backing away from legacy job search strategies, and adopting tactics of developing innovative approaches, disruptive approaches, thinking outside the box, and being visionary with identifying diverse career opportunities, with the goal of being more prudent and beneficial over time. Keep in mind, hiring managers and recruiters will also change along with businesses and customers.

The possibility also exists that you, as an employee, or a business owner, could be directly impacted, and left on the side of the road, along with one of those failing businesses, all due to not evolving with the ever-changing needs of the community and targeted markets. Once again, this puts a spotlight on the need to actually get out to know your customer, and not just say it as a slogan.

Those organizations seeking to maintain constant focus on corporate and organizational social responsibility *beyond* just being compliant with regulatory requirements, should be recognizable by their activities focused on facilitating employee engagement with communities through volunteer work and participating in community events, allowing them to maintain an open ear to the ground so they can focus on staying in-tune as communities, not just their own, express their expectations. This trend of increasing opportunities to strengthen the community relationships and keeping up with social responsibilities by engaging communities face-to-face through participation in activities where employees can understand first-hand what are concerns and what might be the needs of the community they serve, has been proven to work toward building brand names, creating a positive image in communities, and helping to avoid being one of the companies left on the side of the road for not being attentive to their corporate and social responsibilities.

Notable Social Concerns

Here are a few notable concerns expressed by one or more communities which later spread to others:

1. There is an increasing call to have clean energy.
2. To have more food products that are natural and without additives. As a result of increasing needs for natural foods there has been an increasing need for transparency with product labeling of ingredients. In addition, some businesses are open to developing healthier food choices while existing businesses are making more natural food products available for their customers.
3. There is an increased concern about global warming, and yet there continues to be some businesses that ignore the existence of global warming, and as a result, they ignore the growing call for social responsibility by continuing to be unwilling to change how they've been running their businesses. There also are some politicians who continue to

be reluctant to support regulatory changes which would support the protection of our world as one of the social changes being called out by an expanding community voice.
4. There has been a consistent up-tick around businesses doing more with securing data to protect individuals from personal identity theft. With the public becoming increasingly more aware of database hackings, and breaches into customer files, the call for businesses to have strong controls in place to protect an individual's personal and private information is getting louder and louder. Organizations can no longer expect to gather personal information on customers, without simultaneously investing in having measures to protect the information they gather. I would suspect as a result of the outcry, organizations who can't display they have stringent measures in place will begin to face a growing reluctance for individuals to provide truthful information about themselves.
5. There are increasing concerns about drilling and dumping practices related to the contamination of land and water. This is clearly an area where the community has become more vigilant with vetting where drilling for oil is allowed, demanding the removal of lead pipes being used for delivering drinking and bathing water, having oversight for companies who dump chemical and waste by-products in secluded areas and into our water supplies, and having more controls over secondary smoke and air pollutants. In some communities, people can experience smoke-free zones as a direct result of community outcry for businesses to be socially responsible for the health of people. All of these social concerns are coming at the desires of communities seeking to experience longer and healthier lives.

6. Safety and Respect. Another real social concern that might be prevalent in one community but not in another is whether or not customers and employees feel safe and respected while at certain locations. There are communities that may have unique situations that make customers uncomfortable. As a result, they might choose to go to another location or shop with a competitor that can provide them with more safety and respect. Some organizations choose to "fly over" those communities, completely avoiding providing any service, creating underserved communities, food deserts, diminished mental health facilities, trauma center hospital deserts and more. Other organizations recognize that each community has its own distinct needs, and as such, each location is designed to better meet the needs of the communities they serve. Being innovative should not be an obstacle to be able to support communities seeking to feel safe and respected, or having unique needs. The use of innovative solutions can be put in place no matter the location or the customer. For example, I recall going to sports and entertainment events that were well lit, secured by surrounding high gates used to control entry, and had security personnel posted at entrances. And although those events were located in communities I probably would not casually walk around, I felt totally safe and employees respected customers the entire time upon entering and while watching the events.

7. Having a visual presence or office location in the community, hiring those who live there and reinvesting in those communities are some of the social concerns that have been expressed, but ignored by many organizations. As a result, some organizations have brand names known as being

friendly and accommodating only to one segment of our society. They also find it difficult to build market share beyond the one segment of people, while opportunities continue to exist for other organizations who are comfortable with having a visual presence in all of the communities they service. Those seeking to gain market share in communities where they are not present can also face the challenge of not being able to hear the voice of social outcry until their competition begins capturing increased market share and creates an issue with their viability.

In the absence of information related to understanding how people who live outside of your own community, feel, you are left with a lack of input, sensitivity, and forced to make decisions related to products or services, while wearing blinders. You could be making decisions based on only the needs of your own community, and not knowing how one community is being adversely impacted, which may be totally different to the needs of other communities.

For example, you might reside in some community where smoking cigarettes is popular, so public establishments would probably have minimal concerns about secondary smoke. If you were a parent concerned about the health of you and your kids, you probably would decide to frequent only the establishments where you could enjoy smoke-free zones. As a result, the establishments that actually acknowledge a social responsibility related to the need for smoke-free establishments, will see a growing client base as others become more and more knowledgeable about the dangers of secondary smoke, and probably other health issues. As you might imagine, those having a lack of social responsibility potentially increase the risk of losing customers with families who desire to find establishments with smoke-free zones, and also increase the risk of their brand increasingly becoming thought of as socially irresponsible.

In conclusion, avoiding a better understanding of groups that you may not have direct contact with could hamper your ability to help, develop, build, or enhance existing products or services beyond the ones that only benefit your own group or mindset. You could also miss new opportunities or understand gaps in existing products, services, or processes.

And yes, it may take some time, but stars do fall.

Chapter 16: Preparing Your Stand Against the Face of Deception and Avoiding the Five Major Risks

The five major risks are:

1. Financial risk.
2. Strategic risk.
3. Compliance risk.
4. Operational risk.
5. Reputational risk.

As you move along your diverse career path, you may encounter other risks, but these five are universal ones which you should be aware.

I define a risk as being the awareness of something that *potentially* could happen, and if it does happen, is expected to result in a negative impact to you and/or others. You may ask, why is this important to you. Because in addition to you putting yourself at risk from decisions you make or actions you take, others, including your employer, can also put you at risk of being impacted in each of the five areas of risk. And that requires you to be vigilant in looking for signs that your employer is putting the business at risk, or you specifically are being put in situations where you are increasingly put at risk, in any of the five major areas. I highly recommend you consider putting safeguards in place, as best you can. And if you become aware of one or more risks going un-managed, you might want to be poised to implement your exit plan, to avoid being impacted.

I define an issue to be a negative impact that occurs *after a risk has actually transformed into an event*, and is now, actively real. Here's a scenario to help you gain more understanding. You purchase auto insurance to: 1) Comply with municipal regulatory laws (compliance risk), 2) To minimize your out-of-pocket expense if your vehicle is damaged (financial risk), and 3) To provide options should an accident occur resulting in the inability to drive your vehicle (operational risk). If you have an accident at some point in the future, some or all of those risks could become real issues. So, although the accident has not happened at the time of purchasing insurance, you buy insurance as a risk mitigation plan to minimize the level you are impacted if you are involved in an accident. The *accident* itself would present one or more issues.

Buying an auto or home alarm system is another type of risk mitigation plan focused on first, deterring thieves from breaking in, secondly if they do, alerting you of the breech, and lastly, minimizing the amount of out-of-pocket expense you'll need to pay to replace the loss of your property. Early warning severe weather alerts, technology disaster recovery (DR) plans, fire drills, and aircraft pre-flight safety presentations are all risk mitigation plans focused on minimizing or mediating negative impacts or outcomes.

The Two Conflicting Perspectives When Considering Risks

Over the course of my career, I've had a number of discussions regarding risk mitigation planning. I consistently find there are two distinct camps when it comes to allocating time and effort to identify risks, and then creating risk mitigation plans.

Those aligned to *Camp 1* are comfortable seeking feedback and asking for suggestions on what can be done to design efficient controls to ensure minimal impacts while increasing confidence that property, products, and services remain safe. They might even create a log and assign individuals to be risk owners in charge of monitoring the risk, come up with plans to protect against the risk from happening, and if it does, ensuring there is a plan to minimize the damage.

Those aligned to *Camp 2* will often view discussions focused on identifying, controlling, and developing strategies focused on minimizing negative impacts if a risk becomes an issue as either a waste of time, or just an avenue for people to *complain* since during risk discussions, attention is given to making improvements and identifying missing processes (gaps) or capabilities. The process of managing risks could also be perceived by some as being personal attacks on their capability to manage responsibilities under their authority.

Unfortunately, those managers who tend to label individuals in Camp 1, as complainers, don't realize they have innovative thinkers in their midst. The innovators are often the ones who can see the forest from the trees, and come up with ideas on how to make something easier, or more efficient. And I have to ask, who really wouldn't want their work to be easier and at the same time, being more efficient while delivering higher performance?

I caution you to be aware of organizations led by someone who does not take the lead in seeking a commitment from *all employees* to participate, in their perspective roles, with managing the five areas of risks. For these are the organizations which are often peppered with turbulence as employees are forced to regularly address unexpected 'ad hoc' issues beyond real emergencies. Employees will often hear those infamous words, "We need this right away," which in the absence of real emergencies, exposes the lack of pre-planning that can facilitate the ability to multi-task and minimize chaos. If you are hearing these words often, there's a good chance you are in the belly of an organization that doesn't manage risks, but instead waits for the risks to become issues, and then everyone finds they are constantly in reactive, not proactive mode. I can pretty much guarantee upon hearing the battle cry of "We need this right away" before you go home, is not something you are going to feel good about. And if you are constantly in reactive mode, it's often very difficult to complete planned efforts on time, due to 'ad hoc' efforts, which can only be disruptive to your previous plans. And when you are consistently in catch-up mode, stress becomes you.

Recommendation: I highly suggest you take some time to do all you can to identify, mitigate, and control risks by developing appropriate risk mitigation plans that have a goal of stopping risks from becoming an issue. And if a risk does evolve into an issue, having a plan to control the damage.

Recommendation: As part of your risk mitigation plan, I highly suggest that you develop *more than one source of income* as an integral element to your career strategy. In addition, this could reduce the risk of feeling the need to make decisions that could *compromise* your reputation, values, or morals, in order to maintain employment with your current employer.

Will You Be Compromised?

What would you do if you became aware of a company practice, or have been put in a situation where you know the actions will falsely report on individual employee performance, hurt customers, or the public? Would your response be, "I need this job?" We have seen municipalities put its citizens at risk with lead-tainted water, car manufacturers with defective air bags, organizations covering up safety controls and reports, financial institutions creating loan products, and accounting practices that mislead customers and stock holders. There have been aggressive managers who introduce unrealistic sales goals that force employees to falsely report sales figures or conduct business in a way that unfairly takes advantage of its customers. In some instances, managers have been known to implement strategies using headcount reductions to strengthen the value of their company stock.

In each of the situations listed, I believe *there was always someone who knew about the deceptive or abusive practices*, but for some reason, chose to go along with the plan, or keep silent, in order to receive a reward or ensure they maintained their job security for that moment, over the needs of public safety and hurting real people. Some even might have chosen to risk being legally summoned to testify in a lawsuit, about their awareness or involvement. That risk could result in individuals being fined or imprisoned, because they didn't speak out on something they knew would hurt people. And of course, knowing that if they did speak out, they face the risk of being ostracized and receiving retaliatory attacks from managers, face receiving false annual reviews, or ultimately needing to find a new job. Yes, you should be aware that at some point in your working career, there's a high probability you will experience one or more of these types of scenarios, in which your morals, reputation, integrity, or common decency could be compromised. And you'll ponder, which way do I go. And let's be real, there are organizations which will actually seek to hire individuals who can keep their mouths shut, look the other way and ignore something wrong, unfair, unethical, illegal or immoral, but I'm not encouraging or condoning that career path.

When planning this guide, I considered if there might be any value for a chapter to spotlight some business cultural practices that are unspoken, but standardized and engrained in the workplace. Then I recalled an actual work-related experience that was very troubling to me, mostly because it had never happened to me before, it was totally unexpected, went against one of my core values, and even more troubling, because I was naïve in believing someone in management, would knowingly put me in an adverse situation, that was also against my core values. So, I decided to share this actual event.

There came a time when I was directed by my manager to send an email to a group of business stakeholders that identified specific members in their group as having some negative data performance results, essentially to publicly shame some specific individuals listed. In reality, this was a totally false report, and the individuals did not have negative performance results, and so I questioned it. It just didn't make sense to me why I was being directed to send out a report that really was not correct. I internally reasoned that maybe the manager had just somehow had a misunderstanding of what he had instructed me to send, so I alerted him. However, he insisted that I send the report as is. But this report would be coming from me, not him. This was *my* reputation and image that would be called out if people actually dug into the data. In addition, this was an unfair public shaming. Up to this point in my career, I had never contemplated being in this type of situation. As a result, I had no plan for how to respond once this situation was a real issue. And since I was already aware of the character of this manager as one who often flew unbridled, I had concluded if I chose not to comply with this directive, I would soon have to defend myself against false charges of my insubordination. For me, I felt as though someone had taken something from me, my integrity, which I held, and still hold as valuable today. Fortunately, only one stakeholder openly challenged the data, and I immediately let him know that I was told by my manager to send the report, even though I did not support or agree to what was in the report. Given my reputation compared to his, they found my accounting as creditable. And that was spread to others that I was ordered to send out a false report. Later I thought, could it be that I was unknowingly in the midst of a personality conflict between two team managers? And the false report was an attempt by my manager to turn leaders against the other manager by disseminating false performance data, which if believed, could have damaged the reputation of the other manager and diminish the confidence leaders had in his management capabilities. Given his character, this probably was the case. So, in combination with my disclaimer given to one of the stakeholders, the heat went to the manager who had ordered me to send the false report. That evening I reached out to some trusted friends to get their advice. After some soul searching I realized what I would do the next time, and as a result today, I'm a stronger person, and have a flaming sword at my side, should something similar to that happen again. However, the personality conflicts between my manager and myself only escalated. Eventually I was presented with a severance package, which I joyously accepted.

Unfortunately, in this day and age, the risk of you encountering a similar scenario, challenge, or practice, which tend not to be publicly discussed by business leaders, can be a jaunting emotional experience if you had not previously considered the risk of something like this happening to you. What would you do if your employer strongly encouraged you to deliver a communication focused on convincing the public that weapons of mass destruction (WMDs) exist, when they actually did not? What would you do if you became aware of a product being released or process being rolled out that you knew would put the public at risk? (E.g.: sub-prime mortgage products, lead contaminated water, defective electronic products which haven't been thoroughly tested.) What would you do if your manager often expected you to lie on their behalf? It could begin with something seemingly innocent like telling someone they are not in their office when they actually are, or providing other managers information that is just not true. In some organizations, these small lies to protect the whereabouts or adverse decisions could be deemed as normal expectations and responsibilities for administrative assistants.

However, if you decided *not to* 'cover' for a manager, or carry out what you've been instructed to do, you would have to take into account the probability of your manager not having loyalty or trust in you, accusing you of insubordination, being fired and then facing an inability to pay your bills and support your family. On the other hand, *if you decided to comply* with what you've been instructed to carry out, *or ignore* that a product is being released that *could potentially harm people*, for some, this decision might leave you with remorse or guilt having the knowledge of doing something you know is morally wrong, that could damage your reputation, impact your future employment opportunities, and/or result in potential criminal charges.

Recommendation: If you find you are working with someone who regularly makes your work environment uncomfortable as a result of unethical or immoral behavior, their lack of integrity, sexual harassment, or offensive language, just to name a few, you may want to document the time and date of each event in writing, and use your cell phone to capture verbal proof of each offense. And if your manager gives a verbal direct order, or suggestion, insinuates, or implies what they would like for you to do, or hopes you will consider something that could benefit your career, and the action is unethical, immoral, dishonest or illegal, I would suggest that you try to obtain any type of confirmation from your manager via an email or recorded phone call, where your request might be phrased something like, "I just want to confirm you would like me to do <insert description of the request>." (Note: In some states both parties must give consent to be recorded.) It might also add some validation to your situation if there is a witness. Without tangible evidence, the offended employee is often left in an even more adverse work environment. Since a primary focus of human resource departments, which the offended employee soon learns, is to protect the company, you should not be surprised if a complaint you submit will not result in a resolution. Reportedly, a number of surveys of past whistle-blowers reveal the offending manager had been allowed to initiate retaliatory actions, conduct on-the-job harassment, block advancement, and get away with unfair disciplinary actions, that often resulted in the employee being fired for unsubstantiated reasons. Unfortunately, some HR and business leaders have a propensity not to punish managers who reciprocate against employees who have filed complaints, despite having language included in their code of conduct, against such an act. And many publicly outed whistle-blowers report it to be difficult finding work as a result of public shaming. Also, the court system usually tips the scales in favor of business owners *unless* there is a group of people filing a complaint, in the form of a class action suit. And it has been done successfully.

Here's another true experience. During an early point while on my career path, I made a decision to change direction and began pursuing a career in the food service industry. I recall as part of my training, I had to learn about food safety. And on one sunny, summer day, while working on cleaning the soda fountain dispenser nozzle, I discovered small, green mold plants growing in the aerator nozzle.

Evidently, the combination of sugar water and bacteria provided a fertile breeding ground for mold. According to the cleaning guide, this nozzle should be cleaned every week, so I brought the nozzle to the manager, as proof it was not being cleaned, and as a result was creating a potential health risk to customers. But for some reason, instead of being acknowledged for my thoroughness, and eliminating a potential health risk that could then be followed by a potential lawsuit (financial risk), I started receiving retaliatory type assignments, which made me feel that I shouldn't have let the manager know when safety procedures were not being done on their watch. There it was: Camp 2. Afterwards, I adopted a new policy. When eating at a restaurant, I avoided purchasing any beverages that you get from soda dispensers. Later I relaxed that policy, to now accept beer dispensed from a tap.

    It's not unusual to find yourself in a situation where you have deal breaker personality conflicts with your manager, resulting in a decision to seek resolution with a higher manager, human resources, ethics hotline, legal remedies, or just leaving when all else fails. Historically, business managers tend to rally behind managers involved with unethical behavior over complaints from their direct reports. HR is often found to be without power to enforce punishments without the blessings of a senior leader. So, in each case, you'll need to determine the climate for whether managers will police their own, or will they take a blind eye and label you as someone who just doesn't fit the culture, or somehow suddenly is deemed as an under performer, and a strong candidate to be let go. When you look at business compliance rules, usually a mandated course is required for all employees to complete. In this course, unethical behavior is always called out, but often overlooked depending on the level of political capital one has with upper management. Businesses also speak of all employees being mindful of identifying risks that could negatively impact the brand. This could be a:

1) financial risk, 2) strategic risk, 3) a compliance risk, 4) an operational risk, and yes, 5) a reputational risk. I can attest as earlier mentioned, that I've experienced a manager who put my reputation at risk which required me to take corrective actions. Over some time, the ordeal was eventually resolved, and I was glad to receive a severance package and the opportunity to start over somewhere else, but a lot wiser.

Will you be prepared to tell a manager that, this is not acceptable and take the risk of losing your job at a time which will probably not be a good time, when bills are due or you have a child coming? I've seen people choose to allow themselves to be compromised, and stay because they weren't prepared to take a stand, or to move on. It's also common that businesses attack and demonize whistle-blowers despite HR policies which speak against that type of behavior, but rarely seem to be able to protect whistle-blowers. So many women have had to tolerate sexual harassment in the workplace and suffer years before reaching a tipping point or psychological breakdown. And during their ordeals, their significant others and children also suffered, while not really knowing why their relationship was crumbling. Take heed; I would suggest that you consider what you would do before having to do it. Talk with your loved ones and those who you would share confidential thoughts, to strategize on options to take in advance of finding yourself in the middle of it.

You will need to protect yourself from being put in a compromising position that leaves you at a fork in the road where you need to decide to accept, tolerate, or refuse. To refuse could possibly negatively impact your political capital, your ability to work with others, your potential for advancement, or impact the viability of your current job. On the positive side, it could increase the level in which people trust you, fortifying your reputation of being a person with integrity and being known for standing for positive principles and values.

Make a plan now. And please include as part of your plan, discussing with friends, what they think would be solutions given hypothetical scenarios before they actually materialize and become an issue. This could be an interesting conversation over drinks which can facilitate how you might respond given current situations like family and your economic state of affairs.

If a woman was sexually assaulted at work, some ladies may feel reluctant to discuss with their significant other and also feel reluctant to file a workplace grievance for fear of losing their job or being blocked from advancement, and being kept out of the loop. If you are paying for a car or mortgage, you may be reluctant to risk losing your job, and as a result, not be willing to defend the need for you to be respected and the need to protect your name and honor. Feeling uncomfortable in the workplace is a clear sign of unethical behaviors. And these are the types of scenarios you should discuss from various hypothetical perspectives, with those close to you, *before it happens*, because you can bet, if not sexual harassment, there could be other scenarios where you struggle with a decision that could result in you losing your job. Also, keep in mind that having tolerance in an adverse work environment, can come hand in hand with emotional distress. And emotional distress could materialize in a diminished ability to effectively do your job, and could impact personal relationships.

I can personally confess that after experiencing being the target of antagonistic behavior, and having thought about my alternative tactics and options, I've become much more confident with being able to walk without concern for being unfairly targeted. In this day and time, it's no longer unusual to hear of racial, sexual, and whistle-blower bias. Or hear of major businesses taking unfair advantages in the marketplace, or putting customers at risk. It's literally impossible that no one within those offending companies didn't see something or was not aware of unethical behaviors, but looked away in fear of losing their job or opportunities for high pay and bonuses. Keep in mind, if your name becomes associated with a story that reaches social media, your reputation could be impacted so severely that it may be difficult to get employment in your area. And so, you pull up roots, remove work experience from your résumé to hide the trail, develop a cover story for the gap in your employment history, and move far enough away where you hope no one will know who you are or associate you to the event. But social media has an uncanny sense of catching up with people years later. So maybe you should do what many businesses do, and that is work to avoid the five major risks which could introduce serious obstacles into your career path.

The Downward Trend Needs a Strong Push Upward

In these days, more and more leaders, businesses, politicians and organizations are being exposed as unethical, deceptive, lacking integrity, and having little concern with putting people at risk. There is also a probability that *some* of those who supported the efforts of those being exposed, made a decision to provide support because they were compromised in some way. As a result, they may face repercussions at some point in the future.

In each case, you can bet there were individuals who stood up and chose not to compromise their integrity and principles, but the odds are you probably will not hear their story. They are rarely acknowledged. Not many know the name Frank Wills, the security guard who discovered the Watergate break-in. But if you conduct an internet search, you can find stories which impacted large numbers of people. For instance, there was the false claim of weapons of mass destruction where young men and women lost their lives in the war that followed the false claim, but we don't know of the ones who proclaimed WMDs were not there. There was a movie made about the renowned whistle-blower, Erin Brockovich which exposed water contamination. And there was the sub-prime mortgage loan crisis which preceded the 2007 to 2009 recession which damaged the finances of millions of Americans of all colors. There was the 2014 Flint, Michigan water scandal, and in 2016, there was a cell phone model that began exploding unexpectedly resulting in the FAA prohibiting the phones from being turned on during commercial airline flights. There have been companies charging high insurance fees or mortgage interest loan rates based on race or where you live. And there was the Serpico corruption scandal, which exposed police corruption in the 1960's, and the 2014 Laquan McDonald scandal where dashboard video exposed the shooting by a police officer followed by alleged cover-ups. For some reason, the good cops and police superintendents continue to ignore and refuse to report the criminal acts of bad cops who commit crimes ranging between obstruction of justice, perjury, and murder. They also must consider repercussions from their fellow officers having guns and who are supposed to have each other's back when going into dangerous situations. Unfortunately, we don't hear the stories of all those who refused to allow their morals and principles to be compromised, but they are there. And we should know of these stories today. But in order to pad yourself from being compromised, you'll need to have risk mitigation plans in place, or face falling into the abyss. Yes, there are and will continue to be people and businesses who put the public at risk.

I think for some, they could be indifferent when asked to support an unethical, immoral, or illegal action, until they actually experience how it feels when the action of someone else negatively impacts you. If you were to discover your annual review contained false statements from your manager, and as a result, you did not receive a bonus, a promotion, a raise in salary, or possibly had your job eliminated, you may have a stronger reaction, and maybe the next time, you'll consider pushing back against supporting a negative climate, and allowing your values or integrity to be compromised. Some managers might tell you 'off the record' that having their resources in a compromising situation is a very old practice used by deal negotiators and managers to get more work out of their employees, or to punish employees when there are personality conflicts.

But what recourse do you have? Unfortunately, employees believe their recourse against adverse actions by managers is to speak directly with the offending manager, and if there is no resolution, to file a complaint with their human resource (HR) department. Unknowingly, employees don't realize a key responsibility of HR and legal departments is to keep the company out of court and protect the company. Aside from identifying candidates when hiring managers are seeking to fill an open requisite, HR managers are also the ones who are responsible for communicating the rules documented in the employee handbook, obtaining legal confirmations from employees, and carrying out any punishment to employees as directed by business leaders. They rarely have any authority to disperse punishment to managers for their bad behavior without first receiving approval from senior leadership. And punishment to managers are rarely seen until their misdeeds result in the team imploding, like an erosion of team morale, an increase with insubordination, employees seeking to transfer off the team or there is an upward trend with attrition/quitting. Or maybe the public has become aware of the misdeeds and as such, begins to negatively impact corporate reputation, brand image, or stock prices. Then you may openly see HR implement punishment as corrective measures approved by leaders, and as part of crisis management damage control.

There is another recourse that employees believe is available to them called ethic or compliance hotlines, which are communicated to be a way to report unethical behavior anonymously. But once again, this is a process setup and paid for by the company. And I don't know about you, but I've never heard of any punishment, fines, or criminal charges for leaks from ethic hotlines, to company leadership. In other words, there is rarely any transparency, or visibility into any governance that ensures complaints are kept anonymous. Instead, you are just supposed to believe every complaint submitted will be anonymous. And yet, somehow whistle-blowers are somehow outed, then attacked by their managers and/or peers, and at times fired despite companies publishing they will not tolerate managers creating a hostile work environment by harassing, retaliating and attacking employees for filing complaints. By the way, this is one of the key reasons why corporations fought to eliminate unions, which provided representation or negotiation on behalf of the employee.

Here's another true experience. I once received a call from an HR compliance specialist as a result of another employee filing an anonymous complaint against our common manager. In the complaint filed, my name had been mentioned as someone who could confirm some of the practices I personally experienced or observed of the manager who was the target of the complaint. Approximately a week after my phone interview with HR, who assured me my conversation would be kept anonymous, my direct manager, who was not part of the complaint, my manager's manager, and the manager who a complaint had been filed, all began verbally attacking me on the same exact day. I found this coincidence to be quite interesting. Since I was not the one filing a complaint, and I was assured my responses would be kept anonymous, it seemed really odd how these three managers became aware of what I had said. And then approximately one month later, I received a raise in salary and a change to my job title citing, I and others were recognized as being part of a group of employees who based on established advancement criteria, should had received promotions. We had surpassed established leadership goals, but had not received approval by the manager in the filed complaint, to be given the appropriate promotions based on our achievements and scope of responsibilities. However, there were a couple, not included in the impacted group, who *had not met the criteria required*, but had somehow been awarded and promoted. In addition, they were friends of the managers who were the target of the complaint. Since the team was rapidly imploding, senior leadership determined they should take corrective actions. Damage control.

    I also experienced an incident where, as part of an annual performance review process, I provided feedback for one of my matrixed direct reports where I had complimented and documented how well he worked on my projects. However, the employee's direct manager provided contrary feedback, stating the same employee didn't do any work well. The range between the two reviews raised questions at the senior leader recalibration reviews and triggered an additional review by a senior leader committee. The results of this review concluded the employee's direct manager had not thoroughly reviewed the outcomes of this employee's assignments over the course of the year. And this meant the feedback was not factual in that false information was posted, resulting in a negative performance rating. To my dismay, the employee's rating was not revised accordingly, which resulted in a negative financial impact in light of unethical behavior on the part of his manager.

I share these specific experiences, which involved individuals across race, gender, and culture, to say unethical behavior on the part of managers will happen. In the 2007 to 2009 sub-prime mortgage crisis, a number of leaders linked to creating the crisis received substantial bonuses and escaped criminal prosecution. In reality, you will see cases where managers are given a pass by leaders, boards of directors, compliance, and HR. In other cases, unethical behavior on the part of some managers is dealt with quietly in ways to protect the manager's reputation. In some of these situations, employees are negatively impacted, and if that's you, you'll probably need an escape path.

Recommendation: Just like you have a doctor to address changes in your health, you should consider joining professional social media groups, engage alumni association advisers, or career experts, where you can submit questions or request advice from the group members on how best to resolve work related conflicts.

So, at this point, you should be quite aware of some challenges that are rarely spoken of publicly. My actual experiences and third-party observations led me to believe you should prepare for these negative aspects encountered over one's career.

Policy Change Needed

Unfortunately, high schools and colleges often shy away from talking about ways to prepare yourself if you have to make a stance on your reputation, morals, values, or honor. I've never had the opportunity to enroll in a Moral Values or Corporate Social Responsibility 101 course since they were not offered at any educational institution I attended. Instead, many will have to rely on some various options focused on influencing one's foundational principles of sound, morale, and humanistic values.

But What Now?

God's spiritual favor, one's family values, church upbringing, friends, peer pressure, role models, or trusted mentors could help you develop and establish the foundation of your integrity and values. If you grow up without any moral training, you might lean toward whoever is the strongest influence in your formidable years.

But there are many who are not afforded the same level of grounding and support as those fortunate enough to have a strong, positive family support system. Regardless of how you develop your value system, there is a high probability, and risk, that while on your career path, you will be faced with a challenge to your integrity, morals, reputation, and future employment opportunities. If you have developed multiple sources of income, I believe you will be in a better position to minimize and pad yourself against the ability for someone to compromise your decisions, and hopefully, avoid having your dreams deferred. Keep in mind, it's a challenge to not be compromised in some way, so your goal should be to minimize the ability to breach, while simultaneously fortifying your defenses.

Recommendation: Continually work to diversify your skill set, similar to how businesses diversify their product and service offerings to ensure they remain viable and able to keep up with market trends and changes to customer expectations.

So, the question I pose to you is what will you do when you become aware of a manager or business involved in actions that could hurt or kill people? Will you opt to remain silent because of fear of losing your job, or you don't believe that you have any options to get income except the current job that you have? Will you stay silent and accept the course of action, or will you stand and say this is just not what I signed up for, this is not acceptable?

Career Themes

One strategy you can consider for helping you to decide on a diversification plan is to create a theme to use as a foundational root to build upon. I and others have found by using a theme, this strategy can become a central focus point out of which you can plan a progression of growth activities. Essentially, you could develop a diversification strategy by adding to your existing skills based on the theme, instead of adding skills without a specific goal or purpose, potentially leaving you with a mishmash set of skills.

For instance, you could focus your career planning on a 'creative business' theme, 'financial business' theme, 'food service' theme, 'fashion industry' theme, 'education-related' theme, 'healthcare-related' theme, 'hospitality services-related' theme, 'fitness athletic' theme, or 'STEM-related' theme. Once you have selected one or two themes, you now can have a better idea of the types of skills you logically should add as a diversification strategy.

Now, let's drill down into a few themes to give you some hypothetical diverse career path possibilities. For a potential 'creative business' theme, the initial root or foundational skills could begin as a musician, artist or dancer. A secondary diversified skill set could be adding on the skills required to be a creative coach, trainer or teacher while maintaining the root skill. Another diversified skill set could be adding on commercial creative production organizational management knowledge for advertising or marketing agencies, artistic direction, artist coordination for live performances, stage productions, broadcast, online delivery or cinema. Another diversified skill set could be talent scouting for business managers seeking new talent. Another diversified skill set could be creating works for artists to purchase or perform. Another diversified skill set could be focused on creating new content to sell to the growing online streaming services market. As you can imagine, at some point after diversification of your root skill set, you could be utilizing a variety of your developed skills simultaneously, which would also afford you with multiple revenue streams, multiple *"work-for-success"* opportunities, a couple of professions requiring extensive training, and the formation of a risk mitigation plan to pad yourself from compromise.

    For a potential 'food service' theme, the root could initiate as a short order cook or completing training to be a sous chef. A secondary diversified skill set could be adding a specialty cuisine cooking style and becoming an executive head chef. Another diversified skill set could be teaching culinary students. Another diversified skill set could be publishing a collection of special menus or recipes. Another diversified skill set could be becoming a nutritionist for designing individual health plans or population health plans. Another diversified skill set could be a commercial food product conceptualist creating new food products for underserved communities or in preparation for space exploration. Another diversified skill set could be becoming a distribution strategist for distributing food commercially, or for world health organizations.

    For a potential 'education-related' theme, the root skill set could be a tutor or mentor. A secondary diversified skill set could be obtaining a teacher's certification needed to be a S.T.E.M. teacher or adding on the ability to develop innovative pedagogies for specific groups or populations. Another skill set could be a designer focused on creating specialized curriculums for specific populations, in the absence of, or in addition to public education.

For a potential 'fashion industry' theme, the root skill set could be a model. A secondary diversified skill set could be those needed to be a specialized clothes or couture designer. Another skill set could be a fashion show producer or commercial product buyer.

Although these are all simulations on how one might hypothetically use themes as a focus to diversify one's initial foundational root skill set. In reality, each person can ultimately create a unique diverse career path and unique themes based on a number of optional considerations motivated by one's individual needs, desires, commitments, capabilities, collaborations and available economics.

Back-up Financial Considerations

Before accepting a job offer or while you're negotiating your employment agreement, it's not unusual to negotiate, in addition to the benefits you'll receive while employed, some benefits you'll receive in the event of a separation, like a layoff or divestiture. These post separation benefits are sometimes referred to as "golden parachute" benefits. And there's no reason why anyone can't negotiate various benefits which will continue over a period of time, post separation as part of their total employment benefits package. You might consider if they can maintain your healthcare for a determined number of months, pay salary for a determined period of time, provide outplacement service for a set number of months, or other benefits you might need to help pad you from an abrupt change to your finances and living status. This is the best time to obtain a good financial deal, while both parties are hoping to build a good relationship. Actually, many organizations have standardized benefits available to offer but usually don't discuss during the negotiation, in the event at the time of a separation, the climate is classified as an unfriendly separation, or they prefer not to offer any benefits. And off you go with your bag in hand.

Another financial precautionary measure, you may already be aware, is the standard recommendation from financial advisers to save money to cover seven or more months of bills as protection if you lose your job. But the reality for those who are living paycheck to paycheck is the ability to amass that level of funds is deemed as an unachievable goal for that population (Run an internet search to learn how S.M.A.R.T. goals are defined). But the ability to have multiple lines of income is very possible when considering you don't have to wait for a crisis to take on a part-time or seasonal job, work on developing a creative skill that could become valuable, starting a community, self-help, advocacy, or training service. Becoming a researcher gathering and selling special or unique bits of information, creating cell phone apps, or maybe creating a service where you make yourself available as a liaison to handle tasks for someone not able to get around or having an overload of responsibilities, and needs help with completing simple tasks. And of course, there is always the option to take individual courses to add on additional marketable skills.

Recommendation: Yes, financial advisers often recommend putting away approximately seven or more months of savings to handle bills just in case you have a personality conflict with your manager, choose not to compromise your value system and decide to quit your job, or your job is eliminated as part of a re-org, headcount reduction, or you are just plain out fired. In this day and age, there are some who have been out of work for extended periods of time as a result of unique contemporary (E.g.: recessions, extreme weather conditions, fire damage, terrorism) or personal reasons. Hopefully, those facing any of these types of scenarios have a risk plan or skill diversification strategy implemented to minimize the impact. Knowing that, it may be to your advantage, while you are employed, to contact an insurance company, and pay monthly premiums for 'supplemental unemployment' insurance or 'income protection' insurance. For any employee having some type of 'disruption of income' insurance it could be extremely beneficial seeing how the majority of employees will face a couple of disruptions over the course of their careers. For some reason, we rarely prepare for a work-related event which could result in being left financially at risk.

Policy Change Needed

In the age where business re-orgs are a common occurrence, taking place one or more times each year, employee income and job tenure can be put at risk, *each and every time* there is a re-org. The risk could materialize in the form of a change to reporting structures, a change of your responsibilities, or a headcount reduction resulting in roles being eliminated completely (a.k.a., a layoff). Knowing re-orgs have become common place and headcount reductions can be a consistent practice, done quietly and not publicized by those impacted due to legal language in their separation agreement, employees should *encourage their employers* to offer some type of 'loss of income' insurance as part of their *standard employee benefits package*, where premium deductions are pulled, pre- or post-tax, from their payroll checks.

In addition to having to survive re-orgs, what would you do if a fire or flood severely impacted the location where you work? Or if there was a chemical leak or terrorist incident, and a large area was destroyed, quarantined or became a crime scene? Do you think your employer will continue to pay you over a long period of time while business has been disrupted? And if you are self-employed, an independent contractor, or running your own business, you might also consider seeking a 'disruption of business income' insurance policy. You could keep this type of policy in place until you have saved up enough funds to cover your bills for seven to twelve months. Ultimately having an exit agreement negotiated before you agree to start a new opportunity, along with having a 'loss of income' insurance policy included with your standard employee benefits package would be a good start to having a risk plan focused on mitigating financial, operational and strategic risks.

And although many adhere to a belief that you should not talk about the negative things, it is my hope that your awareness of these scenarios and actual experiences will be of some benefit to you in helping you prepare for negative events which you may encounter over the course of your career. With awareness of these potential risks, you will have the opportunity to prepare yourself so that the impact will be minimal. And it's very important that you don't fall prey to those (Camp 2) who may classify these experiences as those of a 'complainer' but instead those of someone trying to warn you so that you can adequately prepare should the storm reach your front door and water begins to seep in. You will begin to see the two camps I spoke of earlier. A group of people who plan to handle risk, and those who choose not to put any protection in place. Which leads me to a story.

I was fortunate to understand the lesson of *"The Three Little Pigs"* children's story. The one who built his house with straw, and the one who built his house with twigs, were both allegedly eaten by the big, bad wolf. But the one who built a house of bricks, survived the wolf's attack by first taking extra time, which would have cost a bit more, to build a house of bricks, which the wolf couldn't blow down. He also had a back-up risk plan to build a fire in the fireplace in case the wolf tried to enter from the chimney. The third piggy had a well-thought-out risk mitigation plan. One might deduce that the other two pigs didn't listen to the third pig's warning, citing he was just a complainer or a whiner. Given that story, which camp would you prefer to be a member of? But wait, there's more.

In business, I've often heard management communicating the need to complete projects faster and for less money. Piggy one and two probably decided, we'll build our houses quicker, save time and money and then have more time to chill-ax and more money (profits) to play with. Well, in this story there was only one piggy that lived happily ever after and enjoyed viability and the benefits of longer life. It was the one who managed risks. And in the real world, I hope you won't be naïve in thinking you won't run into a figuratively speaking, big bad wolf at some point along your career path. I would guess that you sure don't want to be the piggy with the straw house or house built of twigs.

All businesses must manage their risks or face the possibility of compounded issues which could at some point result in total business failure. Every project should identify any risks that could cause the project to fail, and then have a plan to avoid them or handle them if risks get real, becoming issues. And as someone developing plans to enjoy a successful career, you are no different. I highly suggest you should always consider a back-up plan and plans to avoid needing to implement your back-up plans. Let them call you a complainer, while you reside comfortably in your brick house.

Recommendation: All businesses should have risk management plans, and everyone planning their careers should also maintain continual and constantly adjusting risk management plans. Don't be misled by someone labeling you as a complainer, when you are focusing on risk mitigation to avoid peril and handle it if a risk turns into an issue.

There's a reason why on every commercial flight there is a pre-flight announcement focused on what you should do should there be a problem. Could you imagine astronauts not using every option available to identify what could happen to them while in space and what could they do? Well in business, managers normally don't conclude that if a project fails, people will die. They also don't consider what would happen, if not only the project they are assigned failed, but other projects failed simultaneously or sequentially across the business. That could ultimately result in a huge economic disaster. And, that could also result in people being let go, and continual layoffs, depending on the depth of the financial impacts and if competition began to capture substantial market share.

And for business leaders focused on having a rapid speed to market strategy that relies on having the lowest cost and high return on investment (ROI), be careful of the risk involved if all of your products and services hang on these principles. Many business leaders may not be aware that around 1951, a scholar named W. Edwards Deming worked with Japanese businesses to utilize Total Quality Management (TQM) in changing a vastly accepted and false image that anything made by the Japanese would equate to cheap products. This perceived generalized image impacted those having reputations for high quality as well. Later, Six Sigma and Lean process improvement concepts emerged. Today, customers worldwide consider Japanese products like automobiles, computers, and televisions to be quality, viable products. So, speed does not always equate to quality. When thinking about your career, take some time to map out a path, possibly using themes that can provide you avenues of focus and direction. And for liberal arts majors, there are many opportunities for you, just take some time to develop a diverse strategy.

Chapter 17: Conviction, Strong Faith, and Confidence

One thing I can assure you is that during one's journey of traveling along their career path, there is a high probability of facing the type of challenges that will require critical decisions to be made. Some of those decisions could potentially evolve into, or initiate additional challenges or roadblocks. If one or more of those challenges ends up being a fork in the road, and the decision you choose to take results in a considerable setback, it's at that time when your level of conviction, strong faith, and confidence in yourself, not necessarily in that order, may be tested. The introduction of doubt can lead to one abandoning previous plans in exchange for less thought-out or researched plans. But if you acknowledge and accept the strong probability that at some point while moving along your career path, there will be unexpected challenges, your awareness should alert you of the need to really take time to gather as much information as possible in developing your career plans so that you will have a high level of confidence, conviction, and strong faith, at the time when you encounter challenges.

And although career strategies will have uncertainty, you can reach a level where you feel good about the information you've gathered, the steps you plan on taking, the risk planning you've put in place, and the people you've spoken with, collectively combine into a consciousness that will help you feel that you will be able to overcome most challenges.

Although these psychological tools often are overlooked in favor of completing tangible action items like taking additional training to increase your confidence, it might be difficult to believe that through conviction, strong faith, and confidence these psychological tools can help you when you hit the proverbial wall, or feel as though you won't make it, or have doubt in your previous plans. If you face multiple failures, the normal reaction is to begin to wonder, what do I need to change, is this worth it, or what's the point of putting in more effort. Ideally, you want to consistently have more victories than failures, but every diverse career path will have different types of challenges.

For many, conviction, strong faith, and confidence are tools that can assist with increasing your viability, endurance, ability to build upon long-term plans and strategies, and increase your confidence with traversing cultural boundaries. When used as a triple threat package, it can potentially help to expand your available opportunities worldwide as you increase your ability to get along with a variety of people across cultural boundaries far beyond the traits and practices you've learned within your own neighborhood and circle of close friends.

If, and when you do end up having to make a decision that results in you taking a totally new path, make sure you are willing and able to make a substantial level of conviction and dedication to work hard enough to validate if your new path was a good decision. With this new path, you'll need to ask if you have enough faith to believe you can achieve your goals and be successful. You'll need to have enough confidence that you believe your decision is actually achievable in the time you set to see results. In other words, give it a good chance before giving up or changing to a new direction. Always account for the probability that the roll out of new plans can take time to show results.

Using Sports and Fitness as Motivating Tools

When thinking about the triple threat tools, I sometimes like to refer back to my own experiences with playing sports and doing physical exercise, as my psychological motivation to aggressively apply a substantial level of effort, dedication and conviction focused on increasing the odds of being successful with achieving career goals.

For those who have not played sports or have not engaged in physical training or physical therapy, I can tell you that in each case there are *phases of success* you experience when playing sports and working out to stay in shape. As you realize you have reached a new level of success, more motivation appears. Motivation results in an increased drive and hunger to achieve. This is very similar to the phases of success you experience when striving to meet the goals set in your career strategy.

For instance, if you are starting a workout program, at the beginning you might need to overcome a mental roadblock to get started. Your mind tells you that working out is not fun, is too difficult, painful, boring, and requires someone like a trainer to coach and encourage you to maintain a regular regiment. This mental hurdle can also happen while working through your career strategy.

But then surprisingly, if you can keep your conviction with working out, for at least three-months, you may begin to feel and notice some very slight, almost unnoticeable differences that let you know your workout is doing something. And then at some point past the first three months, after beginning to realize those slight changes, you begin to recognize other notable benefits that now validate the value of working out. With that proof, you might become self-motivated to continue working out, and the psychological challenges lessens.

You might ask, how can the experience of working out or playing sports provide you an example to follow and motivate you to apply consistent efforts toward building a successful career? My answer is, first, you have to *overcome a mental challenge* that says this is too hard, you can't make it, try something easier, or since you may not know what are the steps you need to take, just chill. Secondly, you must have conviction, dedication, and be consistent *over a period of time* before you can begin to see results, validate your plan is solid, and begin to recognize notable achievements.

When comparing working on your career to sports or working out, it's easy to draw similarities to the physical and mental challenges, and the highs and lows you'll experience when you are in a game. In sports, there are emotional swings, back and forth, but you keep playing until there is a clear decision. The same should be true when working toward your career goals. And for both, you must have a thought-out game plan to follow designed to get you to predetermined goals. Also, in sports, there is a determined time period to play the game. When working on achieving your career goals, you should set a reasonable period of time to assess if you are on the right path, or need to revise your path. The body-mind connection, which is needed to achieve success with athletic activities, is the same discipline needed to achieve success with obtaining career goals.

Conflict Resolution Skills are a Must

Empowering yourself with conflict resolution techniques will be extremely helpful as you navigate your diverse career path. You may recall there are a number of reality shows where conflict resolution, problem-solving in combination with overcoming individual personality conflicts are key to being successful. In each case, the balance between all three varies based on the challenge.

Unfortunately, many educational institutions have not found the need to *make conflict resolution training officially incorporated* into their curriculum, and yet employees will continually find the need for conflict resolution skills pretty much every week. Employees face some very similar scenarios to the ones seen in reality shows. Without being versed in effective conflict resolution skills, employees could face the risk of having adverse outcomes after engaging in verbal battles. The result of conflicts gone bad could be the loss of opportunities, total separation from the organization, or violence.

Given the high volume of conflicts individuals will need to resolve in the workplace, in their personal relationships and when dealing with the public, I really don't understand *why* conflict resolution training *is not a standard course.*

Here are a few considerations for building your conflict resolution skill set:

- Discussions should center on having mutual respect for all parties involved. *Without* having respect for all parties, there will continue to be conflicts and tarnished reputations. Some managers may believe the easiest solution for solving a conflict is to remove the individual, but they overlook others become aware of their reputation and their inability to manage personality conflicts, which is essential to interacting with people.
- Listen to gain clear understanding, and avoid reaching conclusions or assumptions before hearing all points of view. Afterwards, try to summarize what you believe has created a conflict. Then seek acknowledgment of the summary from all of those involved.

- When working on a compromise, parties should agree on a fair set of rules for mediating the conflict.
- Be open to compromise, avoiding a "my way only" stance (More probable with manager-to-direct report conflicts.)
- Avoid stereotyping, name calling, disrespectful, confrontational, inflammatory, embarrassing, inconsiderate and dehumanizing communications (E.g.: social media or vocal exchanges). All of these could result in an equal or escalated reciprocal response.
- Focus on calm, measured, well thought out written and/or verbal communication.
- Learn faith-based or other personal guidance foundational principles that you can refer to when interacting with people.
- Utilize meditation techniques and other tactics to calm your emotions to help you avoid an exchange from escalating into an emotional, unfair, unreasonable, or violent response.
- Recognize unfair rules do, in fact, exist and are created to maintain control, exclude equal rights, take advantage of a targeted group and have a tendency to be written without seeking diverse and objective input or feedback, which is often seen in politics. Relying on unfair rules to win a dispute does not always resolve the dispute, but often results in an escalation of conflicts.
- Finalize a compromise with some type of acknowledgment like a handshake; a written email or announcement that confirms results; some verbal thanks; or an agreement to use a similar approach for resolving future conflicts.

After looking back at some of my own experiences I truly believe, when you put in place the tools of conviction, strong faith, and confidence, it will be extremely difficult for adversaries and antagonists you encounter along your career path, to stop you. I can wholeheartedly concur, it's a really good feeling to look back and recognize each time you overcame a roadblock or obstacle that was put in place by someone nipping at your heels, or involved with focused or misguided efforts to negatively impact your success. They were your opponents in a game which you may or may not have known they were playing.

Having confidence and having fun with overcoming the challenges helped me to drive, and keep driving toward my goals. But without clear plans and set goals, you may be unclear on your next steps, and can be easily disrupted by pretty much anyone. As long as you have your goals defined, and remain focused on the tools of conviction, strong faith, and confidence, I believe you will find good results, even if you are unaware of the games being played with you, or around you.

Conviction, strong faith, and confidence are strong materials for mixing the cement needed to build long-lasting roads leading to achieving your career goals.

Chapter 18: The Blame Game

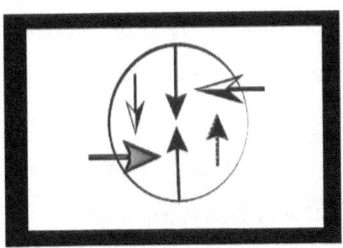

There could be some point in your career when your income is diminished or possibly cut off temporarily. And if that time comes, it's important to move quickly away from taking all the blame. Or assuming your change in economic status is the result of your performance, or lack thereof. Yes, there may be a time when things have not been going well or you've been having personality conflicts with someone and a decision has been made to move you out. But, in fact, there are actually many scenarios where your actions may have had nothing to do with your loss or temporary impediment.

This chapter is about making sure you are *aware of the need to prepare for uncertainty*, from day one, not about blaming anyone, which is what many will want to do.

Acquisitions, mergers, and decisions made to fortify the value of stock can all result in employees losing their jobs no matter how well they have performed in the past. There are also a number of external actions which could impact jobs, one of which being a loss of market share resulting in less annual profits.

And then, how can anyone ignore the possibility of a manager reaching a point where he or she is tired of seeing your face, or just doesn't like working with you because of personal prejudices? Rarely will anyone admit that they decided to eliminate someone's job because they just didn't like them, but that actually happens, and historically senior management has displayed an indifference with enforcing controls to stop unethical behavior by managers.

Managers seeking to gain upper management support when they are actually guilty of unethical behavior might use simple tactics to negatively tarnish targeted employees. They might demean, bad-mouth and spread disinformation, combined with either communicating false claims of incompetence, insubordination, low performance, or claims of the employee not being a good fit with the business culture. For some organizations, if any of these claims were put through an ethics validation process, I would predict most would fall under the realm of being deemed to be unethical behavior on the part of the manager. But unfortunately, with 'no-fault' employment laws in place, many organizations don't bother enforcing governance controls that should be met when a manager makes a derogatory reputational claim against an employee. And so, a manager can get away with making false statements without any validation of truth.

The Company Pays Twice

If an employee is actually a talented resource whose only issue is having an unhealthy relationship or personality conflict with their direct manager, the company actually loses in a couple of ways.

First, the company will lose the time and cost spent initially to train the employee, and the doubling of that time and cost for training and possibly hiring a totally new employee. *Secondly*, the business loses an experienced resource who has domain knowledge and expertise that could benefit other business segments. Without internal retention efforts, now the separated employee can become a benefit to a competitor, or be hired back as a consultant since they have domain knowledge. Plus, a consultant being hired back can charge an increased rate, and now the company is once again paying for a resource they helped to train. If the company had only chosen to retain the initially trained employee, they would only need to separate the manager and employee, retain the talent and investment costs in training, and offer a transfer to another team instead of encouraging unethical behavior on the part of a manager who created a false narrative to get the employee eliminated, especially if the role is actually needed.

Be Prepared for the Unexpected Boot

Sadly enough, some traditional scenarios when employment could be severed comes in the form of headcount reduction, layoffs, or re-orgs. When it comes to a layoff or re-org that results in you losing employment temporarily or permanently, you will be really lucky if managers are considerate enough to actually take the time to honestly tell you, and others, why they decided to cut jobs. In many cases, you should expect to get no explanation which will leave you guessing if it was something you did, or something you could have done better. You also stand the chance of having the type of leadership that will create a false narrative to direct your attention away from a mistake they made, or *a business decision* they made *to increase the company's viability and value*. Needless to say, employees are often deemed expendable resources, below the value of the brand name and stock value, if it's a publicly traded company. But always keep in mind there are organizations where the employee is considered to be the ingredient for making the company valuable to its customers.

But Wait, There's More

Another reality is businesses will need to make course corrections and adjustments focused on maintaining strong business financial health. And their decisions could impact their employees as a tactic for cutting back on their benefits expense. For instance, they may choose to offer early retirement for certain employees, or decommission job titles only to replace them with new titles responsible for the same work, but now having lower salary ranges. They may change the criteria aligned to their bonus structure in a way that makes it more difficult to obtain higher bonuses. There also can be strategies implemented for lowering the amount paid out for employee benefits through annual re-negotiation of the price the company pays insurance companies for group rates, and/or eliminating the types of benefits made available, thereby increasing the premiums paid by employees. And then there is the possibility that a company may choose to reduce a large portion of their full-time payroll line item by obtaining a 'fixed' cost support contract package where an external staffing firm guarantees to provide resources for defined levels of support, thereby eliminating the benefits line item for a number of full-time employees.

And Just a Bit More, For Your Reading Pleasure

And now, for your awareness and reading pleasure, here are other scenarios where employees could experience a cutback on work, forced days off, or lose their jobs due to no fault of their own.

1. There is an external event like a fire, natural disaster, infrastructure disruption, health safety quarantine, or crime scene closure.
2. Your employer has utilized a large amount of money as a result of defending and then losing a legal dispute.
3. Your employer needs to allocate funds for an extensive public relations campaign as part of a damage control effort

deployed after experiencing a negative impact on their brand name and company image (especially if the legal dispute went public).
4. A major competitor is capturing increasing amounts of market share resulting in lower profits for your company.
5. Your company failed to meet the profit expectations communicated to convince investors that they are going to receive increasing dividends.
6. Your company needs to gather adequate capital to diversify and support the expansion of products or services.
7. Your company needs capital to finalize an acquisition.
8. Your company needs to pay off punitive regulatory fines.
9. Expected municipal or federal funding has been cut-back or eliminated as a result of a change in political policy.

Each one of these scenarios could impact your job security even if you have been an exceptional performer. Ultimately you may never see a cut-back or layoff coming, unless of course you work in the finance department or are privy to executive discussions.

Job security is one of the unpredictable risks that always exists for employees. If you are a business owner, you have the advantage of knowing when a staff reduction is needed. And the various "not-your-fault" scenarios I just highlighted are some of the reasons why I truly hope, and highly suggest you initiate *a back-up strategy to protect yourself from an unexpected loss of income.*

Since there are so many variables in play, aside from the personality conflicts that can occur between employees as one of the normal experiences of being in a work environment, I would highly suggest that you avoid blaming yourself for *events and decisions you can't control.* But on the positive side, you can have multiple risk protection plans, insurance type strategies, back-up plans, *contingency plans* or strategies to handle "what-if" scenarios.

I think this is one of the most highly emotional experiences that many will face at some point during their career. Public school teachers and federal employees can face forced days off every time funding or municipal budgets are not approved in a timely fashion, or when employees decide to *go on strike* when they can't reach a negotiated benefits contract agreement with their employer. And these types of turning points will be experienced either from the perspective of the *employer* having to give a directive to department heads to let people go from their team, slow down, cut back or halt on-going projects, cut headcount by a certain percentage, or from the perspective of the *employee* who, shortly after arriving to work, unexpectedly is asked to come to a room or office where he or she is informed that his or her job has been impacted or eliminated. Afterwards, they are instructed to collect their things, and then are escorted out of the building without time to say good-bye to anyone.

It's at this point, where there is uncertainty related to how you might respond, so the tactic is to get you out of the building, and close that door behind you for fear you might go off, delete critical files, decide to inflict physical damage on property, copy intellectual property, or seek retribution in other ways to express your anger, or possibly your glee. But for the most part, I believe it's to the employer's benefit to conduct this as quietly as possible to keep others from having an empathetic emotional response. Obviously, it will be a bigger effort to manage if there is a major unexpected layoff on one day, or a rolling layoff that happens over a period of days.

But how many would stop to think about who really takes the blame when head count is reduced? When one employee or multiple employees are let go, we rarely consider layoffs are an in-your-face, tangible, and visual end result of something decided to be implemented by management, and possibly due to no fault of their own.

Businesses do fail. And getting fired is often viewed by employees as aligned to poor performance or un-mitigated personality conflicts. But layoffs point to business leaders and how they manage protecting their employees, business viability, risk, issues or cold-hearted failures. Will you ever know what they did or the options they had available to choose from? Probably not, unless the cause slips out and is plastered throughout the media as a badge of shame and a warning for customers and jobseekers, to beware.

I've had firsthand experience where after a headcount reduction decision was handed down, decisions were made to identify the critical projects that must keep running and the projects that needed to stop immediately, impacting everyone assigned to those projects. Managers began creating a short list of employees they wanted to keep, but not realizing they too were on the short list created by their own managers. And then the Human Resource (HR) department presented recommendations to encourage managers to transition impacted employees to other areas that had bandwidth to take on employees.

But headcount reduction also opens the door for managers to eliminate anyone they had personality or political conflicts with. For those employees, they probably never received any discussion about available options. They were called in for a meeting, and informed their job had been eliminated, even though there were actually opportunities available. I remember feeling fortunate that I was called in more than once, and offered a continuation offer, while simultaneously feeling sad that others were not given offers. And so, the headcount reduction cascaded through the entire targeted business segments, from individual contributors, to mid-managers, ending with senior leaders, who after the headcount in their teams were reduced, they no longer had a team, but instead were reassigned or merged into a totally new team. But in some cases, their job was eliminated too. These are the types of events that impact the entire organization, physically and emotionally. And although your role may have been eliminated through no fault of your own, those left after the carnage, often find a much harder challenge in facing daily instability and insecurity, constant worry if they will be the next to go, increased complaints, a possible freeze on wages, and the need to take on additional workload as a result of having less available resources, due to attrition.

I have discussed more about back-up plans which you might consider, in the *Preparing your stand against the Face of Deception* chapter. But, what I realized after my first experience of being impacted by a layoff is the value of having a back-up plan. Many employees wait. But, *you have now been warned* to get your back-up plan in order. For most, being laid-off is not something you would consider when you are negotiating the terms of a new job or initially after you have received a job offer. And it's probably the last thing you consider will happen after you get hired. For those who have felt the impact of being laid-off, you will always acknowledge the possibility, and as such, seek to negotiate exit plans at the same time when negotiating the details of the job offer.

Here's a thought. Since a key benefit of insurance companies is to provide risk protection, they should be able to offer *companion products* to state managed unemployment insurance, which actually should be considered a minimal supplement. Employees should begin to encourage a change to their employer benefit packages to include the addition of independent job loss protection insurance products, just like additional insurance you can add onto your payroll deductions. The high hurdle for many employees who are in their early through mid-portion of their careers is often a steep uphill effort to be able to put away seven months or more of savings if you have a modest salary, especially if most of your income is already allocated for basic staples and bills.

Just like auto insurance where you pay a monthly or annual premium amount to protect yourself against potentially more costly expenses resulting from damages to your vehicle, there should also be similar types of insurance available for loss of one's individual income.

So far, I've never known of employers offering as part of their benefit package individual income protection insurance that may pay out seven months or more of salary, just like they offer individual life insurance that works as a companion to corporate paid life insurance. And if this was a group rate the cost could be lower and easily paid as part of pre- or post-tax payroll deduction. What do you think? Something you might want to speak about with your insurance company or alumni services organization.

When it's all over, taking the time to blame someone will not do much for you. I would suggest after experiencing a loss of income, take a few days to gather your thoughts, develop next steps, and begin running your plan. The sooner, the better. The Blame Game only breeds more pain and emotional stress, when honestly you will not really know who to blame, even though it's so relieving to just blame the messenger. I know, not fair, but they are the only ones out in the open. In many cases, the cause was the result of someone or some event nowhere close to you. So why bother trying to hunt down the culprit?

The one thing you don't want to do is sit and do nothing. If you were a very active person before you had a change in income, I would suggest you consider replicating your active patterns. Find activities to keep yourself busy and active while working to replace your loss of income. I've even heard advisers say *your job now is finding a new job* and re-establishing your income. That should be a full-time job.

Chapter 19: Increasing Your Odds of Having a Successful Career

Some of you will not like what I'm about to say here, but I'm one who believes if you truly want to put yourself in a position to make the best decisions, design the most opportune approach to effectively meet your needs, or be empowered to make productive adjustments to existing career plans, you will need to come to grips with, *address, and resolve*, as many of the *areas in which you are lacking information*. Some might refer these as being deficiencies, gaps, or missing capabilities. Sounds bad, but with awareness, they can be minimized or eliminated completely. But you need to know about them first. You'll need to identify them.

There comes a time when your thoughts begin to turn toward wanting things and seeking ways to acquire the things you believe will make you happy. At that point, first you might ask someone to provide items for you at no charge, free and clear. Later, after coming back to the wishing well multiple times, facing the need to repeatedly convince someone to just give you things for free, you begin to wrestle with what you can do to make money to purchase those things you want, without having to justify why you want or need them. Ultimately, and hopefully sooner than later, your introduction into your personal "*Age of Acquisition*" blends into your need to begin wrestling with what exactly can you do to get your own money so you can fulfill those desires to acquire things, without needing to ask or convince someone to fulfill your acquisition desires for you. To make this even clearer, at some point, your parents are going to say, if you want it, you better go out and *get you a job* so you can pay for it, and not them. This scenario is the same for other "quid pro quo" situations where you have an arrangement to get something, after doing something. Your personal *"Age of Acquisition"* should lead you into an extensive search for an answer to what do you want to do (as a career) in life.

An interesting realization is there is a common pattern for many people. Once they initially begin to fathom thoughts about wanting things, they quickly conclude the best solution for resolving their need and urges, is to obtain those things sought, *by any means possible*. And now the "easy way out" planning phase begins. For many, that approach, results in unfortunate outcomes, very early in their lives. The "by any means necessary" approach combined with the "easy way out" concept comes with the risk of criminal, psychological, physical, and long-term reputational damages, and is often tried at a point when you may not be aware that other options exist. Also, at this point, the short list of proposed solutions often leaves out the understanding of what might be *the consequences of using these solutions*. But normally focuses more on what is the easier solution and/or which ones can return some type of results, quickly. But fast is not always better.

The "by any means necessary" approach can evolve into a broader set of behavioral principles you might use when personally interacting with others. It can influence how business leaders interact with customers, and how employees are treated by managers. This early and potentially foundational approach taken by individuals as their solution for acquiring things, is at times recognizable in various aspects of the work environment, particularly in the practices by decision makers who might use "by any means necessary" tactics to capture higher revenues, or dividends and to increase stock values. Unquestionably, the "by any means necessary" approach used for personal acquisitions, can taint an entire business culture if decision-makers have a lack of concern if their decisions result in negative impacts to their customers in targeted markets or communities. And of course, the on-going public debate for fair practices, transparency and morality, may be facilitated and nurtured early in life if youth are not taught how to play with others, and have respect for others. A lack of behavioral training in these areas can later provide misguided justification for these behaviors, and culminate into discriminatory practices.

Needless to say, the "by any means necessary" approach is easy in the absence of morals, personal values, regulatory compliance, having social responsibility, respect, and consideration for others. This is the path where people can get hurt, which might include you.

Community Influences

However, when you consider your opportunities are considerably defined by what you perceive as being 'your world', and if that world is defined by the community where you live, where you go to school, go shopping, go to church, the places you and your friends hang out and all that you experience when you travel along the various paths you use to move between those destinations, then you can bet those community defined boundaries will influence and limit your thinking of what you believe to be your available career options to get money for paying for the things you believe will make you happy. Odds are you will work within the boundaries defined and/or most definitely the boundaries will influence your view of the world. (More about this can be found in the World Cultures chapter.)

In addition, the areas where you live will have a huge psychological influence on how you treat those internal and external to the boundaries determined by your world view. You could be a champion for, or against one group or the other. The culture within that community, or the behavior of those living in that community could all impact your choices.

So, when considering it will be your own perception of what you perceive to be your geographical and psychological boundaries that leads to defining your available career opportunities, I ask you to think about this now, what is your vision of the world? Is your world flat? Is the extent of your world limited to the area where you live, go to school, go shopping, go to church, go to your friends' homes, or the places you hang out? And what about all that you experience and actually see as you travel along the various paths you use to move between those destinations?

How Big is Your World?

Now, right now, please take a minute to think about and assess how big is your *view* of the world. Please be honest to yourself, keeping in mind no one will ever know your inner thoughts. When thinking about how big is your view of the world, consider the following. What are the physical geographical borders where you have not gone past, or prefer not to go beyond (streets, neighborhoods, towns, countries)? Are you comfortable with hanging out socially with people of other cultures? How many blocks can you travel from your home before you feel uncomfortable? Have you been downtown? Have you been to the city, town, village, or neighborhood adjacent to the area you live, and are comfortable? Have you traveled beyond the state or country you live? Do you feel as though your world is getting smaller, and your personal view of people from other cultures influence you to conduct most of your activities close to where your own kind live? Are there specific types of people you don't want around you? If you are honest to yourself, you should now have a short list of some of your own personal boundaries, psychologically and physically. And I might add, we all have some, but should be aware how they influence our decisions, good or bad. And those influences can impact how you perceive your self-imposed boundaries within the entire world of career opportunities and experiences.

The Outsiders, They Keep on Coming

As the population of the world continues to expand and people from various cultures continue migrating across various physical or culturally imposed borders as immigrants, and refugees are seen more and more frequenting previously segregated local establishments, does that make you feel uncomfortable? Are you increasing your support toward politicians working on keeping them out, maintaining exclusive areas and strengthening the physical and psychological borders around you? Would you consider including in your career plans to seek employment in a different state or foreign country? Is your fear of the unknown influencing how much confidence you have in believing you can survive and thrive when you travel beyond the borders and paths you have previously used to move between your safe zone destinations?

In answering any of the above questions, hopefully you will begin to identify and visualize some key influences that are filtering how far you will feel comfortable seeking and applying for available opportunities. Variety and diversity are woven into the available career choices you might and can consider.

In retrospect, when thinking about how my view of the world influenced the opportunities I believed were available to me, I recall how my view of the world *was initially shaped by the distance where I could walk*. During this point of my life, the available opportunities were determined by the jobs that existed within walking distance. I actually worked as a life guard at a swimming pool located two blocks from home. Doing yard work for neighbors, selling candy, and delivering newspapers, presented other opportunities available to me at that time.

As I began to venture out, ride public transportation, my opportunities were shaped by businesses relatively close to the public transportation routes. Next, when I purchased a used car and began to drive, the available opportunities were shaped by my confidence in going into areas I was unfamiliar. But how far did I want to drive round trip, and how much gas I could afford to pay for, now were influential. When I obtained a passport, my opportunities were shaped but not totally restricted, by my language skills.

For each scenario, the opportunities available to me were shaped by my view of the world. Having a large world view equates to a vast amount of opportunities. And in looking back, my world was once just my neighborhood, and my opportunities were limited by my world. And every new family that moved into our community presented what I thought, was a danger to me getting jobs. When I went to the neighbors and asked if they needed any work done, they might answer that some other kid just left here. But now through technology, my world is virtually without borders; it's unlimited.

Recommendation: A key element for developing a successful career path is becoming and then remaining aware of what's needed by individuals who exist beyond your personal geographical and psychological boundaries which you have determined to be comfort zones. If you have decided, you don't want to span beyond the area you are comfortable, you should consider what will you do if those comfort areas diminish, implode, or due to other external influences the number of customers diminish within those areas.

On the street, this exact scenario is associated to 'turf wars' and those within the defined borders begin to fight for control of this limited market, a *market defined by distinct, physical boundaries*. But for those who decide they need to prepare to *avoid being restricted to a geographical and psychological boundary*, you will need confidence, a sense of curiosity, adventure, and you'll need information. You will need to overcome your fears. You will need to expand your knowledge of the world, and then scope it, scout it out to educate yourself. And there's no reason why anyone working on their career shouldn't at some point, have their own transaction-capable website and a social media account.

Missing Information

Now, aside from the physical and psychological boundaries that shape how you view the world, there's another consideration. When thinking about your career goals, and someone asks, what do you want to do in life, and your response happens to be, "I'm not sure," then you have some learning to do. But no problem. Many have and will be passengers on that bus going in circles, along with you.

When I first began to wrestle with coming up with a respectable answer, I soon learned the difficulty with having some idea as to what I wanted to do, was the result of lacking the kind of information I needed to express the one, or two goals in which I felt comfortable with betting on, boldly proclaiming, and then committing time, physical effort and finances. Rest assured, this type of uncertainty is not unusual.

But you can erase your uncertainty by gathering focused information that works toward eliminating your open questions. And as you get more information, your uncertainty should *decrease* inversely with the *increase* of information. The more information, the less uncertainty. When you see this work, the mental rewards feel like your glass is full and you have more than enough to drink. And the vision of your career goals should become clearer, and your level of commitment with physical and financial resources increases as your confidence in achieving success also increases.

I believe this is one of those, "If only I knew then, what I know now" moments. With knowledge, we probably would have made a number of different decisions. With that understanding, for you, I would first suggest taking the time to think about and then list out your open questions, fears, and expectations. In doing so, I expect you will quickly discover a slight hurdle: specifically, not *knowing enough to be able to formulate an exhaustive list of questions.* I call this one philosophical logic, in that I wouldn't expect you to be able to create a list of questions about a distant planet that you don't know exists. *If you don't know the planet exists, how would you have questions about it?* So, when it comes to your open questions, in addition to the questions you can think of, you also need to take into account *there are questions you will not know to ask* without awareness. How do you address this? You'll need to have a 'discovery' concept. One of your open questions you'll need to ask is, "*Is there anything I* (the interviewee) *need to know more about?*" This is the open-ended question that motivates the need for discovery of the unknown. When asking this it presents those you ask, the opportunity to impart wisdom and possibly tell you about something they think you should know.

I believe the more answers you have gathered to a majority of your open questions, known and not yet realized, the more you'll find that you are empowered to make informed decisions, *before making commitments* to pursue a profession or career. And if you are already moving along on your career path, you should constantly maintain an 'active' checklist of questions you need to work on solving. Keep in mind there will be areas you don't know exist as well as constant changes and influences within career markets.

Recommendation: If you are uncertain about what you want to do or achieve, create a list of your open questions on your mobile phone or tablet, and begin to get answers by asking your teachers, adults in your family, and people who might already be working in areas you are interested. I highly recommend arranging some time to speak with people who are actually working in the area of interest since they will have real experiences and know the pitfalls. Be sure to ask about what they like and don't like about their jobs. Ask what could be any positive and negative impacts on one's personal life.

Note: This strategy actually helps you to build a couple of useful skills. That of an interviewer (E.g.: media reporter or investigations), and that of a requirements analyst (E.g.: business development, project management, analyst, or innovator).

You must not be afraid to admit, at least to yourself, the areas you lack knowledge, so that you can then proceed with finding the information you lack, ultimately making you a wiser person. And please don't label yourself as being dumb, but instead recognize that we can't possibly know everything. A wise person will seek to answer questions and learn by gaining answers. Also, it's your inner strength that you possess when you recognize your weakness and then begin to strategically move or take actions to eliminate it. You should feel proud of your ability to be honest with yourself, although this confession really *only needs to be to yourself.* Your actions after your self-realization should be manifest in efforts to research various resources to find the knowledge you seek, Kung Fu Grasshopper. Actions could be in the form of speaking with family members, seeking out mentors, and current and former instructors.

You should want to be aware of, and identify as many challenges, risks, and potential influences, as well as determine who are your allies and what support will be available to you. All these should be considerations on the table when formalizing your plans while also taking into account your own character type and needs.

When you begin focusing on the goal of increasing your odds of having a successful career, you are not alone. We all will have to face, head-on, our limited amount of knowledge needed to decide what steps we need to take which will hopefully, guarantee our success.

Many will initially just make a decision based on their current knowledge, exposure to options, or awareness of what might be involved to obtain what we believe is success. Maybe just accepting what our parents suggest.

You should keep in mind, you can gain wisdom from others who are far along on their career paths and who can provide you warnings and suggestions. (This book can assist you with that, but don't stop here.) Secondly, we all have to face the fact that we need faith and knowledge to support the next steps on what to do, to get somewhere, and to assist in making decisions on something we might be struggling with. But *no one can guarantee* that what you learn, will be productive. What you learn can only *provide you clues* and suggestions. Ultimately, you have to rely on faith and some bits of information that seem to make sense or fit in with something else you've learned.

Also, *one of the warnings* you might hear more than once, and from so many sources is about the need to save some money for various reasons. That warning comes from our fear of the unexpected and unpredictable. The list of reasons can be perceived to be endless depending on the various influences in your life. The needs could span from building your savings to get a nice place to live, to funding a start-up business so you can be self-employed, or just having backup money in the event one of your decisions turns sour and something just goes wrong. Ultimately, only you should be the decision-maker on determining what your lifestyle will require.

Another warning I would give is for you to protect the specific details of your diverse career plans. I don't think there should be concerns for publicly communicating your plans to go into a certain career, like if you told your friends you were planning to go into the medical field or that you plan to focus in a certain concentration. But, I would suggest you keep your plans on *how you hope to achieve* your goals, close to your vest, except of course with those you believe you can trust.

Why? Because those who might seek to derail your plans could insert any influences they might have with the goal of hurting you for reasons which are unknown. There is the "crabs in the barrel" syndrome where the other crabs attempt to pull down the one getting the closest to climbing out of the barrel. And of course, there are those who might simply be jealous of you, who will seek to derail your efforts. And jealousy can expand across family, friends, and coworkers. Another reason would be that your plans appear to be so well thought out and researched that someone you share those steps with could hop on the same path you planned out and then utilize some of your contacts, or connections *before you can utilize them*. And of course, there are the haters who may, for other reasons beyond jealousy, become your antagonist by doing all they can to impede you from achieving your goals. If they know what you need to reach a next step, they might work directly on blocking you to get that piece of your puzzle. For instance, at work, if you needed to document a certain number of hours or get a certification to be promoted, anyone knowing that could do all they can to make sure you don't get the hours needed, certification, or certain job title, thus effectively hindering you from reaching your goals.

I once remember arranging through a friend to set up a summer job for me, only to find out that a close relative who was at my house before I got home, picked up the phone call, got the message for me, went in for the job interview, and was hired. I was left without a summer job since it was filled by my relative.

Recommendation: Another element of your risk mitigation plan should be to always protect the specific details of your plans, and the steps you need to achieve your career goals. The risk is the more others know, the more you put yourself at risk of others having the knowledge of what they can do to impede you or block the things you need to achieve.

When it comes to accepting job offers, beware of making quick decisions without thorough vetting. The results of engaging in impulsive quick decisions are often regretted. The odds are against you. Sorry, I hate to be the one to tell you this, but from the very early stages and throughout your career, you will have more and more impulsive yearnings. They just keep coming. But either you control them, or they will control you. So there, that's the truth of it. Mark this as another *lesson learned*, or a lesson soon to be learned.

Be Your Own Coach

Everyone has some type of potential. Each day you see sunlight is another day to create opportunities, no matter how small.

Glimpses of Innovation

Why not make some plans and put your own controls, rules, and boundaries in the game? How about today you develop some personal goals, where only you determine the steps and the path. But of course, for those of you who are 'free spirits' I say, *be you*, but know there is a high probability that others might potentially have a high influence in forging your path. And know that their controls, rules, and boundaries are designed to benefit, guess who, *not you*.

Maybe, and hopefully that will turn out good for you, as our cultures continue to blend, evolve, and innovate. Be aware that with innovation, new games will develop, with new rules. And that my friends, is why people innovate. To introduce a new game that the innovator can control. Diversification changes the opportunities and potentially disrupts the game in favor of the disruptor. Lesson learned, who do you want to be? The innovator, the disruptor, or the one who has to catch up because of someone else introducing new controls, rules and boundaries? *Will you own and set your finish line*, or will someone else own your finish line? Keep in mind, they can keep moving the finish line, just out of your reach.

External Feedback

Now, let's turn the wheel. Here's another hurdle that has a high probability of adding a bit more to your stress level. This bandit comes *after you land a job,* and it falls under the category of *annual performance reviews,* a.k.a., what does your manager think about you based on officially defined company goals, but unofficially and off the record, is based on your manager's personal views, which, if smart, they will never be spoken of openly or fall under any company governance? Yep, off the record reviews are a norm and can result in no raise, no promotion, or get you canned. So, over time, as you begin to realize the unofficial review is normal criteria, and 'brown nosing' is a hit or miss tool without any guarantee of returning successful results. At some point you begin worrying about what will you need to do to keep your job and receive promotions. Come in early, stay late, say yes to every request, don't complain, don't get pregnant because you'll need a leave of absence and during your leave, you are hoping that nothing changes while you're gone. Yep, here comes more worry clouds sitting over your head. The game of staying on your manager's good side continues to be a moving finish line, so you take whatever requests that come your way, and you might accept invitations to non-business or off business hour activities to show that you go beyond what you were hired to do. These are the types of hoops you might choose to jump through, and they go on and on, and are often motivated by *your fear of losing your job,* or for what you believe will be necessary to stay in good graces of a manager. Pay good attention for when you hear yourself saying to friends, "Sorry, I have to go to this event because my manager wants me to be there." You'll know it's not what you really want to do with your spare time. You really want to have some 'me' time, be with your best friend or friends, or just want to relax with a good book and a glass of wine.

I once read an HR survey that found many employees quit their job *not* because they don't like the work or the company, but because *they don't like their manager.* Unfortunately, it's not uncommon to have *personality conflicts* with your manager, or have a manager who is inconsiderate and lacks personal or humanistic skills. And it's not unusual to have a manager who makes up their own rules and ignores company ethical policies, or for leaders who could do something, actually look the other way when company policies are breached. And what happens if your manager creates an adverse or uncomfortable work environment? Well your protection mode will kick in, and you will hear that inner voice telling you over and over and over again, "I need a new job" or "I hate my job." Another common phrase is, "I can't stand my manager." And there you are, once again, returning to that sacred crossroad in life, the challenge of landing a new job.

So, what can you do? This will be easy to remember because there are only two choices:
1. Accept the situation and take the pain until you can facilitate behavioral changes, which could result in psychological and/or personal impacts, or
2. Look for a new job (internally or externally) so you can eliminate the stress and focus more on a healthier psychological state of mind. Some choose to self-medicate, but that will probably end up bad for you in the long run.

But before you reach this sacred crossroad, you have the opportunity to begin planning well in advance of reaching that corner where you'll need to make a decision. Starting from your very first career opportunity or if you have already landed a role, I highly suggest you begin developing a strategy focused on addressing this decision point and to ease the stress each and every time you find yourself needing to return to your sacred crossroad. In addition, I would suggest you try to be a collaborative resource in presenting your best image, consistently. Whatever happens, you want to feel good about your contributions throughout your career experiences. With what I've brought to your attention, believe it or not, a veil has been removed from your perception, and you now have new choices. Suck it up and take your medicine, or make some plans to add your own controls in the game. And if done well, you could begin to welcome each visit to that sacred place.

So, what can you do? Especially knowing that it can be a challenge to find a career opportunity and remain satisfied and happy with it for years. You can begin to plan for a career in which each opportunity you land has some association or is similar in skill set to each other related opportunities. I've referred to this earlier as career themes. Why is this powerful? Because each return to the sacred crossroad and subsequent landing of a similar role tends to increase your career market value, which translates into potential higher income, ability to make demands on your working arrangement, and most importantly, higher return on your investment, which is the time you are giving to your employer, making them successful. And at some point, you might become an employer. Yes, self-employment or running your own business, if your character type aligns. But I caution you, despite many may aspire for it, everyone will not be suited for managing their own business or having the discipline for self-employment.

Be Your Own Coach

Learn how to work with people, and you'll be on your way toward learning how to run your own business, providing a product or services to others. But keep in mind your character types. Believe it or not, everyone will not be able to have their own business. Some people are not good with helping others, providing customer service, or being able to promptly respond to actions needed. I know people who have trouble returning phone calls after you've left them a message. Would you really want to rely on them if they were repairing your car? Running a business requires a specific type of person. If that's you, train and learn from others who are successful doing it.

Complimentary Skills

A good plan for success would be to begin preparing for your next opportunity, after landing the first. *"Work-for-success"* opportunities can tie you to another if the skills are related. As an example, I provided the following *"work-for-success"* example in the "Purpose" chapter. You obtain an airplane pilot's license. You can expand from working support at an airport, to being a charter pilot, test pilot, commercial pilot, move into air traffic controller, airport supervision, airplane design, air safety, outer space transport, or aviation related training. All of these could be considered careers within the aviation industry, with transferable complimentary skills centered on an aviation career theme.

Through using a strategy of building related complimentary skills as an ongoing strategy, you could position yourself for new opportunities. And each time you need to return to your sacred crossroad, you could potentially find a variety of opportunities to choose from and your market value increases.

Chapter 20: Acknowledge Those Who Help You, Your Business and Your Career

In today's work environment, there seems to be a continuation of a historic trend in which business owners, managers and senior leaders are reluctant to share profits and give acknowledgment to *all employees* who have contributed to the success of their teams and/or organizations. Instead, there has been a trend that leans more toward communicating selective acknowledgments or honors in the form of assigning leadership roles to individuals (at times due to selective favor), granting change of job titles to ones sounding more prestigious, awarding monetary rewards and bonuses, or allowing a select few to have their work location moved from an open, shared workspace to more private office space. Other honors come in the form of exclusive invitations to events or outings that allow attendees to enjoy special amenities and closer engagement with senior leaders or executives. And although leaders like to say acknowledgments are given to those who have done exceptional work, that criteria *ignores all others who regularly work as a collaborative team* focused on delivering successes, like those who achieve expectations every four to six weeks in Agile sprints, or those who successfully implement small to medium sized projects every three months. Also, the bar can potentially change related to how they choose to define what are exceptional accomplishments. And changes can also be aligned proportionally to how much they are willing to shell out to their employees.

However, some managers who understand the efforts of collaborative teams more than those from individuals, are consistently the cause of success, and as such, may arrange small lunch outings, or for lunch to be supplied on-site as a way of showing recognition of the combined efforts that consistently result in delivering success that ultimately moves the business forward throughout the year.

For customers, there should be various types of acknowledgment from businesses for their loyal support. But what we often experience is a pattern and practice that shows when a business captures a higher percentage of the market share and customer's purchases of products and/or services trend up, we see increases in the cost of products or services, not a decrease. And we also may see a reduction in the quantity, net weight or level of product or service rendered per cost. Passengers receive snacks on a plane despite each year there are multiple predictable times when ticket sales increase for air travel. The cost of gas goes up even when people are driving more and automobile sales have increased. And although there are some businesses which offer free or extreme discount days for "reward club" members only, as more automation and technology results in lowering the cost of doing business and increasing the return on investment, somehow there continues to be a lack of acknowledgment transferred back to their customers for loyally supporting their business and being essential to the business achieving greater success.

We now live in an age where businesses are paying out tremendous executive salaries and benefiting from tremendous returns on their investments (ROI) where ROI = the Gains from total investments, minus the Cost of the total investments, divided by the Costs of the investments. Some businesses are actually paying salary packages and "exit bonuses" to their senior managers and executives that are more than the operating expenses of many Fortune 500 companies.

I would *encourage you*, very early in your career, to adopt a regular practice of *acknowledging those who help you*, no matter how small the benefit. I remember receiving a coffee house gift card after completing a project, which at that time, made me feel acknowledged. When considering how does one achieve success, many believe it comes as a result of a series of focused efforts, not just one action. (Gambling would be the contrary belief that relies more on chance, and the odds of achieving success if possible by odds are more in favor of failure with this approach.) Something basic like saying thank-you or acknowledging an employee's efforts for contributing to achieving targeted goals, through their work that may have required late nights or working on weekends, can be valuable and appreciated by those who give up their non-business hours and put in the overtime when needed. But one should keep in mind that at some point, the number of late nights and weekends begin to add up for the employee making the sacrifices. And it doesn't take long for employees to develop a perception of not being appreciated, which their managers have reinforced through the lack of rewarding or acknowledging each employee. If their workdays of giving without receiving appreciation and acknowledgment continue, the probability increases that a change of some sort will begin to be visualized and justifiable. That change could materialize into a reduction in their level of effort, quality of work, increasing demands for a more favorable work-to-life balance, and increasing push back to protect a separation between work time and non-business off time. This can introduce a negative workplace dynamic that could develop into excuses for managers to punish employees seeking to protect their off time. For these managers who have grown to expect being able to issue assignments that cut into their employees' non-business hours, this employee push back often introduces more justification for managers to punish their employees *by not providing acknowledgments*, rewards, bonuses, or promotions, except maybe just to the employees whose non-business hours are respected and considered off-limits.

Is Expressing Common Courtesy Bad?

When we view our society as a whole, one might begin to witness an accepted practice where managers, senior leaders, and people in general appear to be losing any *value for common courtesy*. This loss of common courtesy is not just something unique to business organizations, but I believe it a sad glimpse into how we engage each other as people.

For example, while standing in the check-out line at a grocery store, I noticed no one provided a simple "thanks" to the young men and women positioned just past the cashier who were working feverously to place customer's purchased items into shopping bags. When it was my turn, I made a point of giving a "thank-you" with a smile. The response is usually, "You're welcome." An effort so small, and yet the bagger saved me some time and gave me a nice service, for free. And it didn't hurt me one bit to say thanks. Maybe there's a reason why the check-out lines where there is a cashier and bagger, still have longer lines than the self-service lines. For me, sometimes I will choose to wait in line because there are days when I just enjoy, or prefer to have service. And yet, after items have been bagged appropriately in separate bags which makes it easier for you to carry and unload at home, so many walk right by those individuals without saying two simple words, thank-you. If you are one of those people, ask yourself why do you choose not to thank someone who just did you a favor. And now when thinking about your career path, have you chosen a profession where you will rely on others to provide you collaborative assistance in order to maintain your support and maintain clients, or will you be working alone?

And yet, many will continue this lack of courtesy for small, medium, and large efforts of work, holding out to only provide acknowledgment to a select few, overlooking the larger group of individuals who are making efforts that when looked at in totality, all helped to move the team and organization toward success, on a daily basis. A thank-you costs nothing. Small denomination gift cards are now sold at the check-out line of grocery stores.

So, in reality, is there really any meaningful defense for not acknowledging someone's efforts each time they deliver a successful effort at that time, instead of tabulating the efforts after four to six weeks, 3-months, 6-months or 1-year? So, what is a more accurate reason why managers and senior leaders decide to plead a case for only a select few to receive a thank-you, acknowledgment, or value-based reward? I would guess it's purely based on each individual and unique business culture that has been created. Regardless of the reason, this could be a cultural behavior that can grow dissention throughout the work environment.

What's Your Expectation After You Help Someone?

I want to re-assure you there are individuals out there who are bright shining stars when it comes to acknowledging each and every one of their family members, friends, and coworkers. And there are those who couldn't care less about thanking people for helping them. Some people may think you are rude and poorly raised. Others may think you are inconsiderate, cold, showing no signs of weakness. But no matter how you are perceived externally, the other factor is *how do you feel* when people are rude, inconsiderate, or cold to you? Are you okay with it, have no real issue if you helped someone get out of a jam and they just walked away? Your response to that question might put a spotlight on how you will feel while in various work environments. You may be the type that feels acknowledgment should be received but not given. I would guess you might have some friction with your coworkers and peer.

I have personally experienced business leaders who made the decision to shell out funds to take their entire business segment within a corporation, to an island resort for a few days of good eating, open bars, relaxation, fun and games, as well as providing time for leaders to update their entire group of employees about future business plans. This appreciation trip included administrative assistants through senior leaders. But I don't doubt this trip probably created some jealousy from many employees whose business segment never took them to an island resort, or anywhere for that matter.

I've also experienced one business giving out bottles of champagne, fruit baskets, and tickets to local sports events to every employee. Another small business made a point of having a monthly food, wine, and cheese party. I also worked for a business that provided free breakfast, lunch, and dinner every single day. This appreciation also motivated employees to arrive early for work and stay late. And the meals weren't shabby; a wide variety of food options were always available. Eventually, this practice lost out to deeply discounted meals, but was still a good deal.

I would suggest that everyone working hard deserves some type of acknowledgment, even if it's just a thank-you, communicated during meetings. I recall during a quarterly update meeting I gave acknowledgment, calling out each name, of an entire team, assigned to support one of my projects. Seeing the looks on each of their faces as people around them were shaking their hands and congratulating them, was priceless. They clearly were not accustomed to receiving acknowledgment in such a high-profile setting. Afterward, a number of employees approached me to let me know they would like to work on my projects in the future. Could this be just because I was one of the few managers who gave credit to those who contributed to our success? Simple words returning increased engagement.

Is there anything you can do for your clients and customers to let them know that you appreciate them? Of course, there are numerous options to acknowledge benefits your organization is receiving that don't have to break the bank. And ultimately, you begin to build a favorable reputation that can translate into an increase of dedication, support, and opportunities. The lack of acknowledging your customers can result in increasing segments of your customer base who can be easily captured by competitors who are acknowledging them. Customers could begin to have lower expectations for common courtesy (which could hurt you), have diminished allegiance to your brand, or less desire to return for your service.

What Might Be the Benefits of Courtesy?

It's my premise that the very simple pattern and practice of *courtesy can help you* to be successful with moving along your career path by increasing the number of *individuals who feel positive about you, and want to work with you.* If they feel positive about you, you stand to get pushed to the 'top 5' of candidates during external hiring and internal employee promotion processes. You also increase the probability of individuals willing to helping you. And it costs you nothing. It also potentially could empower individuals by making them stand out from others, especially when so many have forgotten what are the characteristics of being courteous. By displaying courtesy, you should expect to attract others whose core values and morals are similar. So, when it comes to building productive networks, your courteous manners could strengthen the foundations for future partnerships and business opportunities. As the trend of people becoming colder and less caring for clients and fellow employees emerges, you can display a character that others having respect and consideration, will want to emulate and gravitate to.

As I continue to practice the art of being courteous, having manners, being polite, showing respect and consideration for others in public and the workplace, I've also found some seem to be thrown off balance in not seeming to know how to respond to courtesy.

Here are a few real-world scenarios related to courtesy which hopefully might stimulate some thoughts regarding cultural etiquette, current and past:

- A birthday gift is sent. The recipient provides no acknowledgment that they have received the gift, and doesn't communicate a thank-you to the sender for doing something special, no matter the cost of the gift.
- A young man wearing a baseball cap enters a restaurant to meet his friends, but doesn't remove his cap. Families are no longer teaching the etiquette or what is also a sign of respect that a man should remove his hat or cap upon entering a home, public buildings, sitting at a table, or in the presence of a lady. This courtesy is greatly diminished.
- A couple of friends decide to meet up after work for some snacks and drinks. The bill comes, and one of the friends offers to pick up the bill. The other person

doesn't thank the other or offer to pick up the bill next time.

- A former classmate who is aware their classmate is looking for a job. A recommendation is made to the hiring manager resulting in the former classmate getting an interview and hired for the job. The new hire doesn't thank the hiring manager for the job offer or give a thank-you gift to the former classmate for giving the recommendation.

- On a rainy day, you are walking outside to your car or to another building with your umbrella, and you see a lady standing at the doorway, who clearly doesn't want to get her clothes and hair wet. You offer her the use of your umbrella, or to walk her to her car or location so she can keep from getting wet. This courtesy has faded away, except in small towns having less safety concerns, but this act should warrant a thank-you with the offer. In larger cities, you will not see this anymore due to personal safety concerns. Has chivalry fallen?

- A driver is navigating toward a roadway entrance ramp that merges into a freeway having heavier traffic. Another driver who is already driving on the road and having the right-of-way, slows down to allow the driver to safely merge onto the expressway. The driver who received courtesy from the driver who had the right-of-way, gives no common courtesy thank-you wave to the driver who slowed down to allow the driver to safely enter the expressway. This type of acknowledgment is happening less and less.

- A young man and woman coming from different locations of a parking lot, both heading into the same store, reach the doorway at approximately the same time. The young man gestures to the young lady to go first, acknowledging his "ladies first" training. The young lady goes through the door without giving any thanks for the courtesy. And although some families continue to teach young men to always let a lady go first, it also appears that some families living in certain regions are overlooking the teaching of young ladies that it is also proper to respond to courteous gestures with an appreciative 'thank-you' response.

- A manager contacts their direct report regularly a few minutes before the employee is preparing to leave for the day to request the employee stay late to complete a task that is needed ASAP. The employee communicates reluctance, but calls their family to make arrangements. The manager notes that salaried employees are expected to work extra hours as needed. As a result of the regular pattern, the manager builds an expectation that working late does not require any special acknowledgment or act of appreciation since in many settings, putting in unpaid overtime past an eight-hour day, has evolved into normal expectations, and is the result of continual behavioral modification implemented by employers focused on getting more output for less pay.

The point of these real-world scenarios is to highlight what seems to be a trend that as society slowly becomes more indifferent to basic courtesy, mannerisms, and etiquette, business leaders and managers, being part of society, also will track to those same changes, specifically in whether or not to give acknowledgment to each employee who has successfully completed assigned efforts focused on moving the business further toward meeting objectives, goals, and achieving success. We are increasingly experiencing varying sets of requirements being put in place in order to control who can receive acknowledgments. This pattern and practice ultimately *excludes* the larger numbers who are *regularly performing.* Along with the practices of some organizations annually changing the criteria for how individuals are scored to the performance review categories (consistently exceeds; meets expectations; needs improvement; does not meet expectations) and their need to implement damage controls over managers whose review assessments may include personalized discriminations, one can easily understand why some organizations are facing more scrutiny, seeking objective and consistent ways to fairly capture individual accomplishments and acknowledge their collaborative efforts. I believe they realize their people managers are responsible for working with their teams over the course of each year, to correct performance concerns, and not just wait out an entire year to use the annual review process to punish those they don't like and acknowledge those they do. If people managers are engaged year around with their employees, there should be small numbers who haven't contributed to the success of the organization.

How Does Acknowledgment Fit Into Your Character Type?

And so, when someone holds the door for you when you have bags in both hands, would you wait until next week to say thanks? Or would you wait until the same person held the door for you fifteen times before you say thanks for helping out? And yet, employees could just show up each day, handle their assigned responsibilities, go home, and get paid. But instead you will often find employees in addition to doing their assigned responsibilities, also providing feedback and contributing to 'process improvements' with the goal of helping the business or team they are on, to increase their previous levels of success.

What I've seen is the overwhelming number of employees work toward making the product or service the business owns, more valuable, as though they actually own the business. So, when employees are moving the ball further down the road each and every week, one has to wonder why only a select few are acknowledged after weeks of being focused, when actually, the majority of employees are doing concentrated and focused work, day after day. In some organizations, it will be easy to recognize those having a culture where there will be a large number of employees who will not feel appreciated when they think about their dedication and hard work, but are consistently overlooked and not acknowledged for their consistent efforts.

I remember a time when *all* students who had good attendance would be acknowledged in some way. *All* students, not just specific ones, who achieved a specific grade point average were recognized and honored as being Summa Cum Laude, Magna Cum Laude, Cum Laude, or for being on the Dean's List. Unfortunately, in the work environment, there will be employees who are consistently completing small and medium sized efforts on time, having a consistent string of successful project deliveries, implementations, maintaining business continuity or consistently supporting their clients, but never acknowledged for *providing consistent value*. But when they go on vacation, or decide to leave the company, managers feel the panic while trying to replace the lost value and consistent continuity.

So, I suggest to you not to wait weeks or months after someone has provided a benefit to you to say thank-you and to acknowledge each of their efforts which have helped you. It won't hurt you, and can only work to build a positive character on how others view you. It could also result in creating a group of strong supporters who consistently provide you benefits and value as you move along your career path, just with a simple acknowledgment or thank-you.

Recommendation: Do consider showing appreciation and giving acknowledgment to those who help you. It could do more good than harm.

Recommendation: Always document details of each of your completed projects including stakeholders, approximate initiation, and end dates. Also, send a brief email to the main stakeholders to ask for feedback that can speak to successes, challenges, and issues which still need to be resolved. Ideally, when it's time for a review of your value, you want to have documentation that can be used as proof of your actions, accomplishments, satisfied clients, risks avoided, issues resolved, and any savings realized.

Chapter 21: Leap of Faith

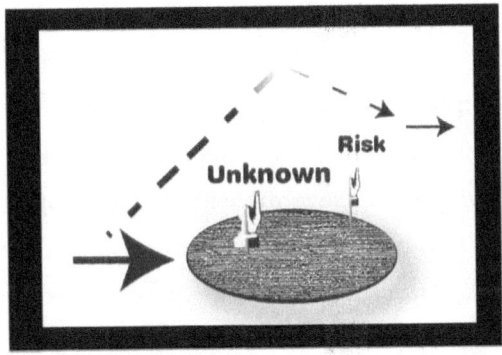

Whether you are in the midst of deciding to make a new career move, changing existing plans, or just stopping everything to go where your desires lead you, these are all situations many will face that may require a leap of faith. It's that moment when you really don't have much guarantee of success to lean on, you know it, but go for it anyway.

Sometimes this moment is facilitated at a point when you feel you don't have any good options right after experiencing a magnitude level emotional event like the loss of employment, the end of a personal relationship, your reputation has been severely damaged, you have been shredded by some type of financial or legal impairment, or you just experienced such an embarrassing moment or other catastrophic event where you decided you've had enough, can't take it anymore, and it's better that you reset, leave town or start over someplace else, having little or minimal plans in place.

The above group of challenges I consider as being in a category called "One of these you will face." As such, you now have the opportunity to think about what could you do before you actually experience any of the scenarios listed. I wish someone had spelled this out for me early in my career. And although, being able to survive emotional impacts will vary from person to person, knowing about them allows you to consider options for guarding yourself as best you can.

Keep in mind, many will face a moment when a leap of faith becomes a viable option. It may come at a time when an emotional situation hits you and you believe there are no real options, or you don't have any solutions you believe that you can rely on. Your back is against the proverbial wall. And, it's now when you have an opportunity to gain insight into how you respond under stress. Do you make impulsive decisions which later you realize, you need to apologize to someone, or you acted without really thinking? And maybe a day later you realize there actually were other options.

So, there's a possibility that some, as a result of how they manage their stress, will experience leap of faith type decisions influenced by how they are accustomed to responding in those moments when they are emotionally impacted.

If you happen to be a "Trekkie," the Commander Spock character is regularly noted as making decisions where he relies more on logic. But because he is half human and half Vulcan, he also realizes there are decisions where emotion needs to be embraced as part of his decision process, which ultimately provides him with an additional set of options and proposed solutions.

It might be beneficial to recognize your own tendencies and processing when you need to make decisions while emotionally impacted. Potentially by considering your emotional personality and tendencies, you can also become increasingly aware when you are in that moment, and can then draw upon your inner self to help you when you believe you are at a leap of faith moment.

If you consider the potential situations I listed earlier, in addition to knowing how beneficial your own decisions are when you're emotionally stressed, I also believe that building a strong support structure sits at the top of my mind when trying to handle emotional impacts. Who can you rely upon for objective feedback?

For some, you might realize your best viable support coming in the form of being an active participant in a faith-based group, being proactive and participating in building a network of trusting family and friends, having an emergency escape bag packed and funded just in case you'll need to go somewhere to clear your mind for a few days, or having available a mobile accessibility plan that allows you to manage your key affairs remotely, 24/7. Although these options vary from being relatively normal to sounding extreme, you never can tell what types of situations you might encounter, so considering only what sounds relatively normal at this time, may not be thorough planning when considering what might be the situation that gets you to a leap of faith moment. I found by having some relatively normal through extreme plans available, I actually had some solace in knowing that I had a variety of options in my toolset.

When looking back on some of the challenges I've faced, I probably would have experienced more issues or greater level of setbacks if I had not had a number of family members, clergy, mentors, and friends that I could confer with on various subjects. I recall some of the decisions I made after experiencing emotional impacts, allowed me to develop counter-measures to insulate myself from recurrence. I can also admit that some of my counter-measures provided such good benefits, that they put me in the position of having self-produced "golden parachute" benefits. And with those types of benefits, you can be back in the position to make another leap of faith, but now being able to incorporate lessons learned or information gathered that had nothing to do with your leap of faith decision process.

But you know, in retrospect, I realized, for me, my leap of faith moments, which included failures and successes, resulted in a new level of confidence and character. I'm not going to lie to you: I believe that the most opportune time to take a leap of faith is when someone else has your back, or you have a financial windfall that can isolate you from negative impacts in the event your move goes sour and does not return the expected results in the time allotted, needed, hoped for, or expected.

I remember spending all of the money in my bank account, to produce some music tracks which I later traveled around the country trying to obtain a creative production deal. It sure was nice that I was living under my parents' roof at the time, when I didn't have many bills, and could always go home to get some food and a place to sleep. But there were also times when I believed so strongly that I would be successful with an idea, that I went forward without knowing how I would make ends meet.

So often we hear of countless stories of starving artists who leave their home town to move to locations where they believe it will be easier for them to get their big break. Their ability to make the leap is a testament to their strong faith, and a belief that they can't fail.

And for those of you who are pursuing a creative or riskier path, you should expect to hear countless recommendations that you'd better get a "real job" to pay your bills until you make it. Probably that internal desire to dedicate more and more efforts toward a risky path, will not go away. And if you decide not to take that leap, or take the risk, you may beat up on yourself later in life, just wondering what would have happened if only you took the leap. Even worst, you may end up blaming someone close to you for your dream deferred.

Sometimes the decision to take a leap of faith may suddenly emerge without warning, due to a series of events built over time that results in enough pressure that you know you just have to do something now. It's time to leave that safe, comfortable, situation and off you go. And there are others who make all types of protective measures or make business plans with the goal of obtaining some level of confidence before taking the leap. Regardless of what approach that gets you to that leap, at some point, those who create their own path, will have to take the leap. And if you talk to those who are successful achieving something others have not, most will tell you of that point when they went forward, without having guarantees.

Chapter 22: Perspective

For those of you who are just getting started and for those who are well along on their career paths, there are some motivating thoughts that I would hope that you keep in mind, or at least consider. This book transfers actual knowledge to you and shares some lessons learned from mistakes, that you can consider or ignore. This book provides recommendations and suggestions, encourages you to dream, think about plans, and derive decisions that are *best for you*, not based on what others insist or tell you to do, but based on your own assessment of various bits of information. If you are preparing to begin your career, or in the early stages of your career, hopefully the information provided can empower you with ideas for designing your own diverse career paths and risk mitigation plans. As such, there will always be opportunities for others to agree, disagree, debate, challenge, and ponder. But the information, experiences, and recommendations provided are focused on providing some assistance with creating your own unique path, and to help you with finding yourself and feeling great about the person you find within you. Ultimately, I've attempted to invoke your higher thinking to facilitate your awareness of things previously unknown, a search for things still unknown, and evoke your abilities to prepare for and manage what you find. Why? So that you have the potential of having an easier time and more enjoyable experience by having the information I've provided, now available to you. This is one of my personal character traits, which is to help others achieve their goals.

Five-by-Five Signal Strength
1. I believe *with planning, you can achieve success* with your career.

2. The needs of the world will constantly change. As a result, new opportunities will develop, while existing opportunities will continue, or be determined to be irrelevant, as a result of evolution.
3. I found my most challenging competition was with me, myself and I.
4. There are unlimited ways to measure one's success beyond power, money, and acquisitions.
5. You should always protect the *specific details* related to the *actual steps you plan to make* that you believe will be needed to achieve your career goals and your career plans.

A Deeper Dive into the Five-by-Five

Planning includes:
- Truthful self-reflection on who you are as a person (character type, values, needs, etc.),
- Determining what success looks like for you (stability, economically, philosophically, emotionally, culturally, and humanistic-ally),
- Regular assessments of current expectations of people around the world,
- Keeping an eye for indicators near and far that could impact your work environment,
- Regular gathering of information,
- Putting in efforts to build viability (lasting value to others),
- Applying lessons learned but not being afraid to dream and commit to moving on a hunch or taking a guess and leaps of faith,
- Achieving a consciousness and respect for the rights for world cultures to co-exist,

- Consistent management of risks,
- Having a minimum of two sources of income working simultaneously,
- Having ability to adjust to change in yourself and around you,
- Having an unwavering belief that you, and we all have purpose which comes through favor from a higher Spirit, from God.

Since the needs of the world will always be in constant flux there will always be new opportunities. What does that mean? It means we will always have increasing levels of needs, proportional to population growth. And that will continue throughout our lives. Someone will always be needed to fulfill those needs. This is a completely symbiotic relationship. So, if you keep in tune to your own needs, and keep your eyes and ears open to recognize the needs of your community, the opportunity exists for you to plan diverse career paths that can support an ever-increasing level of needs.

I found my most challenging competition was with me, myself and I. This realization first came into focus when I was placed in one of my first leadership roles. I was a freshman snare drummer on the Tennessee State University's Aristocrat of Bands drumline. Due to an unfortunate personal situation, the current drumline section leader, nick named "Dirt Dauber" had to drop out of school. My percussion instructor, Prof. J.L. Lane, who I still consider to be one of my most impactful mentors, came over to me, and with no discussion or emotion, told me, you're the new section leader. With "Dirt Dauber" out, I became known as KAT Tyler while others just called out "Hey Chi-caaaah-go!" This nickname gave me a bit of Native American-Indian mystic, but at the time of my sudden promotion, all I remember was being in a constant state of fear and shock, because my awareness of this new high visibility role of being the drumline section leader came with tremendous competition, called challenges. At any time, anyone wanting the role could call out in front of the band, or drumline, "I challenge so and so for their position." And if you wanted to maintain your reputation and avoid the embarrassment of losing in front of your peers and band leaders, who would vote, you needed to practice regularly to increase your skills to play. In addition, there was added pressure associated with every football game where our school played against another school that had a marching band. Each game presented the possibility of having to defend against any challenge from the opposing school's drumline. And for me, there existed a potential 'one-on-one' direct challenge from the opposing school's drumline's section leader. That up front and personal challenge would be in front of the entire student body, professors, alumni, guests, and media who showed up to see the game. It was that awareness which drove me to practice each day, with the goal of being better than I was the previous day. I blocked out the realization that at that moment, as a seventeen-year-old freshie, there were two other freshies in our section, Reno and DT, both from Memphis, who were both powerfully skilled snare drummers, who on any given day were capable of leading the section. And the next year our drumline was joined by M. 'Leroy' Adams from Alabama State, Hot Rod and two new freshies, Craig from St. Louis and Bubba from Nashville, who all came in blasting the snares with innovative techniques.

To manage my fear of potentially facing challenges from the opposing team's drumline section leader, after each Saturday football game, I blocked out that I didn't have intel on the abilities of each drumline and section leader aligned to every band we would face over the course of the season. But instead, *I competed with myself* and applied that same approach by *motivating collaboration* from all drumline section members to innovate routines in preparation for pending challenges. I also learned that staying out of the way of innovators resulted in *team buy-in and commitment* culminating in a team that enjoyed working together and enjoyed the acknowledgment the entire team received. I focused less on competition and more on personal and team expertise. As a result of applying the approach of seeking collaboration among our section, our performances were not based on what other sections were doing, but we were unique, innovative and entertaining. We did things that others had not seen because we became innovators.

In addition to our work as part of the full band, we were thoroughly prepared to perform flawlessly at least four "make them cry" routines, including the passed down and legendary routine named "Stick Control." When challenged, we would run one routine, that we expected to be countered by our competitors. After being countered, we had three others that were equally brutal. We soon discovered our competitors rarely were prepared with more than two show pieces, so when we unveiled number three, the consistent result was seeing them turn and walk away, they didn't have a comeback. And now with the crowd who had encircled us and cheering, we had the choice of running number three to completely embarrass and increase our fame for being innovators. We were campus rock stars. We felt the fame, the roar of the crowd, as a result of competing against ourselves. Not really concerned about our competitors, but more about us *delivering a great product*, performing at a level that we were proud of what we presented, with ourselves being the judge. Ultimately, our audience or customers, highly appreciated our innovation and professionality.

And for me, I believe my focus on challenging myself resulted in others seeing me play something they were not expecting. Not knowing what I was going to come up with next. As a result, my personal product *was not just like the others*, and although I worried about potential challenges from competitors, I became increasingly confident that *I was ready to defend*, my turf, and my brand.

I decided to share this experience to reinforce the idea that your career path can be guided not by *competing with what others are doing*, but with *what you respect and feel good about*. If and when others get acknowledgment or promoted, and you begin to wonder or ask yourself, "What about me and all I did?" Well, unfortunately, you will not be alone looking out the side of your eye at those giving out acknowledgments or promotions, and the recipients. Yes, it's true that acknowledgments are often guided by the subjective values of distinct personalities and varied criteria focused on ensuring everyone *will not* become a prom or homecoming king or queen. We have all experienced the controversy after the homecoming king and queen or beauty pageant winners are announced. Somebody will always shout, "How did that happen? So-and-so should have won!" But that critique would be driven by your own value criteria. Trust me, my criteria for who would be selected as a homecoming king and queen would definitely not be the same as how you would make a selection. So please don't get bent out of shape if you don't receive votes for acknowledgments or promotions. Depending on who actually determines the criteria, the list could actually be designed to ensure you will never get anything. And some criteria are certainly created so only certain individuals need apply.

I recall two separate instances when coworkers confided in me, their beliefs that coworkers should not receive titles 'like ours' until they have completed what we've done or experienced the pain we experienced. I questioned, why should individuals, spinning along, revolving on their own path, given different assignments, having different challenges, all be judged base on what we did? They would never experience the same as unique individuals, nor should they. In other words, they believed until others have completed some assignment which appeared to be the same as some we've done, they should not be promoted to the same title as we currently had. Wow. Unfortunately, that's really how some coworkers and business leaders feel about acknowledgments and promotions.

But, I believe when you focus on competing against yourself, you will have the motivation to continue to excel, increase your skills and value, and be able to present a long list of accomplishments you can be proud of. And that is the type of happiness that you can attribute to being successful based on your own measures for success, and enjoying the fruits from developing successful diverse career paths as determined by your own criteria. You don't need to be in a group who sits at 'table number one' in order to become successful. You can experience success, not based on being compared to others, but as a result of you creating *a value and brand that others don't have*, after which others will want to duplicate, emulate, or recognize they need to compete with you. When you focus on competing with yourself, no one can possibly know what you will come up with next. In this way, you become an innovator, and can build upon your own diverse career paths. You don't have to work at trying to be like him or her. But instead, work at *the evolution of you*, and others will see the difference. Try not to focus on jealousy since that approach relegates you to always being a step behind since *you have to wait* to see what the other person is doing *before you can then imitate*. Jealousy will always result in you being behind.

Success. There are unlimited ways to measure one's success beyond just power, money, and acquiring things. I've seen luxury cars, parked on the street, which were owned by individuals who lived in houses that needed so many repairs it looked like it was tilted to one side. For them it was the car that lauded their success. I know individuals who, because an older family member had built a successful business, were placed in positions of power within the organization as a result of nepotism. Being a business leader was their success. Early in my career, I used my credit card to finance a round trip from the United States to Europe, Bahrain and Abu Dhabi (U.A.E.), and then to Africa, a trip that could be considered by many to be one of their bucket list items. I enjoyed that experience of success at a young age just because I had family members who had considerable knowledge of overseas travel, as such I understood the logistics needed to get there, I had a family member working in Africa, and I wanted the experience. I've seen women working in low wage jobs who had acquired renown "red sole" designer shoes that cost more than their total month's wages, and afterwards needed to ask their family and friends to loan them money so they can pay their monthly rent. The "red sole" shoes were their success at that point. I began purchasing my first auto and first home by negotiating deals with family members. Having that first car and paying a home mortgage felt like success, and the smell of victory, even when my investment savings account had serious deficiencies. But the long-term success plan was underway and active.

My advice is we shouldn't judge one's motivation for how they seek to achieve success, but only acknowledge people have various ways in which they measure success. Some take into account currently available resources that allow them to fulfill some aspirations and achieve immediate levels of success. Others look for measures which target long- or short-term benefits which could be focused on time, family, emotional, philosophical, psychological, philanthropic, or generational wealth or power.

Protect. You should always protect the *specific details* related to the *actual steps you plan to make* that you believe will be needed to achieve your career goals and career plans. A risk exists related to the more others know, the more others will have the knowledge of what they can do to impede you, or block the actions you need to complete. Without knowing your next steps, it will be extremely difficult for others to interrupt your plans.

The Unknown

It has been my experience that some of the most difficult challenges an individual will face when developing their diverse career paths will materialize because it is difficult for most, unless you have prophetic gifts, to predict the future, and therefore be able to determine appropriate steps needed to navigate around challenges and external influences, when they are unknown and yet to materialize. And so our challenge is that we have to formulate various decisions by considering how we measure success, and then rely on our faith, tolerance for risk, and confidence in our skill set, taking into account all gathered information, making regular assessments of our particular personal situations, having assessed the strength or lack of protective measures in place, taking into account all lessons learned from previous decisions, and finally making a leap of faith or using our gut feelings on what we believe will result in success.

Looking Forward

There's another perspective which I believe is easily overlooked when people are developing and then carrying out their strategic career plans. And that is the perspective of seeing oneself far enough into their careers at a time when they are riding along their career path, comfortably, and having minimal worries. We often are so focused on work that we can't see this point in our careers, and when it arrives we may be too focused and occupied with current events to know that it has arrived. This is a point which hopefully, is envisioned well before you publicly proclaim you are retired, and in position to get up in the morning when you want, do whatever you want, and take on projects whenever you feel like it. Many visualize this state as retirement. But why can't this comfortable state arrive before you proclaim to be retired? Couldn't you achieve a kind of mental happiness while you are still moving along your career path? And after reaching that level, would that *open the door for increased innovative thinking and higher productivity*? Who knows what you might achieve if you were *psychologically successful*? That's a whole different concept that could provide different results and opportunities for you.

    I would suggest, as part of planning you career, you also consider extending your thoughts into the future and visualize how you would like to see yourself, in the absence of worry, not so concerned about all of those inputs mentioned earlier, that you will need to consider when making career path decisions. Do you see yourself as respected in your areas of expertise? Are you someone who is confident and comfortable with your skills and capabilities? Are you someone who has established a moral compass that allows you to be in the presence of people having different values and beliefs, but not really concerned with being swayed to comply with requests contrary to your values? Are you a philanthropist? Do you see your financial affairs as having a good number of safeguards which can protect you when you actually decide to retire? Are you someone who will be volunteering your time to champion a cause?

Could you put any of these visualizations in place while still moving along your career path, and well before you reach the state you would consider that you are retired? The answer is yes. You could successfully achieve career goals well in advance of retirement, and enjoy various benefits being realized due to successful career plans while you are still moving along your career paths.

I bring this to your attention to add another tool that could potentially increase your probability of enjoying good results with your career plans. By extending your thoughts toward visualizing how you might see yourself in the future and before retirement, you can engage in efforts earlier during your career, with the hope of achieving visualizations of being satisfied, well before retirement age. As a young adult, I completed trips to the other side of the world because I envisioned international travel as elements of my success, not elements of my retirement years. And once you've achieved an element of your success, you can continue along your career path having minimal worries. But of course, you first need to visualize your future expectations, and systematically seek to address what needs to be put in place.

This is where you *dream to achieve.* You can visualize what would be success to you, when you are not concerned about needing to work to pay your bills. What would be the defining factors as to why people would consider you to be successful if their assessment didn't include the car you drive, the house you live in, or what's in your bank account? Hopefully, you get my point that many people define success as things you have. And in reality, you can rent or purchase things early, but would you feel successful, knowing you are still chasing dollars? Or would your visualization of how you might be enjoying the benefits of successful career path planning be more than having physical things? If success means achieving psychological goals related to how you feel, you might be able to achieve success well before the point when you actually retire.

Something to Think About, For the Dreamers, Wherever You Are

For those who can transport your consciousness forward, beyond today, here's just a little something to consider as an aspirational concept to consider when defining who you really are at the core.

If money had no value, and there was no necessity to pay for anything, or acquire things based on monetary value, what profession would you choose to do? People will need to carry out many of the same work efforts, except maybe in the financial industry, but without money having value, money would no longer be a measure for success, prestige, power, favor, or focus for building economic wealth. There would be no need for salaries, bonuses, and raises. What job or profession would you choose to do? What would really make you happy if monetary value no longer existed?

Can you imagine what it would be like if we lived in a world where money has no value?

What would be the criteria for identifying someone to complete various efforts needing to get done? What would be the measure for success? What would be the means used to negotiate collaboration? What would be the values and principles you would follow in order to ensure you are perceived as someone who could contribute in some way to society? What would you choose to contribute?

Stay Strong, Have Faith and Stay Well, for Hope Dies Last.
Be You, Now's the Time to Fly!

Appendix: Summary of Recommendations

Recommendation: Please run a search on the meaning of S.M.A.R.T. goals. (Introduction)

Recommendation: It may be to your benefit to periodically re-assess your psychological and emotional needs so you can tweak your career plans along the way and avoid needing to make a hard stop. (Your Value, Salary and Income)

Recommendation: If income is your motivation, I highly recommend you should review available salary surveys on the profession or career path you're interested so you can get some idea as to what is the expected salary. (Your Value, Salary and Income)

Recommendation: After you reach a point when there is a firm offer by someone or a company for utilizing your skills, always request some type of written offer letter, employment agreement or a simple statement that spells out expected responsibilities and the agreed upon compensation (hourly, annually, or by specific effort of work). (Adversaries in the Shadows)

Recommendation: I would suggest if you choose to accept a role with a poor work-to-life balance, please consider negotiating in writing, additional benefits like more vacation days, ability to work from home, or anything that can help you maintain your health. (Be Good to Yourself, along the way to success)

Recommendation: Experienced managers recognize that effective project estimation requires a clear understanding of the project requirements, a determination what is the validated solution to fulfill the requirements, an awareness of how many resources will be available to work, and what is the resources' current capacity to work on an effort, keeping in mind that resources normally work on other assignments simultaneously. In addition, less experienced managers should use the S.M.A.R.T. best practice definition as a guide for setting goals, where S means specific in that you understand the goal requirements or details and what will be needed for the solution. M means measurable, in which you determine values that let you know if the goal was successfully achieved. A means achievable, R means realistic, and T means time-bound, where an achievable and realistic amount of time is estimated as being needed to complete the goal when considering all known dependencies. (Be Good to Yourself, along the way to success)

Recommendation: Take all allowed time off and sabbaticals if available. Try not to miss out on opportunities to smile, laugh, stretch out, smell the roses, watch a sunset, or experience a moment you can mentally re-live over and over again. Having fond memories and pictures can help you to re-visit experiences even when you're down. I was fortunate to find out early in my career that rest and relaxation is definitely a beneficial part of your diverse career path, and you totally own this. (Be Good to Yourself, along the way to success)

Recommendation: After a company has given you a firm job offer in writing, I think as part of your initial counter offer, you should also attempt to negotiate a "make whole" agreement focused on encouraging the hiring company to lock in and keep the terms of the initial job description, responsibilities and expectations over a pre-determined period of time. Obviously, over a longer period of time employees should expect the needs of a company to change and evolve, and with those changes, their role and expectations will undoubtedly change. But, you shouldn't expect your role or responsibilities to change drastically shortly after being hired. That would fall into a bait and switch sales or marketing tactic focused on benefiting those implementing the tactic. Hopefully, there will be no need to execute a "make whole" agreement of this type, but think about how would you feel, if you left your current company to join the new one based on the presented job description and expectations, and in doing so, there were moving costs, or other costs you incurred as a result of believing the promises made by the hiring company would be maintained over a determined length of time, and for some reason your role changed into a totally new role from what was initially presented? I think most would agree it would be fair to make some type of adjustment to compensate for the differences between what was negotiated and what actually resulted. A make good agreement could include a confirmed bonus, a change in title, agreed increase in salary, or a severance type payment if you decide to exit totally. (Dead-End Jobs Blues)

Recommendation: I hope you will be mindful of your political capital or lack thereof. Whatever your choice, your decision to engage or not engage in building political capital could impact the amount of opportunities available for achieving your career goals, and speed at which they become available. But, I don't believe having a limited amount can block your success, just potentially impede it. So, be aware, it exists and will be used by others to accomplish their gains, possibly at your expense. (The Rules of Discrimination)

Recommendation: I highly recommend that you keep your eyes wide open for signs of how leaders support their organization's values that they customarily order to be published by the communications resources responsible for socializing the voice of the business leaders. Many unknowingly are unaware the core values are the windows into the business's soul. Either they will be clues into why they believe in their business, or they could be a set of published deceptions. The communicated core values can expose the leaders who are committed or not. Their actions to support, or not support, will unveil if they truly believe in the published values, which together compose the overall organization's culture. (A look into being a Team Player)

Recommendation: Stay alert for new players entering the game (new hires, re-assignments, re-orgs) who will be either a protagonist, antagonist, or seek to be neutral. (A look into being a Team Player)

Recommendation: I highly suggest you take some time to do all you can to identify, mitigate, and control risks by developing appropriate risk mitigation plans that have a goal of stopping risks from becoming an issue. And if a risk does evolve into an issue, having a plan to control the damage. (Preparing your stand against the Face of Deception and avoiding the Five Major Risks)

Recommendation: As part of your risk mitigation plan, I highly suggest that you develop more than one source of income as an integral element to your career strategy. In addition, this could reduce the risk of feeling the need to make decisions that could compromise your reputation, values, or morals, in order to maintain employment with your current employer. (Preparing your stand against the Face of Deception and avoiding the Five Major Risks)

Recommendation: If you find you are working with someone who regularly makes your work environment uncomfortable as a result of unethical or immoral behavior, their lack of integrity, sexual harassment, or offensive language, just to name a few, you may want to document the time and date of each event in writing, and use your cell phone to capture verbal proof of each offense. And if your manager gives a verbal direct order, or suggestion, insinuates, or implies what they would like for you to do, or hopes you will consider something that could benefit your career, and the action is unethical, immoral, dishonest or illegal, I would suggest that you try to obtain any type of confirmation from your manager via an email or recorded phone call, where your request might be phrased something like, "I just want to confirm you would like me to do <insert description of the request>." (Note: In some states both parties must give consent to be recorded.) It might also add some validation to your situation if there is a witness. Without tangible evidence, the offended employee is often left in an even more adverse work environment. Since a primary focus of human resource departments, which the offended employee soon learns, is to protect the company, you should not be surprised if a complaint you submit will not result in a resolution. Reportedly, a number of surveys of past whistle-blowers reveal the offending manager had been allowed to initiate retaliatory actions, conduct on-the-job harassment, block advancement, and get away with unfair disciplinary actions, that often resulted in the employee being fired for unsubstantiated reasons. Unfortunately, some HR and business leaders have a propensity not to punish managers who reciprocate against employees who have filed complaints, despite having language included in their code of conduct, against such an act. And many publicly outed whistle-blowers report it to be difficult finding work as a result of public shaming. Also, the court system usually tips the scales in favor of business owners unless there is a group of people filing a complaint, in the form of a class action suit. And it has been done successfully. (Preparing your stand against the Face of Deception and avoiding the Five Major Risks)

Recommendation: Continually work to diversify your skill set, similar to how businesses diversify their product and service offerings to ensure they remain viable and able to keep up with market trends and changes to customer expectations. (Preparing your stand against the Face of Deception and avoiding the Five Major Risks)

Recommendation: Yes, financial advisers often recommend putting away approximately seven or more months of savings to handle bills just in case you have a personality conflict with your manager, choose not to compromise your value system and decide to quit your job, or your job is eliminated as part of a re-org, headcount reduction, or you are just plain out fired. In this day and age, there are some who have been out of work for extended periods of time as a result of unique contemporary (E.g.: recessions, extreme weather conditions, fire damage, terrorism) or personal reasons. Hopefully, those facing any of these types of scenarios have a risk plan or skill diversification strategy implemented to minimize the impact. Knowing that, it may to your advantage, while you are employed, to contact an insurance company, and pay monthly premiums for 'supplemental unemployment' insurance or 'income protection' insurance. For any employee having some type of 'disruption of income' insurance it could be extremely beneficial seeing how the majority of employees will face a couple of disruptions over the course of their careers. For some reason, we rarely prepare for a work-related event which could result in being left financially at risk. (Preparing your stand against the Face of Deception and avoiding the Five Major Risks)

Recommendation: All businesses should have risk management plans, and everyone planning their careers should also maintain continual and constantly adjusting risk management plans. Don't be misled by someone labeling you as a complainer, when you are focusing on risk mitigation to avoid peril and handle it if a risk turns into an issue. (Preparing your stand against the Face of Deception and avoiding the Five Major Risks)

Recommendation: Just like you have a doctor to address changes in your health, you should consider joining professional social media groups, engage alumni association advisers, or career experts, where you can submit questions or request advice from the group members on how best to resolve work related conflicts. (Preparing your stand against the Face of Deception and avoiding the Five Major Risks)

Recommendation: If you are uncertain about what you want to do or achieve, create a list of your open questions on your mobile phone or tablet, and begin to get answers by asking your teachers, adults in your family, and people who might already be working in areas you are interested. I highly recommend arranging some time to speak with people who are actually working in the area of interest since they will have real experiences and know the pitfalls. Be sure to ask about what they like and don't like about their jobs. Ask what could be any positive and negative impacts on one's personal life. (Increasing Your Odds of Having a Successful Career)

Recommendation: A key element for developing a successful career path is becoming and then remaining aware of what's needed by individuals who exist beyond your personal geographical and psychological boundaries which you have determined to be comfort zones. If you have decided, you don't want to span beyond the area you are comfortable, you should consider what will you do if those comfort areas diminish, implode, or due to other external influences the number of customers diminish within those areas.

On the street, this exact scenario is associated to 'turf wars' and those within the defined borders begin to fight for control of this limited market, a market defined by distinct, physical boundaries. But for those who decide they need to prepare to avoid being restricted to a geographical and psychological boundary, you will need confidence, a sense of curiosity, adventure, and you'll need information. You will need to overcome your fears. You will need to expand your knowledge of the world, and then scope it, scout it out to educate yourself. And there's no reason why anyone working on their career shouldn't at some point, have their own transaction-capable website and a social media account. (Increasing Your Odds of Having a Successful Career)

Recommendation: Another element of your risk mitigation plan should be to always protect the specific details of your plans, and the steps you need to achieve your career goals. The risk is the more others know, the more you put yourself at risk of others having the knowledge of what they can do to impede you or block the things you need to achieve. (Increasing Your Odds of Having a Successful Career)

Recommendation: Do consider showing appreciation and giving acknowledgment to those who help you. It could do more good than harm. (Acknowledge Those Who Help You, Your Business, Your Career)

Recommendation: Always document details of each of your completed projects including stakeholders, approximate initiation, and end dates. Also, send a brief email to the main stakeholders to ask for feedback that can speak to successes, challenges, and issues which still need to be resolved. Ideally, when it's time for a review of your value, you want to have documentation that can be used as proof of your actions, accomplishments, satisfied clients, risks avoided, issues resolved, and any savings realized. (Acknowledge Those Who Help You, Your Business, Your Career)

Appendix: Sample Career Theme

Career Theme Concentration: Financial

Expectations

- Ten years or less completion target.
- Fundamental financial skills are usable across each income stream pillar.
- Each income stream pillar will require some specialized training courses that can be completed within the ten year completion target.

Income Stream Pillars

- Certified Public Accountant
- Certified Financial Planner
- Financial Business or Technology Project Manager
- Tax Adviser
- Underwriter
- International Financial Web Blogger
- Part-time Teaching Professor

Potential financial markets to service if fluent in English plus at least one of the following languages

- Japanese
- German
- French
- Portuguese
- Hindi
- Spanish

Unique Actions Needed

- Register as a foreign agent in each applicable region.
- Fulfill all specific requirements needed to conduct business in the countries you would like to work.

- Acquire industry specific software and communication technology tools.

Potential Results: Seven simultaneous income streams in which you can conduct business face-to-face or video chat in English speaking countries and at least one non-English speaking country.

Theme Development Opportunities: Entrepreneur services, Internship, volunteer work with community organizations, entry level hire, internal or external advancement from current employment role.

Probable individual commitment needed by the financial career themed student: Training equivalent to a Bachelors and MBA degree program combined (three to six years total study beyond themed high school study) should result in the student having met the requirements for at least four income stream pillars.

Sample Career Theme Planning

Career Theme	Financial Theme				
	Plan expectations: 10 year or less completion target; fundamental financial skills are usable across each income stream pillar; each pillar will require some specialized training courses that can be completed within the 10 year completion target.				
Income Stream Pillars	Certified Public Accountant	Certified Financial Planner	Financial Business or Technology Project Manager	Tax Adviser	Underwriter	International Financial Blogger	Part-time teaching professor
Unique Actions Needed	Register as a foreign agent in each applicable region.	Fulfill the specific requirements needed to conduct business in the countries you would like to work.	Acquire industry specific software and communication technology tools.			
Serviceable Financial Markets given Linguistic skills	Fluent in English plus at least one other major financial market using either Japanese, German, French, Portuguese, Hindi or Spanish.					
Potential Results	Seven simultaneous income streams in which you can conduct business face-to-face or video chat in an English speaking and at least one non-English speaking country.					
Theme Development Opportunities	Entrepreneur services, Internship, volunteer work with community organizations, entry level hire, internal or external advancement from current employment role.					
Individual commitment for Career Themed Studies	Training equivalent to a Bachelors and MBA degree program combined (three to six years total study beyond themed high school study) should result in the student having met the requirements for at least four income stream pillars.					

www.ingramcontent.com/pod-product-compliance
Lightning Source LLC
Chambersburg PA
CBHW021117300426
44113CB00006B/188